No Way Back

A Memoir of a Young Man in Search of Home

Bruce Parkinson Spang

Eliot, T.S. "Four Quartets." The Complete Poems and Plays: 1909-1950, New York: Harcourt, Brace and Company, 1958.

Published by Piscataqua Press
an imprint of RiverRun Bookstore
86 Morning Street
Portsmouth NH 03801

Cover photo by Penny Pierce

ISBN: 9781958669983

Also by the Bruce Parkinson Spang

Poetry

All You'll Derive: A Caregivers Journey (2020)
Not Just Anybody, BPS Books, 2015
Boy at the Screen Door, Moon Pie Press, 2014
To the Promised Land Grocery, Moon Pie Press, 2008
The Knot, Snow Drift Press, 2006

Poetry Chapbooks

Tip End of Time, Smyle Publications, 2005
Once the First Berries Dissolve, 2003

Poetry Anthologies

Passion and Pride: Poets in Support of Equality, Moon Pie Press, 2012
I Have Walked Through Many Lives, Young Voices-Scarborough, Moon Pie Press, 2009

Libretto:

Reckoning, the Musical, 2010.

Novels:

The River Crossed, Wisdom House Press, 2024
Those Close Beside Me, Piscataqua Press, 2018
The Deception of the Thrush, Piscataqua Press, 2014

Memoir

No Way Back: A Young Man's Search for Home, Piscataqua Press, 2026
Dear Teen, Dear Poet: Coming of Age in Letters. Warren Publisher, 2026

Dedication

To Ralph and Ann Spang for their resistance and encouragement that shaped who I am; to my husband Myles Rightmire for the life we share; to Erling Duus for his vision of America as a place where people value democracy and where the have-nots can be heard and seen; to Marie Cirillo and the people of Rose's Creek who opened their homes to me and remain in my heart; to Reverend Dick and Pam Schmidt for their lasting friendship; and to Don Beisswenger for his right words at the right time. I also owe much to other real-life figures such as Reverend James Lawson, Baxter Bryant, Dean Walter Harrelson, and Father Flye for their wise and compassionate counsel.

I hope that, as much as I can, I have been faithful to their spirit. Some parts of this memoir are fictionalized, as memory—fragile as it is—can only capture fleeting moments in time. Therefore, imagination must be called upon to bring those moments to life. However, this memoir reflects, to the best of my ability, the spirit of the times and those I knew. The people in Rose's Creek are not meant to represent any one family or individual, but rather to embody the resilient and courageous spirit of those I admired and who taught me much more about religion, faith, and trust than I ever learned from a textbook. Still, I would be remiss if I didn't mention two families in Rose's Creek who significantly impacted my life: the Metzlers and the Kings. In particular, I am forever grateful to Dorothy, her daughter Lois, and her son Bobby, whom I loved as a second family. I am also thankful to Bonny King and her children, who welcomed me as part of their family. Additionally, I am grateful to Nancy McDaniel, Steve Putnam, John Michael Albert, Alice Persons, Dick Schmidt, and John Himmelheber for their guidance, suggestions, and wise editing. Thanks also go to Kellsey Metzger for her editorial advice and dedication in helping make this book what it is.

Contents

Introduction to this Memoir

THIS BOOK IS A MEMOIR with elements of fiction woven throughout. When I originally wrote it as a novel, I wanted the freedom to write about my experiences and many of those close beside me without worrying about upsetting anyone. I disguised some characters by changing their names, while others remained unchanged due to their importance to me and their significance to civil rights and antiwar movements of that time. Their names can be found in history books. Reverend James Lawson and Reverend Baxton Bryant were key civil rights leaders at the forefront of the movement for minority rights. Dean Walter Harrelson, who led Vanderbilt Divinity School, profoundly influenced me both intellectually and spiritually. Father Flye, who befriended James Agee, welcomed me into his home and shared his love for Agee. Others, though not famous, played significant roles in changing my life. Mr. Hook encouraged me to keep a journal; much of what happened at the Folk School was transcribed into letters sent to him and became part of this memoir. Marie Cirillo was a brave community organizer working to uplift the Appalachian people. Erling Duus promoted the idea of a Folk School to honor the indigenous traditions of people dismissed by capitalist society. Don Beisswenger, my advisor at Vanderbilt Divinity School, knew what I needed to do and told me so.

Being with them and witnessing their way of life, beliefs, and the influence they had on others changed my life. Many of the people mentioned in this book also existed, but I chose to change their names so I could tell my story openly without revealing their identities or misrepresenting them.

The line between memoir and fiction is blurry. Many studies show that just hours after a traumatic event—a car crash, a fall, a death—people may have very different versions of what happened compared to someone else nearby. Memory is often influenced by a person's own worldview and life experiences. Even recalling a conversation from minutes earlier can be difficult. Writing a memoir about early childhood or past experiences can never be completely accurate. As psychologist Alfred Adler argued, we often create our lives and build an "as if" reality to shape how we want to be known and remembered.

A recent study of Ernest Hemingway's first novel, *The Sun Also Rises*, showed that the characters and events in the book were taken from his journals and partially, but not convincingly, disguised. What he wrote could have just as easily been a memoir. In either case, his version of the story offended those who believed they were his friends until the book exposed a very different reality, depicting them as characters with deep flaws and devious motives.

Changing this book into a memoir is, therefore, not a big stretch, and is, in fact, more authentic for me than portraying people I knew as characters that didn't stay true to who they were. Calling it a novel, I felt obligated to craft a story with a clear plotline. Ideally, if I did that, the book would feature fewer characters, and those characters would appear throughout the novel, influencing what happened to Jason over the years.

Instead, I chose to stay true to what actually happened. Much of what I wrote, as I've mentioned, came from journals I kept at the time to try, often unsuccessfully, to understand what was happening to me. Like most of our lives, especially when we are young, people come and go faster than in novels. In college, a close friend in a different class moved on after graduation. With a summer program like the Folk School, students who arrived for a few months went back to their homes and blended into the anonymity of their schools. Therefore, for Jason and me, people I became attached to and who were close to me left much quicker than I wanted.

As a result, the novel I envisioned doesn't have the narrative continuity I would have preferred, although the issues Jason faced—the fear of being gay, the need to break away from an overbearing father, the hunger to find a home, some place to belong, a sense of himself as a budding artist, and the courage to stand up against injustice—were also mine. How Jason came to confront these issues was often puzzling because, in many ways, the society in which he grew up was doing its best at that time to dismiss everything Jason and I stood for.

By calling this a memoir, I invite you to see this story as a coming-of-age journey. I retained the protagonist's name, Jason, instead of using my own because, in some ways, he serves as my alter ego—an earlier version of myself. His different name feels natural and allows me to present him honestly, without trying to romanticize him or fit him into a neat plot. It's not the entire story of his life, only a few pivotal years when our nation was battling itself and when civil rights for minorities, gays, women, and Blacks were deeply dividing and tearing at the fabric of the country.

In those times, Jason was blessed, as I was blessed, to have people who took him under their wing, understood that he needed to be challenged, and offered him a helping hand. To be sure, some did their best to deny him and discourage him from being who he was. His story is my story. It doesn't end with a glorious resolution or a final conclusion. It ends, as much of our lives do, with a character having to make a new beginning—one that starts with a deeper understanding of who he was, who he was not, and where, if he kept faith in himself, he might finally find his way home.

The Waking

I wake to sleep and take my waking slow.
I feel my fate in what I cannot fear.
I learn by going where I have to go.

We think by feeling. What is there to know?
I hear my being dance from ear to ear.
I wake to sleep, and take my waking slow.

Of those so close beside me, which are you?
God bless the Ground! I shall walk softly there,
And learn by going where I have to go.

Light takes the Tree; but who can tell us how?
The lowly worm climbs up a winding stair;
I wake to sleep, and take my waking slow.

Great Nature has another thing to do
To you and me, so take the lively air,
And, lovely, learn by going where to go.

This shaking keeps me steady. I should know.
What falls away is always. And is near.
I wake to sleep, and take my waking slow.

—Theodore Roethke

I

In order to possess what you do not possess,
you must go by the way of dispossession.

—T.S. Eliot, "Four Quartets"

Taking Leave

MY FATHER BUILT A WINDING staircase in his house. He probably saw it as a symbol of elegance from a bygone era, when ladies strode down them and gentlemen took their arms, leading them into a ballroom. The problem was that there were no ladies on the second floor. Only me and my bedroom, first on the left, at the top of the stairs, tucked away from my parents on the first floor.

I woke late, nearly nine o'clock, and sat on the edge of my bed, staring at a gray squirrel in the oak tree. Quite acrobatic, he leapt from one branch to another. Most likely, it never occurred to him that he might fall. He paused on one branch and looked at me. He sat upright, his front paws in front of him, almost as if he was encouraging me to applaud. He had every reason to be proud of himself. He knew what he was doing. I wished I had his confidence. I had many doubts. Maybe everyone did. But in my case, it was a concern. I'd spend hours second-guessing what I'd done. "Should I have…" "If I only was…" and "What if I'd…" were regularly on my mind.

The squirrel scampered off.

I rubbed my face.

Time to get moving.

After a shower, I combed my hair. At the hairline on the left side, a cowlick would rise, untamed, and point in the opposite direction. Dab it with water, smack it down—nothing worked. It had a mind of its own. That's how my sex life had been, too.

Other guys had told me I was attractive. "Geez, you could have any girl." But in the mirror, I saw a regular guy, clean-shaven, nice features. I'd tell him, "Hey, go for it. Ask her out." But I wasn't interested in girls. I was more attracted to guys. It's not something I wanted to admit to anyone, least of all myself.

My body didn't behave as it should. When I'd least expect it, I'd get aroused—the young clerk measuring the inseam of my pants, a buddy's knee pressing against mine at a pep rally, the lone boy stripping off his swimsuit in the changing room—and have to hide my erection. Sometimes, the veneer of who I appeared to be and wanted to be was so thick it was impossible to peel it off and expose the truth that lay inside. I was like those insects encased in amber. I could see out at the world around me, but I always felt trapped in a body that wasn't my own.

I couldn't get away from that trapped feeling. It just was. But I could get away from my parents' house. My departure for graduate school marked the beginning.

Who knew where that would take me? I had my doubts, suitcases full of them. Reading was a chore for me. In third grade, Mrs. Dowling noticed I read from right to left. Sentences started with objects and, like a car backing up, bumped into the predicate, then crashed into the subject. Even now, if I hurried, my eyes moved backward, and I'd slam into the wrong word. I'd taken four speed-reading courses, two the previous summer, and learned how to skim and trim down a text. But the truth was I enjoyed reading in the slow lane and rolling the words over my tongue, though I knew at Vanderbilt, I'd have to read in the fast lane.

But at least I wasn't in a body bag on a tarmac in Saigon—not like Tom Duffy, my high school classmate and the best, quickest running back on our football team, who'd been in a hurry to serve his country and was the first in our class to die in Vietnam. A sniper blew his head off.

By luck, and the recommendation of a college professor, I applied to Vanderbilt Divinity School, was accepted, got my 4-D deferment, and, for at least two years, put off military service.

I bade the squirrel goodbye, dressed, and gobbled a bowl of Raisin Bran—only five raisins in it, hard as rocks.

My mom was out in the back garden picking roses to set in a bowl by the kitchen window. I piled my dishes in the sink, brought my suitcase downstairs, and set it by the front door, where the roses' scent would fill the foyer.

I walked through the living room, slid open the sliding glass doors, and stood on the back porch, gazing at the garden, the last of the Shasta daisies, their white faces straining up to catch the early sun. My mother waved at me.

"Lovely day," she called out.

"Good day to drive," I said.

I'd already packed my records, Zenith record player, clothes, and books in the trunk of the new Volvo. It was a graduation gift from my father, a practical car, one that would last, or at least, that's what I thought. Dad preferred an American car, a Mustang. Too flashy for me, but money was no object for him.

"Get a classy car," he said.

I drove one.

"See, it's powerful. And a girl magnet," he said.

"Sure," I thought. "That's all I need." I settled on the Volvo sedan, four-door with a trunk that could hold an elephant.

Dad was off to work as the Vice-President of the Zenith Radio Corporation, where he always was when he wasn't playing golf. That made it easy to leave. No lectures about "work before pleasure." No pressure to date more, find the right girl, one with money.

"If you have a choice," he'd admonish me. "Find one with money, lots of it."

All I needed to do was say goodbye to my mom. When she came back from the garden, she fussed in the kitchen and put dishes away that clanked angrily as if they didn't want to be where she wanted them to be.

She was worried I'd never return. She was right to be concerned. Home no longer felt like home to me. I had nowhere else to go, no place where I could say, "I belong here." I was a nomad, about to leave with no compass, no map, and that trunk full of "what ifs." I had at least a year, maybe two, at graduate school to figure myself out.

"Mom," I called out after checking my room one more time, picking up a journal and a golf cap, "I'm going."

She stepped out of the kitchen, drying her hands on a dish towel, her face drawn, the crow 's feet at her eyes distinct.

"Oh, honey," she said, reaching out to hug me, "Are you sure this is right for you?"

Sure, I thought, *how could I be sure? I was never sure of anything.*

I hugged her. Her hair, frosted but not overdone, was quite understated, with a few light blond waves mixed into her natural brunette color—a simple style that easily fell back into shape after a swim or a round of golf—

and smelled clean, as if it had just been washed. She looked up at me, the squint in her eyes revealing her fear. She'd been crying but managed to wipe away the tears.

"It's fine. I gotta do what I gotta do," I said, smiling. I picked up the suitcase, gripping it tightly in my hand.

She shook her head and smiled weakly.

"Say goodbye to Dad," I said.

"Your dad is proud of you," she said, stepping back. "You know that."

I suppose he was, but that wasn't how I felt. I wanted to get as far away from his expectations as possible. Five hundred miles felt right. No more dealing with his insistence that I find a job with his corporate friends. No more questions about my friends who had been protesting the Chicago Democratic Convention: *Why are they protesting? Who do they think they are? Do they realize Communists support these protests? Are you in contact with them?*

It was as if J. Edgar Hoover were scrutinizing me. Besides giving me the third degree, he was nosy. When I was at work one day, he paged through my journal. I could tell because I left it in a certain place on my dresser with a pen on a page. When I returned, the pen was on the wrong page. The journal had been moved. It contained my thoughts about the war I opposed and the social injustice I blamed on my father's friends. At the club, "Negro staff" (as he called them) only worked in the kitchen, never as waiters in the dining room. After that, I hid the journal under my bed, buried in underwear. I'd had enough of him. I suspected he'd had enough of me.

My mother acted as if everything was fine between us. That was her role. Our being happy was a religion to her.

"Yeah, Mom, I know," I said. "It's just he has strange ways of showing it."

"But he is, you know he is."

"Sure."

She sighed and brushed something off my sweater.

"I'm off," I said.

She nodded, walked out with me, and stood by the front door, the towel knotted in her hands.

When I pulled out of the driveway, past the chokecherries, hawthorn, and oak, I eased up on the accelerator. A squirrel scampered across the driveway and leapt into a tree. He looked over his shoulder as if to say,

"This is fun. Give it a try." Another time, I thought. My mother waved. I honked the horn and waved back. I turned onto Swan Lake Drive, drove down Butterfield Road to the East-West Tollway, and from there, onto Interstate 65, heading south to Nashville, Tennessee.

The Wounded

I DROVE SOUTH PAST Gary, Indiana. The steel mills gave off a harsh, acrid smell like burning tires. My father's friends called it "the smell of money". If it was the smell of money, it was the smell of dirty money. I closed the window and sped past the belching smokestacks. The road turned southeast toward quaint villages, yellow cornfields of southern Indiana, and fresh air.

I drove past Greencastle, where I had attended DePauw University. Three months ago, one after another, my friends said their goodbyes and set out on their new lives. In 1968, some of them went on the campaign trail with their respective candidates—Kennedy, McCarthy, or Rockefeller—while others, later that summer, drove to Chicago to protest the war at the Democratic convention.

Paul, the most politically active of my friends, had been beaten and arrested in Chicago. My father suspected he was a communist. "How come your friend," he'd ask, "is involved with those radicals?" I didn't explain because to do so, I'd have to admit I wished I were with him. Another "what if." I wanted to be on the streets with Paul. But if I had, my father would have cut me off. I couldn't do that.

After the convention, Paul and I sat at the terminal at O'Hare to wait for his plane. His eyes, both blackened like he'd been pounded for fifteen rounds, scared me. It wasn't their yellowish-purple hue. It was the look in them. They appeared wild, dangerous, as if he might be attacked at any moment.

While we were waiting for his flight back to New York, he kept folding and unfolding his hands and glancing in front of and behind him as if he expected someone to accost him and take him away.

"You don't know what it was like," he said. "The cops came at us, a phalanx of them, moving without a word—all you could hear were their boots—so at first, we didn't know what to think. They kept marching at us.

No expression on their faces. Just doing their job. Maybe they were just going to herd us down the street, we thought, block us off, keep us from the convention."

At first, he spoke softly, looking around to ensure no one overheard him. He tapped me on the arm. His voice became more strident, frightened.

"But without warning, they charged at us—steel-toed boots and clubs in hand—hitting, kicking, and bashing. There was no escape. I kept thinking, 'Is this America?' and it wouldn't stop. It seemed like they wanted to kill us, like we were the enemy. Like we were Vietcong. A man with a club raised his arm. I ducked my head—you know, duck-and-cover—but it was no use. He swung his baton at me. I thought I was gonna die."

I put my hand on his shoulder, but he pulled it back, wincing. "Don't. It hurts."

"I'm sorry," I said.

"Sorry," he laughed. "Sorry? Hey. Fuck that, man. *Get mad.*"

"Mad?" I said, querulously.

"Damn right. This is a fuckin' revolution. We *need* to fight back. They don't care. No one cares. It's fucked up. Totally fucked."

His face flushed, his fists clenched, and his jaw gripped tightly; he seemed as if at any moment, he might explode.

"Paul, it's not that bad," I said. "It's *really* not that bad."

I knew I'd said the wrong thing the minute the words came out of my mouth. They were words my mother would say to mollify me when I'd get banged up at football practice.

Paul winced as if he'd been slapped, stood up, and shouted, "Bullshit! You don't know. How can you say that when you sat in your daddy's plush house watching TV? It's not the same. You *don't* understand how it is."

"Maybe I—"

"I met Black Panthers—you know who they are?"

"Of course, Huey Newton and—"

"Not really, but anyway, the Chicago police are harassing them. Fred Hampton, their chairman, wants to form a Rainbow Coalition to support the revolution. He's a good man—really good. Charismatic. He wants food and education for the poor. And the pigs beat them. Death threats. It's madness. You don't know," he said, staring at me.

"Maybe I don't."

"You don't. Trust me. You don't have a clue." His voice pitched higher. "It's so FUCKED UP." He slammed his fist into a pillar.

A couple sitting near us frowned and pulled back. The husband shielded his wife from Paul, who glared at them.

"Dumb fuckin' bastards," he muttered.

I grabbed his arm. "Let's take a walk."

"Get your fuckin' hands off me," he sneered between his teeth and lurched back, nearly falling. I had no idea what to say and gazed at the couple apologetically. The man leaned toward the woman, who clutched her purse to her chest. He whispered to her, patting her hand.

An attendant at the airline gate came toward us.

"I better go," I said, stepping a few feet from him. I had to admit that he frightened me, too.

He wiped his hand across his face and gently pummeled his mouth with a loose fist. "Fuck, fuck, fuck." His eyes, lowered but focused on me, glistened. "Don't go!" he said. He reached out to me and pulled me close to him. "Oh, fuck man… I'm…"

"Is there something wrong here?" a petite attendant in a blue uniform asked.

Wordless, we stared at her. With a bright, friendly face and luscious lips, she was quite attractive in the classic way airlines want their employees to look: every hair perfectly in place and shiny cherry lipstick on her lips. I couldn't tell if Paul was impressed or turned off by her. With her tiny blue cap, perched and pinned on top of her puffed-up hair, she looked silly.

I burst out laughing.

"Excuse me?" she said, tilting her head sideways.

"Nothing," I said, putting my hand to my mouth. "No, we're fine." She stood for a moment, her hands clasped in front of her.

"Fine," I repeated, more severely.

She smiled at me again, glanced at Paul, who also grinned and, reacting to her querulous look, ducked his head and shuffled behind the pillar. She walked back to the gate, glancing over her shoulder at us several times.

Leaning against me, his arm around my shoulder, Paul said, "Did you see the hat?"

"Miss Potato Head," I said.

He laughed, and for a moment it seemed the ghastly spell had been broken. His eyes lit up as if someone had flipped a switch. The pall that had been draped over him lifted. He was back to his old self. Then, he squeezed me by the arm so hard it hurt. His face drooped. A mask of terror came across him so suddenly, it felt as if he'd become another person again. His eyes winced; his mouth drew in a thin, taut line. "Shit, man, I'm scared, really scared. I thought they'd kill me, and there was nothing, *nothing* I could do." His eyes were glassy. Tears welled up and leaked over his cheeks. I held him and felt like crying too, crying for not being there with him, crying for not understanding what was happening in Chicago, crying for all the "what ifs" that got in my way, crying for not having enough courage to defy my dad, for being a wimp, for being the good, obedient son.

The attendant announced that boarding was beginning. He sighed and wrapped his arms around me, pulling me close against his body. We embraced for what felt like minutes. The attendant then called for those in need of assistance to go first.

Paul should be, I thought, *among them.*

The couple beside us whispered and shook their heads. I didn't care. I wanted to be there in whatever way I could for him. If that meant holding onto him for as long as he needed me to, that was fine. They could think what they wanted to think. Fags. Queers. To hell with them.

"I'll be in touch," he said. His hand loosely trailed down my arm. "I'll be all right. Don't worry."

"Call," I said.

He nodded and walked down the corridor toward his plane and waved, his arm barely reaching waist high, a grimace gripping his face.

I haven't heard from him since then. Not a word.

And the other classmates?

They retreated into the folds of their families, demands of work, or the hardships of military service. Some left their families just as I was about to leave, heading to places they'd never experienced before. It seemed as if all of us who had lived through the spring and summer of 1968, with the assassinations of Dr. Martin Luther King and Senator Robert Kennedy, all of us who'd seen the country torn apart, we just wanted to slip out of history and hide in untouched niches, burrowing into them like squirrels in winter, sheltered from the cold until the worst was over.

Crossing Over

THE STUDENT ORIENTATION for new Vanderbilt Divinity School students was on Wednesday, the day before I had to attend training for dorm advisors.

Except for stopping for gas and a coffee, I drove straight to Nashville, crossing into Kentucky over the bridge that spanned the Ohio River, where I'd read that slaves tried to cross during the era of slavery to reach free states. As a Yankee, I was entering enemy territory. I'd seen images of hoses slamming students against cement buildings in Birmingham. Freedom riders' buses had been burned with them on board. Voting rights advocates were murdered and buried in an earthen dam.

❧

My only previous experience in the South was a road trip I took with my mom in 1954. We drove to St. Petersburg, Florida, where we spent half a year on vacation paid for by my dad's company. We drove our red Ford station wagon along small roads in Illinois and Indiana that had been traveled long before the interstate highway system was completed. We crossed the Ohio River into Kentucky and the Deep South. But a flood that year damaged many of the main roads in Georgia and Alabama. We made detours, taking country roads, often unpaved. The images of that region were imprinted in my mind: the rundown shacks, the children half-naked in dirt yards, and the chickens in the front yard. The Spanish moss's gray beards hanging from giant oaks. Rusted-out jalopies piled up under trees; houses sagging under the weight of years; windows gaping with white curtains flapping out. People on porches fanned themselves. Red clouds of dust from our car settled on the shrubs, chickens, and people on the porch.

Mother told me to sleep, but I couldn't. This was a strange world with yards so different from mine. Our lawns were mowed, every one of them. Our gardens were well-kept. People stayed inside air-conditioned homes. Nothing seemed out of place. And nothing was.

Mother only stopped at gas stations. Attendants in bib overalls eyed us warily. Even there, she hurried me to the bathrooms, pointing out which to use: 'White only.' Not the one marked 'Colored.' She never talked with anyone—that was completely unlike her; she loved making small talk with clerks, waitresses, and car attendants. Looking back, she seemed frightened, worried that she (or my brother and I) might do something wrong, might break some rule. Too many choices about where to go. Even the drinking fountains had signs above them—"Colored," "White"—not five feet apart.

When I asked her why we couldn't go in a "Colored" bathroom, she snapped, "It's unsanitary." She shooed us to the car and sped off as if she were fleeing a crime scene. I guess she was fleeing from a way of life that she wanted no part of. She had grown up in a small town on Long Island, where there were few, if any, Blacks. Prejudice, if there was any, was never part of her upbringing.

Her fears of the south were greater than I knew, and probably led her to ask me before I left, "Are you *sure* this is right?" I hadn't been in the South since that trip with her, so I wasn't sure myself. But I kept on driving.

By late afternoon, I'd crossed the Tennessee state line. From the ridge above Nashville, I could see its skyline in the river valley. The interstate was built like a rollercoaster carved into the hillside. For several miles, the highway tilted sideways away from the Cumberland River and obscured the view of the city. After a long curve, several buildings, like the tips of fingers, came into view. Below them, on either side of the hill, there were other buildings and shabby houses that lined the riverbank. At the bottom, one bridge spanned the river.

I drove across it onto Gay Street and from there, followed Commercial Street to Route 70 and Broadway toward Vanderbilt University. On either side of it, lining the street, were country music record shops and adult bookstores. Broadway headed up a hill. The farther it was from downtown, the more upscale the buildings became, and before long, the verdant campus of Vanderbilt University sprawled across a hillside.

Once parked, I raced to the admission building before it closed for the day. It was brutally hot. Sweat drenched my shirt.

The looming façade of the Divinity School, the campus with its brick dorms and academic buildings, as well as the statue of whiskered Cornelius Vanderbilt, hit me with a realization: this was my new life, my new home.

A stout lady with a distinct southern accent helped me. "Here you are, my dear," she said. "My, get yourself some water. It's horrid out there."

I thanked her for the packet and looked up at the paintings of deans in their ministerial robes. I had no plans to become a minister. Religion in my family was reserved for special occasions: Easter and the Christmas Eve candlelight service. Mom loved the candles.

As a rule, if the call of golf was weighed against the call of God on a Sunday morning, we'd be on the first tee. I had no religion, no interest in the church, and no real faith in God.

I worried about my lack of faith. What if some believers or professors exposed me as a fake? Or, even worse, if they wanted to convert me? Sure, I could say I was an atheist, which might make them pause. And it was true. God never interested me. I couldn't understand the idea of God, a being who's out there, hovering, invisible, hearing everything we say, knowing everything we do, but when push comes to shove, isn't really there. I wanted to ask people who believed in Him, "What's He like?" Maybe they would know: "What does he tell you?" "How did you get introduced?"

But, maybe, as a divinity student, you weren't expected to believe in God. It wasn't like signing a loyalty pledge, as you had to do when enlisting in the army. Besides, there might be others like me—ones who came to graduate school to avoid the draft and are not bent on making a career out of it.

My other "what if" hit me as I looked at the book lists for my classes. What if the workload crushed me? I'd have to head back to Illinois, my tail between my legs, to face enlistment and serve in a war, maybe end up like Duffy, stuffed in a body bag, awaiting a flight back to Glen Ellyn for burial.

With packet and keys in hand, I headed to the Bishop dorm complex. The walkway to the dorm was festooned with magnolia trees. Their blossoms were the size of soccer balls. I lugged my books, record player, and clothing up to a small third-floor dorm room.

I unlocked the door—thick, blond, heavy. It swung open. Three feet from it, a couch jutted out into the room. A bed at night. Across from it, there was a closet with three wire hangers. Next to it, inserted in the wall, a desk. By it, a cabinet with five drawers. It, too, was built into the wall. Above it, a counter with a mirror. Facing the door, a window revealed an expansive lawn and, beyond it, the law school. Five hundred yards from it, the Divinity School.

My books on shelves, clothes in drawers, jackets on hangers, this space was now mine.

I played Simon and Garfunkel's new album Bridge over Troubled Water. Dizzy from the long drive, I sipped a Coke, put my feet up on the couch, stared at the clouds, seemingly unhurried, steaming across the sky. Simon and Garfunkel sang.

When you're weary feeling small
When tears are in your eyes, I will dry them all
I'm on your side when times get rough
And friends just can't be found like a bridge over troubled water

I'd crossed two rivers into this new life. I had no friends. I'd left my old self, or parts of it, behind. My whole body, from my neck to my feet, felt sad.

I thought of Tom, a fraternity buddy, who, along with his boyfriend Tim, was working with the Rockefeller campaign. They had moved to Greenwich Village. Tom had told me he was gay. It scared me. For all the years I'd known him, I thought I was the odd one with strange desires. I never told him, not even when he told me about his boyfriend, how I felt attracted to him. I wasn't about to let it show, because I had an image to maintain, and it was the only one I knew: the straight guy. And maybe I was straight. The more I thought about it, the longer I pretended to be what I wanted to be, the more it seemed to be true. Or, if not true, at least something I could accept in myself.

Tom told me Paul had joined an antiwar group—not sure of its name—and organized protests at Nixon's and Humphrey's rallies. True to his word, a revolutionary.

My room, the size of my mother's walk-in closet, was small, but it was mine. My carefree days at Depauw with old friends, when I could get up whenever I wanted and stay out as late as I pleased, were gone. The record kept playing. The window was open. A breeze came in and brushed against my face.

❧

The retreat for new students was held at a church camp in the woods, approximately ten miles from the campus.

New arrivals were to register at a lodge. When we entered, a perfumed lady at a table asked my name; I gave it, and she smiled and said in a thick southern accent, "Mr. Follett, yes, here it is, honey." She handed me a packet and told me to fill out a name tag. I milled around and surveyed what others were doing.

Some headed to a table with sodas on ice. Some sat in folding chairs, packet in hand, perusing it. Some greeted the faculty, who mingled among us, asking our names and where we were from. *Illinois, yes, I know it well.*

Soon, as more arrived, the volubility in the room increased. Groups of two or three broke apart and came together and talked of nothing of substance, nothing of interest, nothing at all. I met a short fellow from Tennessee, a Baptist, *Southern Baptist*, who wanted to know my church affiliation. He pointed to a guy from California, a hippie, who seemed to be stoned. He told me a girl he met from New Jersey was a revolutionary. Groups gathered and dispersed. *Excuse me, I need to talk with*… or *I think I'll get a soda.*

I sat in a chair by a window, watching them mix drinks instead of doing what I should be doing—socializing, introducing myself to others—but, happily, what I stopped doing years ago when I got tired of my parents' high society and the emptiness of small talk at cocktail parties. I waited for someone to tell the others, who were mingling, to stop, take their seats, and for the program to start.

The trees had the faintest yellow tinge, well behind the maples in Illinois.

Several long-haired hippies with beads in their hair, wearing purple vests and sandals, looked remarkably like Jesus. They regarded me cautiously. I was dressed in Docker slacks with an orange golf shirt and a blue sweater, looking as if I were about to tee off for a round of golf. One hippie asked if I needed a caddy.

I said, "Our tee off time is in fifteen minutes. Hope you can join us."

Professors wore turtlenecks and brown sports jackets. Most had pipes that they puffed on with a sophisticated air. Students gathered around the smoke like it contained an intellectual secret.

Would-be preachers in suits and ties acted as if they were on a political campaign, shaking everyone's hand. Several noticed me in the back and came over. One grabbed my hand and asked if I was a Baptist. I said, "No. I'm an atheist." He smiled wider. His teeth showed. He said, "Oh," and made small talk, hoping, I suspected, to find out what an atheist was like. Then, he noticed someone else in a suit and tie and excused himself.

Ivy Leaguers with buttoned-down Oxford shirts, fancy slacks, sweaters tied around their necks, and loafers (no socks) circled together, mostly hanging around with the professors. They even smoked the same types of pipes.

One guy, handsome with long brown hair that kept falling into his eyes, so he had to brush it back, was talking with a professor. He cupped a pipe in his palm. He looked at me with a slow-to-form grin that crept up one side of his mouth and then spread into a smile. He had an easygoing charm. His marble-blue eyes kept focused on me. He sidled over to where I was sitting and took a seat beside me.

"I'm Bob," he said.

I laughed. "I can't believe it. That's my name too."

His brow furrowed. "Really?"

"No, not even close. Name's Jason," I said.

"Oh, the one who's after the golden fleece," he said, appraising me from head to toe.

"I prefer brunettes," I said.

He laughed. "I think we'll get along, Jason. I *must* find out where you are living."

"Bishop Hall, third floor. Room 15."

"A dormy. That's cool," he said. Taking me by the arm, he pulled me aside, away from the crowd. "Most of these guys are so damn serious about religion. I mean, have you met any of them? It's like they believe all that bunk in the Bible and I…"

I interrupted him. "We are going to get along. This whole thing grosses me out."

"Hey, wait. It's not all bad. There are a few cool dudes here. Very cool. Wait until you hear Reverend Lawson. He'll shake up some of these religious types."

A professor tapped him on the shoulder and whispered something in his ear. "Gotta go," he said. "Master of ceremonies thing."

He conferred with several professors and the Dean of the Divinity School.

While he was talking with them, I noticed that the few women students kept to themselves. One had plain brown hair and big black glasses, dressed in black slacks that were quite wrinkled, as if her appearance was incidental to her. She seemed to be the one person who was entirely herself. Her jaw moved back and forth. She squinted at the crowd as if assessing whether any of them were worth a moment of her time. I smiled at her, but she turned away and walked to a seat on the other side of the room.

She opened a book and read, sticking her feet out in front of her.

I could relate. I wasn't sure if I belonged or wanted to belong. Whatever self I had always escaped me in these gatherings. Maybe academia wasn't right for me. Maybe Mom's worries were justified. Maybe the Divinity School was a bad choice.

❧

After the Dean welcomed us, Bob emphasized the importance of the class of 1968 in keeping the civil rights movement at the forefront of everything we did. Reverend James Lawson spoke in a gentle, deliberate manner about the Divinity School's involvement in the 1960s sit-ins at Woolworth, S.H. Kress, and McLellan Department Stores. Students at lunch counters were beaten and bloodied, but they persisted. He argued that Christians are called to reach out to those who are oppressed. This remains a core principle of the Christian tradition.

Next, Don Biesswenger, a professor responsible for community outreach and field experience, told us that each of us would participate in "The Plunge." Its goal was to teach us about the underprivileged in Nashville and to give us a brief understanding of poverty and disenfranchisement. "The Plunge" was what Reverend Lawson had mentioned: a way to be engaged, to reach out to the oppressed, and to develop some empathy, brief as it was, for their situation.

Biesswenger, a short, stocky man with salt-and-pepper hair, asked if we had any questions or comments. Several students stood up and applauded this idea, but one student took a more critical stance.

"I don't think we need to be on the streets to understand poverty," a tall, red-haired student said. "I've come from poverty, and I tell you this: I'm not going back." His voice had a snarly edge to it, like a chainsaw—the same kind of voice I heard from high school teachers that would stop a student in his tracks. Dressed in a blue suit and red tie, he boasted that he'd earned a Ph.D. in anthropology. He scanned the room to see if anyone would challenge him. He'd caught the instructor off guard and enjoyed doing it.

I immediately disliked him, but I didn't confront him. The scrubby girl I'd seen earlier jumped right in. "Hey, Mister Ph.D., why don't you just sit down and listen to what the man has to say? Stop bemoaning what's going on before you even know what's going on."

The redhead turned sharply and barked, "Why don't you learn how to dress?" There was a smattering of chuckles.

She didn't miss a beat. "I'll do that, carrot head, when you learn to shut your mouth."

A hush fell over the room. Professor Beisswenger hesitated, bit his lower lip, and took a slow inhale before pointing directly at Carrot Head and calling him by name. "Jack, I understand your resistance," he said. "But this isn't about going back. It's about diving into Nashville right now and seeing what it's like on the streets when you only have your resourcefulness to get you through. It's not about your past. It's about September 1968."

Not willing to give in, Jack argued that it truly was about his past and an insult to him and how far he'd come. He finally relented and agreed to give it a try, but he wasn't happy about it.

Professor Beisswenger said, "Good. You don't need to like it," and the meeting ended.

Jack grumbled about it throughout dinner, complaining to anyone who could hear him (and most people could).

❧

After dinner, I sat on a chair at one end of the porch. At the other end, Jack kept up his argument like a skilled orator, one point stretching out as he kneaded and spread it until it dominated every other conversation, leaving him and his disgruntlement as the only topics of discussion.

I sat with Professor James Herd, who introduced himself and, to my surprise, informed me that he would be my advisor. We sat with the woman in the wrinkled clothes and with a second-year transfer student, Dick Schmidt.

From where we sat, the dense woods lined a lake like a frame of a painting, except for a narrow crack in the frame where a path led to it.

Dick muttered, "I could use a drink." Dr. Herd echoed his sentiments. I agreed.

To my surprise, the woman, who introduced herself as Penny, said, "There's a good bar several miles back." We plotted how to disguise the liquor; the retreat was supposed to be chemical-free. Penny said that she could buy some Coke, empty most of it, and mix in the bourbon. Did we mind Jack Daniels?

"Anyone want to ride along?" she asked.

I volunteered. She drove an old Volkswagen Beetle, faded blue, the back seat stuffed with books and clothing.

"Where you from?" she asked.

I told her and asked her where she came from. "Oh, shit, from all over. My dad was a career military man. Army brat. I can't call anywhere home."

She drove down a road that twisted like the laces in a shoe and finally unraveled on a ridge. She took curves like a driver at the Indianapolis 500, downshifting as she came in and shoving it into high gear as she came out. The car slid. I held on to the door. She laughed. "Not to worry, I know this road."

She slammed on the brakes, shoved open her door, and strode purposefully to the bar, clearly familiar territory to her. She pulled a six-pack of Coke from the cooler and went up to the bar. "Hey, Rocco, give me black," she said, slapping a twenty on the bar.

"Sure, Penny," the bartender said and reached under the counter.

She was no-nonsense. Her face didn't look feminine at all, but didn't look masculine either. It was pudgy. Her hair fell over her head as if it was poured from a bucket; she walked like a man with a long stride, her arms thrust out in front of her.

On the way back, she told me she wasn't a fan of the military, nor, for that matter, was she a fan of religion. Her father was drunk primarily. She came to Vanderbilt because of the faculty's commitment to activism. She wanted to be a journalist, but she also enjoyed studying theology and was passionate about the civil rights movement. She appreciated how the faculty invited students to call them by their first names and were actively involved in organizing civil rights protests.

My undergraduate professors maintained their professional distance and adhered to the academic rules. They saw themselves as experts, while the students saw themselves as novices. Professor Herd blatantly violated these old rules, wanting to drink with us when drinking was prohibited. I told her I was surprised by his willingness to break the rules.

"Oh, come off it," she said. "Look at him. He's only maybe 4 or 5 years older than we are. He's a puppy. With that long, stringy hair on his shoulders and wire-rimmed glasses, he's more interested in looking like John Lennon than a university professor. He wants to enjoy life. Fuck authority. He's more like us than those older codgers who are supposed to be his peers."

❧

When we came back with the liquor, we all sat on the porch swigging our bourbon and Cokes, our feet on the railing and our drinks rapidly unscrewing our heads. The atmosphere had a sour mash tint to it. Penny grew quiet and slugged down one can, then another.

I asked Professor Herd what he studied. "Call me Jim," he said. He worked with the Lakota Indians, researched their rituals, and their connection to the earth. He expounded on some of their practices. He went on and on.

My mind drifted.

A silver-haired gentleman came over to him and whispered in his ear. Disappointment spread across Jim's face. A meeting of the faculty. He pulled out a little aerosol container and sprayed it twice in his mouth, and set his Coke on the railing.

"Save it for later." He straightened himself up and shook out his hair.

Penny scrutinized him. "He's a pompous ass," she said after he left.

"I think he's nice," I countered.

"You would," she said, and took another can, opened it, poured out some of its contents, and refilled it with Jack Daniels. "To the good life," she said and took a swig. "I'm going for a walk." She headed into the woods, following a path that quickly swallowed her in the dark.

Dick and I were left on the porch.

"She's quite a character," he said.

"Yeah, but I like her."

"Don't get me wrong, so do I."

He informed me that he was an Episcopalian and came from Louisville and, just this last year, was married. His words, honey-coated, drew out his "O"s and "A"s in a lovely southern accent. His mind was sharp, his wit quick. He scoffed at Jack and his pretensions.

"Jack has an attitude a mile long," he said. "Being close to God for him is proportionally correlated to the level of income. Salvation has more to do with a triple-digit income than God. I suspect that for God, if He values income, it's not the dollar and cents worth, but the sense worth."

"Jack got shortchanged when it came to sense," I said.

Dick told me that he'd like to have me over for dinner. His wife made a mean roast beef. I got his telephone number.

❧

Later, Penny was sitting on the back step looking at the moon that was perched on top of the pines.

"Pretty," I said.

"Yeah. But I'm not the romantic type. It's just the moon. It's there almost every night and is going to continue to be there no matter what we do," she said, shrugging her shoulders.

"I suppose. But it's still pretty."

"'Pretty'—that's a word I hate."

"Why?"

"Do you pay attention to anything?"

"Yep, I think I do."

"Well, buddy, take a good look at me."

I didn't know what to say, so I shook my Coke to see how much was left in it.

"No need to respond," she said. "I'm used to being who I am."

"I like that," I said.

"Good," she chuckled. "Are you sure? 'Cause that's all you're going to get."

"I'm sure."

"Well, handsome, that's a surprise. But I'll take it." She reached over and shook my hand. "It's not often a guy like you just takes me at face value, especially with a face like mine!"

I laughed. She did too. She gave me her telephone number. "Call sometime," she said. "Friends is all. A deal?"

"Sure," I said. She leaned forward, snugged her chest into her knees, pressed her head between her knees, sighed, rocked back and forth as if in a trance, pulled herself into a tight knot, was totally absorbed, and then stood up. "See ya'." She clinked her Coke against mine and headed to her room.

A deep darkness drew over the porch. Crickets chirped. I sipped on my drink. I wasn't good at sleeping in dorms. If another guy moaned, I woke. My radar was tuned in to any movement, any sense that maybe another guy was aroused. I leaned back in the chair, curled up, and dozed.

"What're you doing?"

"Huh?" I said, startled from sleep.

"What're you doing out here?" Bob, the preppy guy I'd met earlier, asked.

He sat next to me.

"Thinking."

"This time of night?"

"Not really. Little drunk is all."

"Really!?" he said, leaning toward me. "Have any left?"

"Sure," I said and sat up. I offered him Herd's leftover can. "Here."

Bob sipped from it. "Nice. Perfect. I could get to like a guy like you." He patted me on the shoulder. We talked as he finished the can. He came from the East Coast for the same reason as Penny: to be where the action was. He'd been involved in Eugene McCarthy's campaign right up to the Democratic Convention.

He asked about me, and I told him that I, too, had been involved with the campaign.

The moon, veiled behind the mist, rose over the pines and cast a milky glow across the porch.

The soft features of Bob's face, his heavy eyebrows and strong jaw, his squinty eyes, and long wavy hair reminded me of the wayward look of the actor James Dean. He leaned close to me as we spoke. His voice, calm and assured, made me feel at ease. He scribbled his phone number on a card. "Once classes get started," he said, "call me."

We found separate bunks at the dorm, shed our clothes, and curled up under the sheets.

The moon had the rest of the night to itself.

The Plunge

ON THURSDAY, THE orientation for dorm advisors outlined my job responsibilities: monitoring activity in the halls, reporting disruptive behavior, providing support for students with personal or academic issues, and being on duty at specific hours.

❧

Friday morning, Dr. Beisswenger, who asked us to call him "Don," explained the logistics of "The Plunge." It would last three days and two nights. We would return at noon on Sunday for a debriefing.

Jack scowled through most of the session. It didn't deter Don. "Most of our lives," he said, "we have props that we rely on to give us a sense of who we are. Just look at your wallet or purse. You have identification cards with a street address and photographs. That's one kind of identification. But we have others. The clothes we wear reveal a great deal about our social status to others. Look around the room at the other students. Some wear coats and ties and have shiny shoes. "Some"—he laughed— "already look as if they'd been on the street for days, and some look as if they're about to play a round of golf." He smiled at me. His eyes glanced over at Jack. He wore a new dark blue blazer, a white shirt, and a matching blue-and-red tie. "Well, what if you didn't have those props? What if you had no place for a few nights to call your own? No place where you really belonged? How would you find your way? Would you lose your identity? Many people, for no fault of their own, live such lives. Many people live hand to mouth right here in Nashville. They are called the dispossessed. We want you, in a small way, to experience what it may be like for them and see how such an experience, however short, might change your way of thinking about your ministry and who you minister to. Do you focus on the well-to-do or do you reach out to those who, because of racism, family violence, alcoholism, or poverty, have been cast aside?"

Jack raised his hand, "Are you saying these clothes?"—he pulled on his blue blazer— "Are props?"

"Yes, to some extent, yes, they are. They're what we wear to signal that we're of a particular class and have a certain social standing."

"I don't see it that way. To me, they are more a sign of who I am and part of who I am."

"That's the point, Jack," Don said. "We're asking you to consider what it's like *not* being as you are and seeing what it's like to be like someone else."

"I don't want to be like anyone else. I'm happy with who I am."

"Fine."

"It's not fine," Jack continued. His voice rose. "Are you saying we have to wear street clothes?"

"No, Jack. You can wear your suit and tie, if that's what you want to do. But it might be uncomfortable for you. You might want to dress more comfortably."

"I'm perfectly comfortable in a suit."

"Then wear it."

"I'm sure you will," Penny observed. "And you'll probably have it pressed and cleaned every day."

"And I'm sure, by the way you dress, you'll be quite at home on the streets," he sneered.

"At least I'll be at home somewhere."

"Bitch!" Jack snarled and rose out of his seat.

Don took four quick steps across the room, took Jack by the arm, and said, "That's enough! Have a seat, Jack. We'll discuss your concerns in private, later." He patted his arm and whispered something in his ear. Jack nodded, gave a glance at Penny, and bowed his head, staring at the books piled on his desk.

With Jack quiet, Don told us to dress in warm clothing. We would be given $5.00 and our driver's license, along with a phone number to call in case of an emergency. We would each have a small journal—he passed them out—to record our thoughts and observations. For two nights, we'd roam Nashville, find out what makes the city tick, and learn what it's like when we didn't have money, when we must make do, and when we have to live off the streets.

Jack asked, "Is the $5.00 all we have to subsist on for those two nights?"

"That's right."

"What if we want to earn more?"

"Your choice, Jack. Whatever you need to do. But, as I said, that's not the purpose of 'The Plunge.' It's for you to allow yourself to experience what it is like to be one of the have-nots."

Jack grimaced and was about to say something else, but glanced around the room at the faces of the other students and decided not to.

"Can we go now?" he asked.

"No, not now," Don said. "You'll be dropped off in different parts of the city. That's part of the project: to see how your experience differs based on who you met and where you were, and, before you go on the street, to make sure you're not in any unsafe areas, but you know where they are and keep away from them. So, please bring some warm clothing, decide on your outfit, and arrive here by noon. We'll have a meal together and you'll be off."

I put $5.00 in my front right pocket, headed back to the dorm, changed out of my golf shirt, and put on a more casual pullover and jeans. I grabbed a heavy jacket and a wool hat. The news had predicted a cold night.

Lunch felt eerily like a meal before marching onto a battlefield.

First Nights

TWO UPPERCLASSMEN, one of whom was African American, introduced themselves to me, drove me around the city, and advised me to stay away from the lower south end of the city at night.

"That's no place for a white guy after dark," the Black man said. "Believe me. It's rough. I wouldn't be caught dead there."

"Dead," I joked. "Not a good word."

"It's not funny." He turned in his seat to look at me. "I'm serious. Be safe, man. Stay as far from there as you can."

They pulled next to a curb. "This is the historic district. But don't be fooled," the white guy said. "It can be rough. A student from my class got confronted here by a guy and had to run for it. But during the day, it's fine and it'll give you a chance to check out the music district and the Ole Opry"—he pointed across the street—"and if you get in trouble, get to a phone booth and call. We'll be on call 24/7 to help if necessary."

I crossed the street to explore the Grand Ole Opry, the Carnegie Hall of country music. For such a historic building, it wasn't elegant at all. It was a brick structure that peaked three stories up, giving the appearance of a church without a steeple. I wandered around it and pulled on its imposing wooden front door. Locked. I browsed in several country music stores down the street, unsure of what I was doing since I had never listened to country music before. I peeked into the adult bookstores that looked like the ones in Chicago. Same dimly lit rooms with shelves of magazines and an entrance to peep shows for twenty-five cents. I wasn't going to risk getting caught there, not my third night in Nashville. I went up a steep hill to the state capitol, a white building with a circular dome, surrounded by a marble tiered promenade with gardens, its late-fall mums in bloom.

This apex of the city was quite lovely, with a view in all four directions: across the valley to the other side of the river, where the interstate strung along the river south, to the Black district snug by the river, to the university up on a ridge, and to barn-like structures near a railroad yard by the tracks that crossed the river by another bridge.

The bridge over the Cumberland River was a good location to see the city from below. I'd never stood on such a large bridge over a wide river. I ambled down one street, crossed another, and found a narrow, metal walkway on one side of the river.

The murky Cumberland River surged under the stanchions of the Woodland Street Bridge. Cars roared by me. The deck beneath my feet shuddered. A gust of wind lashed at me. Cars were headed somewhere: to work, home, or dinner. The river, too, had a destination. It meandered westerly through forest and fields, in and out of valleys, to the Ohio River and, eventually, to the Mississippi River and south to the Gulf. I had nowhere to go and nothing to do. Several massive trucks rushed by. The bridge groaned. A cold wind swept under the girders. I steadied myself and grasped the railing with two hands.

I needed to go back to my room, put on a record, and relax.

That's when it struck me: I couldn't go back to my room. I stared at the river; its current roiled and twisted far below me. "Plunge" came to mind. How many people had stood where I stood and jumped? Perhaps they'd given up, had no place to go, lost love, been forsaken. From such a height, they'd never survive.

This wasn't the place I wanted to be. With my hands on the railing, I sidestepped until I got to the end and sprinted toward downtown, putting as much distance between me and the bridge as I could.

It was getting toward dusk. I had no idea what to do. If I were home, I'd turn on the TV. If hungry, I'd open the fridge. No asking. If sleepy, go to bed. Everything was there. This was different. What would I eat? I had money for one meal, at best. Maybe even a candy bar or soft drink. After that, I'd have to fend for myself. Where to go? What to do? Where to sleep? No car to drive. The words of my mother came back to me: "Are you sure this is right for you?" If she were here, parked by the curb in her Lincoln, I'd have said, "No, it's not right." I'd slip into the front seat, and we'd drive away. We'd stay in the Best Western motel. Everything would be all right.

❧

The heavy lid of night was closing more quickly than I had anticipated. I needed to find a place to eat. But I'd had a good lunch. I could wait until the next day to get a meal. On Sunday, I would eat when I returned to school.

For several hours, people went by me as if I were invisible. They were assured of where they were headed, their eyes intently focused ahead of them. Other people who seemed lost muddled along, hands in pockets, caught in the grip of the night.

I, too, was caught up in forces beyond my control. Scraps of headlines from *The Nashville Tennessean* hailed the rising national polls for Richard Nixon. I thought about Bobby Kennedy, the morning after he was shot, how I'd heard it on the radio and briefly wondered if it was a repeat of the announcement of John F. Kennedy's assassination. They kept saying, "Kennedy was shot." Then, I heard his first name, "Robert." I pulled off the road and cried. Something was wrong with our country.

A man in a frayed suit and scuffed-up shoes interrupted my reverie. "Got any change?" he asked.

I looked up at him. Any change? I reached into my pocket. "No," I said. "I'm short, too."

"God bless," he said and passed on. He headed toward the railroad tracks.

I followed him, past the commercial district, toward the buildings by the tracks.

On one side of the street, off an alley, a barn with cows and horses in stalls smelled of manure. Warmth radiated through the slats. From the stalls, the eyes of horses, large and translucent, glared at me. In an empty stall, there was straw to bed down in.

I slipped through a slat and pushed the straw into a pile, nestled in, and dozed. I woke to the voices of several men twenty feet away. I listened to their muttering. A police car passed by slowly and stopped, its spotlight flashing. Its long light licked against the boards over my head. Too many people were too close to me. My hands shook. I traced my fingers over my face. My skin was drawn taut against my cheekbones.

I crawled back to the opening. My right hand sank into something soft and sticky like Elmer's glue. As I pulled it out, something oozed through my fingers—horse manure. I rubbed my hand on the straw, scrubbed it right and left, and splayed out my fingers to wipe it off. I sat back on my heels. I smelled like shit. Perfect.

The police car passed by again, its light darting back and forth. I ducked and I hurried up the alley and walked toward the Grand Ole Opry. I searched for a piece of paper to wipe the manure from my fingers. Nothing seemed to be going right. I had no sense of what to do next, and I wanted someone I could talk to, ask if there was any shelter or someplace to go.

A few people were on the street. A faint light came from offices in the tall buildings. Night workers cleaning up the day's mess. A few taverns opened. Young couples, arm in arm, went in.

Cold, as if poured from a funnel, descended into the river valley.

I shivered and rubbed my hands back and forth. I didn't bring gloves. Stupid. Stupid. I couldn't put my hands in my pockets. I found a cast-off Opry program and used it to scrape off the manure. I spit on one corner to wipe my hand clean. The smell, however, didn't go away.

Past the Opry, a brick building down an alley had a metal fire escape dangling from the first tier. I jumped, pulled myself up, and climbed the six stories to the top.

From the edge of the flat roof, I could look down on the city: Broadway ran up toward Vanderbilt, and, in the other direction, the Cumberland River wound around the city like a grungy scarf. Beyond the city lights, the hills flickered with suburban homes. I nestled against the interior wall, pulled my coat over my head, folded my knees into my chest, and tried to sleep. The roof was uneven. The tarred surface rippled like hardened lava ridges. I nestled my arms under my head. My shoulder soon became sore, so I turned over, scrunched my knees up, and put my head in my hands.

A few clouds slipped by another building. Above it, dim stars blinked at me. I'd never just looked at a night sky, at how serene and contained it was, its blackness as impassive and inviting as a pool of dark water, unhurried. My legs shivered uncontrollably. Spurts of chilly air nipped my face. I tossed one way, then another, back and forth, slipping into a sleep, then waking, then back to sleep, waiting for a hint of dawn.

The next morning, I wandered up and down seven streets (I counted them to occupy my mind). I came to a desolate neighborhood. Many homes were abandoned, the windows shattered, as if hit by a bomb. On the crest of one hill was a small grocery, Loretta's Place, with a deli and a picnic table outside. With five dollars and another twenty-eight hours on the street, I wanted to get something to eat. I ordered a tuna sub and a carton of orange juice and went outside to the picnic table to eat.

An older African American man, lean, with a partially graying beard, sat at the far end of the table. He wore a gray jacket with torn sleeves and woolen trousers. A winter cap, pulled down over his forehead at a rakish angle, gave him the appearance of a hustler. He didn't make eye contact.

I asked, "Could I join you?"

"Fine," he said and scooted to one side of the table.

"How are you doing?" I asked.

"Me? I'm fine. You?" He looked at my sub. I offered him part of it.

"No, no. That's for you," he said. "Eminent domain." He raised his large hand in a circle like a preacher blessing his congregation. The skin on the underside of his hand was chalky white.

I insisted and ripped the sub in half, passing him half.

He ate it and asked where I was from. Not wanting to disclose that I was in the Divinity School, I made up a story about how I'd been against the war and my dad had thrown me out, and I'd come to Nashville hunting for work.

He nodded his head in sympathy and admitted that he was also out of work. "Rough times, these are," he said. "I used to have a good job. I worked in a parts factory here in town. But it closed several months back, and I'm still looking, still looking." His eyes drifted down to the city below us.

We talked for some time. He told me how he grew up in Nashville, where his dad worked in the stockyards, and how they owned a lovely house overlooking the river. But when they built the new interstate, they took the house, "eminent domain," they called it, but he thought it was stealing. Just outright stealing. His dad, who'd built the house, never recovered from losing it. He died and left his mother on her own. She got cancer, "the liver, bad case." She died a year later.

He offered me a cigarette, but I said no. I had to move on and check on some jobs. He stood, thanked me for the sandwich, and shook my hand with a firm grip that swallowed mine. He held onto my hand and said, "You take care, ya hear? And don't let your daddy get you down. A kid like you is gonna do fine—no doubt about it. You'll end up fine. Trust me."

I knew he was right. I may not have liked being on The Plunge, but I had it made. Being on the street was not my fate.

He was only the fourth Black man that I'd met. I lived in a bubble of white people who never thought about race. Never had to. No one called me "cracker." No one mentioned my color. Race was a subject we discussed when we talked about other people.

But for the man who'd lost his job, race—the color of his skin—was not incidental to who he was, but something that led some people to hate him, to fire him from a job, and possibly to assassinate him. He had to pay attention to it because his life depended on it.

All morning and well into the afternoon, I wandered the streets like a somnambulist. My shoes felt as if they were caked in cement. Up one street, down the other, walking.

Shoppers came and went in and out of stores. Consumers did what they were supposed to do: spend money on the luncheon specials, on the latest LP, and on the discounts at the department stores.

I always had cash in my pocket. If I wanted something, I could get it. Not now. I was cut off, irrelevant. Ostracized. I saw what distressed Jack: I was no longer who I thought I was. He was telling the truth in a way. He already knew something I was finding out: that self-worth and identity in our society were based on the ability to consume. That's how he belonged: a capable cog in the wheel, one who could do what he wanted, buy what he liked when he wanted to, and dress to play the part, to look successful.

I spent the day like a man waiting for his paycheck. I noted the department stores, restaurants, bookstores, and movie theaters where I could patronize once my wallet was back in my pocket. A crowded department store, with clothing on racks, and a cafeteria filled with the smells of hamburgers and fries reminded me of the life I was used to.

By late afternoon, I meandered up Broadway toward Vanderbilt, filling in time, making do. I had time to think. I realized that for much of my life, I had been bent on becoming someone important—making grades, competing on a team, earning a degree, finding a job, achieving success, proving myself, and being liked. Without something to do, I was lost. I sat on the curb and counted the cars. Two hundred came by in an hour, more leaving than coming into town.

"What are you doing?" a voice asked.

I looked up. Dick, a divinity student I'd met at the retreat, stood over me. "Counting cars."

"That sounds like fun."

"Don't bet on it. I'm bored, really bored."

He sat next to me and pulled out his pockets. He'd run out of money, too.

Broke. There were twenty-two hours left on The Plunge.

"What are you planning to do tonight?" he asked.

"Go back to where I was last night," I said.

"Any good?"

"Froze my ass off. You have a decent place?"

"It smelled but was warm," he said and, taking a whiff of me, added, "You smell like you've been in the same place."

We strolled back to town and noticed a small liquor store on a side street.

"Be nice to have a drink right now," he said.

"Let's do it," I said.

"Do what?"

"Pick some up."

"I have no money," he said.

"So?"

We sat on a bus bench to plan our strategy.

❧

I went in the front door and asked whether they had a type of gin—Gordon's London Dry, the one my parents preferred. Dick went to the back and acted as if he had dropped something, swiped a pint, and started to walk out.

The clerk, a stout man with a double chin, noticed Dick.

He called out, "Hey, bud, can I help you?"

Dick fumbled under his jacket. A pint bottle fell and shattered. Dick sprinted out of the store.

The clerk, more than twenty pounds overweight, dashed after him. He was no match for Dick. I ran alongside the clerk.

When he pulled up short and bent over to catch his breath, I said, "That's too bad."

"Bastard," the clerk said.

"I'll see if I can catch him," I volunteered.

"Don't bother. Happens all the time—no use putting yourself at risk. A friend of mine got knifed trying to be a hero," he said. "But thanks." I shook his hand and walked off in another direction.

When he'd walked fifty paces, he turned and called out. "Hey, buddy, tell your friend to watch it. Police patrol these streets."

I started to reply. Instead, I raised my hand, waved, and jogged as quickly as I could to our meeting place. Based on our plan, I changed directions in case the cops were already on our trail and took a detour through the campus.

Dick greeted me with a frown. "Close call," he said.

"Hurry." I grabbed him by the arm. "The clerk knows." We trotted for several blocks to get as far as we could from the liquor store.

Safely downtown, Dick asked, "How'd he find out?"

"Beats me. Must have put two and two together. Customers probably don't chase thieves."

"Never thought I'd ever do that." He was upset with himself.

"Hey, desperate times," I said. "Come on, we'd better get off the streets in case he called the cops. All we have is a broken bottle for the trouble."

"Don't be so sure." He pulled out a pint of bourbon.

That night, we huddled in a stall Dick had found between the stalls of two huge heifers. Their body heat warmed us as we passed the bottle back and forth. The liquor worked its magic. He put his arm around me—being taller than I was—and told me to get comfortable, to use our body heat to keep warm.

"That's okay," I said. "I'm all right."

"What's wrong? Afraid of a little contact?"

"No, it's just…"

"Just what?" His hand was on my shoulder, gentle, tentative.

"It's weird," I admitted. "Snuggling, you know."

"Better than freezing," he offered.

I snuggled against him, my head on his shoulder, my arms curled up next to my body, my hands between my legs. It felt warmer. The alcohol left me lightheaded, content like a boy under his daddy's arm.

A cow belched. Farted. A police spotlight swept the stalls every few hours.

Other men, incoherently drunk, woke us.

But I felt close to someone. And that felt good.

ॐ

The next day, we wandered, as if caught in a labyrinth, down the same streets by stores with the same lettering on their windows: a jewelry store, a department store, a shoe store, a movie theater. We called them out as we walked by them. We raced up the steep hill to the capital, explored the complex of Roman colonnades, and took in the view from the portico overlooking the park. We rolled down the grassy slopes of the hill, staggered to our feet like drunkards. We noted the different films we wanted to see. Charly, with Cliff Robertson, was supposed to be a good film.

Mid-morning, before we were to report back to school, Dick invited me to meet his wife, Pam, who took one whiff of us and said, "You're pretty ripe. Wash up."

She served us hash browns and a bacon-and-cheese omelet. "Slow down, boys. The food won't run away," she said.

By the time we finished, the clock on their mantel read eleven-thirty.

ॐ

Thirty of us were served a delicious meal by the upperclassmen—fish in almond sauce, heaping mashed potatoes, green beans, and salad. A second hunger overtook Dick and me, and we ate as if we'd been starved.

Afterward, Don asked us to discuss what happened on our nights on the streets. Several admitted that they refused to do it—too afraid—and went back to their dorms. Five guys, including Jack, found work and rented a room. Most stayed on the streets. Dick and I talked about sleeping in odd places—the roof of a building and the barn. We spoke of our loneliness and fear. Our lost identity. That was a common theme.

"What was it like," Don asked, "not having your props, like a wallet with money?"

Jack pounced on the question. "It was stupid," he said. "One damn weekend doesn't amount to anything. People need to live as I did—"

"You're right, Jack," Don interrupted. "But some may have learned something. Let's hear from them."

"But I, for one, don't think they're props," Jack asserted. "We *earned* them. We have a right to them. I'm not giving them up, not for a minute."

"I don't imagine you would," Penny chimed in.

"As if you would know," Jack shot back.

"Penny, please," Don said. "Let Jack finish what he has to say." He swiveled in his chair to face Jack. "For you, are they essential to your definition of who you are?"

"Of course!"

"You've made your point. How about others? Anyone find it liberating?"

"I did," I said. "I realized that I don't have a clue about being a have-not. I never thought that I'd been given a passport to success. Without the props—money in my wallet, a car at my command—I was lost. Strangely, I agree with Jack. I count on them to feel worthy. I've always lived with a purpose, with goals, with things to do, with places to go. I just assumed that was how it was. It's as if I were given a passport to success. I never questioned it. It's sad to say—and that's where I disagree with him because I wish I didn't feel that way—but I do."

"That's because you're some rich kid," Jack interjected.

"No," I countered. "It's not because I'm rich. But I do know that I have never wanted for anything. I bet others in this room can say the same."

Others agreed with me. Bob said that he'd not expected much from The Plunge, but once he couldn't reach for his wallet to pull out a bill, he panicked. He felt embarrassed, or, worse, ashamed. He looked over at me. "Follett has it right. Our identities are tied to our ability to spend, to know we have cash on hand. Without it, we're outsiders. It was no fun. It sucked."

Several Black students joined in, telling how they were familiar with the streets; they'd been there, but found the loss of cash distressing.

Don talked about possessions and being dispossessed, as many of the people on the street were every day. Ours was only an inkling of what it was like for them. He encouraged us to consider how the ministry could reach out to them. Everyone, tired and needing to prepare for classes the next day, thanked Don and went their separate ways.

I walked to my room, cast my clothes in a corner, showered, dried off, pulled back the sheets, slipped into bed, and drifted into a deep sleep.

Undergraduate students arrived on Monday. I milled around the halls, introducing myself and letting them know that my job as dorm advisor was to watch over my floor, keep track of them, note who was chronically out late or seemed out of control, and support or, if need be, reprimand them.

After I called Bob to let him know my schedule, we often had lunch together at the cafeteria. My height, yet with a slighter build, he exuded confidence and invited me to a party on a night I had off as a dorm advisor. He told me to bring a date and suggested I call Ann Stone. A friend of his girlfriend, Ann, was a third-year philosophy student with a preference for older men. I called her and she agreed to go.

Bob lived in a residential duplex, with one side refurbished to make a two-bedroom apartment with a kitchen and a large living room. At the party, I was surprised to see that both students and professors—accompanied by their wives—were present. Many of the professors had been involved in the civil rights movement.

We sat on couches and chairs and sprawled on the floor. We debated about the war. Some contended that President Johnson's Operation Rolling Thunder, a wholesale bombing of North Vietnam, only seemed to strengthen the resolve of the North Vietnamese. The bombing of Hanoi had supposedly killed 185,000 civilians but had cost Americans 900 downed aircraft. Johnson believed such assaults would hasten the end of the war. Herd was skeptical. Bob defended the president. Bob loved the argumentative atmosphere of academia, the rational give-and-take. Yet that didn't last long. After drinking four or more mugs, rationality dissipated into shouts back and forth, but Bob kept his poise, interjecting light-hearted comments to temper the intensity.

At some point, he turned up the music and pulled the chairs and couches back. The room became a wild dance extravaganza, with couples doing the tango and rumba, hopping and jumping across couches and over chairs with complete abandonment. Bob, a terrific dancer, grabbed his date, who, lithe as she was, stuck close to him: her leg, his leg, her body, his body velcroed together.

His parties happened every weekend, and the professors, most of them young, had no compunction about fraternizing with us. When the party wound down, professors stumbled out of the duplex carrying cups of beer, their wives as drunk as they were. Bob and I carried several to their cars.

"It was a great party, one of the all-time best," Herd said. "I'd stay all night, but my damn wife has to teach in the morning."

Once the crowd was gone, Bob turned down the music, putting on Frank Zappa's Mothers of Invention. His free-form improvizations sounded like old times to us. Bob curled up with his girlfriend, Janet, and I nestled next to Ann.

Later, we split into separate bedrooms, where I got to know Ann better.

Bright, taking philosophy courses in metaphysics, and pretty—a girl my parents would approve of—she had long brown hair, parted down the middle, and wore short one-piece dresses. Like silk, her dress felt smooth as a lubricant against my skin. The first night, she shed her dress as if it were an afterthought. With no compunction about making love, already out of her dress, she unbuckled my pants. We held onto one another with no pressing need to make love because we were pleasantly inebriated. We chatted about our childhoods, her horseback riding (she had competed in show jumping events on the West Coast), our fathers and mothers, before giving ourselves over to caresses and making long, uninhibited love, which seemed quite natural to me in ways I'd never expected.

Over the following weeks, I discovered that Ann, a daughter of a pharmacist in Seattle, wanted to get involved in civil rights activities and, as she put it, "to do something with her life." As we lay together one night, I told her about an event that Bob had organized, along with the help of Reverend James Lawson, to march against segregation in a Mississippi town that, despite the Supreme Court's rulings, refused to let blacks shop or be in the central part of town.

Although much of Mississippi had begrudgingly integrated, small pockets of the state remained adamantly segregated. Reverend Lawson selected one of them to test whether, with a large contingency to demonstrate and garner more publicity in support of civil rights, he could force the town to integrate. Protesters came from Nashville in the north, Little Rock in the west, Knoxville in the east, and Jackson in the south—to converge on a small Mississippi town not far from Oxford. The likelihood of success was slim. African Americans who went downtown were arrested, and even worse, quietly disappeared. We were told that it may become violent. It certainly was dangerous.

Bob told us to meet at the Divinity School on Saturday at five AM. I picked Ann up at her dorm, and we arrived to find two buses pulled over by the curb.

❧

Reverend Jim Warren was Lawson's right-hand man. He was a white man who served at the Edgehill Methodist Church, located in the heart of the black community. Warren stood outside the buses, along with 67 students who stood in a circle, waiting to board.

We were told what we needed to do: If someone tried to kick or hit us, cover our heads and pull our knees up to protect our internal organs. On our part, no violence. No name-calling. Stick together, arm in arm. Keep marching from the drop-off area to the town hall.

"Hey, handsome," I heard someone say. It was Penny, who wore a blue baseball cap, her hair pulled back in a ponytail, and bib overalls with a white dress shirt. She grabbed me by the arm. "Did you see who's here?"

"No."

"Mr. Coat-and-tie. Jack himself."

"Really?"

"He just got on the bus."

"I hope he wore deodorant."

Penny laughed. "He probably has a change of clothes."

She eyed Ann. "Who's the girl?"

"It's my friend," I told her and introduced Ann to her.

Penny leaned into me as she was getting on the bus. "Not bad, handsome. You're a quick mover." She swung herself into the aisle, called back, "Later," and slipped into a seat by a nun.

Once we got on the bus, I noticed Jack in his suit and tie sitting at the back. "What's *he* doing here?" I asked Bob.

"Don't let him fool you," Bob said. "He's an activist. Has been one for a long time."

"You're kidding."

"No, I'm not. He's been active in the civil rights movement for years. He knew Lawson and even marched with King. He seems to know everyone of importance."

"Damn. I find that hard to believe."

"I did too. But he's authentic."

Ann and I sat in front, our posters up against the window. "Open the Doors to Freedom." "End Discrimination."

Ken McDonald, a handsome Black student whom I had befriended in an Old Testament class, sat in front of us. Ann asked McDonald about himself, interrogating him to find out as much as she could. Raised in a town in North Carolina, he aspired to teach Black theology, which, he believed, would soon become the "in" topic. An admirer of Reverend Lawson, he wanted to follow in his footsteps, but he also admired Fred Hampton, the Black Panther, and his coalition in Chicago.

I asked if he had met Hampton.

"No, but I have brothers who drove there and who work in his office. It's tense. They're worried about Nixon. His law-and-order shit is fueling backlash in the city."

"What's Reverend Lawson like?" Ann asked, leaning forward, her hand under her chin.

Ken told us an interesting story. The night before, he had dinner with Lawson at the Divinity School's cafeteria. Three other divinity students joined them. Lawson asked them about their experiences with racism and how they related it to the Bible. A Southern Baptist guy believed in a strict interpretation of the Bible. What God said was true. The Bible didn't mention civil rights. That was outside the church; it was more of a political issue.

Lawson heard him out.

Another student had heard God's calling. Newly married, he believed that his mission was to find a good church, raise his family, and preach the love of Christ. Ken suspected that he was not "called" by God as much as by a nice income, since, by his speech, he seemed to come from poverty.

The last one, a hippie, had no use for religion. He was in school to avoid the war and planned to go out west and act in movies, he hoped.

Lawson asked them what the harmful effects of racism in their lives were.

The Baptist had never seen any. Several friends were "colored," and they seemed happy. "Always a smile on their face," he said.

Lawson asked if any Black people were close friends. The Baptist said, "Why yes, one when I was a kid, before school age. After that, he went his way, I went mine."

Lawson continued his investigation into other students' experiences with race. The newly married one said that he'd never encountered any Blacks but had nothing against them. The aspiring actor bragged that he'd played in a rock band with a couple of Black guys.

Lawson asked if he'd been to their house.

The actor said, "Well, no, he hadn't."

"Had they been to his house?"

"Well, no. Never thought of it."

Ken said that he grew up in an integrated community, although mostly white. He had several white friends, but they were not close. They never came over to his house; he frequented theirs. He never felt comfortable asking whites over. It just didn't feel right.

Lawson asked what caused people to be bigoted, hateful, violent, and racist. Most said their upbringing. The hippie said it was unconscious, inbred in society.

Lawson shook his head and said no. He disagreed. It's too easy to blame "society." It's a convenient excuse for not acting. "Society" can't do anything about it.

Then he told a story about two boys—one white, one Black—who grew up on the same street, from different families, and became best friends. As little boys, they fished, wrestled, and played hide-and-seek, spending an inordinate amount of time together. They went into each other's yards and swung on each other's swings. They shared their secrets, coming and going between their homes.

Then one day, before the boys entered elementary school, the white father told his son that he couldn't play with the Black boy and shouldn't be seen with him.

The white boy asked why. The father said that it could cause trouble. That was how it was. His son must not be seen with his friend. Period.

Lawson asked, "What do you think happens to the white boy?"

The students said that he might feel sad.

"True," he said. "But often he feels confused, even angry that his best friend can, for no good reason, be cut off from him. The white boy has no release for his anger. No avenue to vent his frustration. You know what happens to it?"

Ken suggested it became internalized, but Lawson added to his point, "Yes, that's true at first, because the boy thinks something is wrong with him—that he may have done something wrong or that he may be wrong. He feels ashamed. Shame is nameless since no one tells him why he thinks as he does. Shame is a bodily reaction, not a rational one. Shame gnaws at you inside. But instead of coming to understand it, the white boy, along with other white boys, lashes out at the Black boy, the one who caused him to feel as he does. The broken relationship foments rage and anger. That is how hatred and racism start."

Ken asked him what to do about it, if it's so insidious. No one knew.

Lawson slapped his hand on the table and told us, "That's *your* job, your work as ministers, if you believe in anything the Bible says. All people belong to the Kingdom of God. That's what Jesus announced. Race is central to *you* and *your* ministry if this nation is to heal."

After Ken told his story, I looked at Lawson. He sat by Reverend Warren. I remembered what Lawson said at the orientation about keeping civil rights at the center of our ministry. Here, he was not only talking the talk but walking it too.

*

We arrived at the small, single-room church in the Mississippi town and assembled along with those from the other schools, 300 of us in lines of five. Lawson was in the lead row; Warren was at the end. Jack walked alongside Warren, chatting with him as if they were best friends. Several other preachers mixed through the lines. Bob and Ken, right by Lawson, led us toward town. The street was singularly absent of traffic.

On either side of the street, young men in T-shirts sat in open convertibles with shotguns resting in their arms. Other men and women, standing nearby, called out, "Nigger lovers!" and "Yankee, Go Home!"

We sang "We Shall Overcome," held hands, and found assurance in the physical contact and the power of the song.

Ann held onto my arm and whispered. "Geez, this is scary."

I said, "I know." I couldn't imagine how Dr. King had done this over and over, facing the hate and speaking of love. I looked at the eyes of the men in the cars and thought about Lawson's story. Ann held on tighter as some men with enormous beer bellies came up and spat at us.

"Niggers!" "Faggots!" "Jews!"

Two young men in white T-shirts noticed Penny, who was walking alongside us, and yelled, "Look at the dyke! They even got fuckin' queers in this march."

His buddy added, "Hey, lesbo, you like it with girls?" and stuck his tongue in and out.

Penny shouted back, "I bet you couldn't get a piece of ass if you paid for it."

One man, short and stocky, lifted a baseball bat and charged at Penny. Before he reached her, Jack, who had stopped when he heard the commotion, raced up to us and stepped in front of her. He raised his hand.

The stocky fellow stopped in his tracks.

"This is a peaceful march," Jack said. "Your comments aren't appreciated."

The man lifted the bat. The march halted.

The two sides watched the encounter. Jack, a foot taller than the other man, with his suit and tie giving him a professional authority, stared at the man with the bat. "You don't want to do that," he said.

The friend of the stocky man came up and said, "Let the bastards be. He's probably a fag." He took the baseball bat from his friend. "Come on." They backed up and sat on a car bumper.

Jack nodded and gave them a thumbs-up. "Thanks." He turned to Penny. "You okay?"

"Fine. You know, I could have handled it. I'm not a Barbie doll."

Jack smiled. "I'm sure could, but these guys can be deadly."

"In that case, I'm sorry. They got to me," she said.

"They get to all of us," he said, and rejoined the line.

The march continued up the street under intermittent shade from a line of oaks.

Ann pulled on my arm. "Who is that?"

"It's Jack."

"Amazing guy."

"Some might disagree."

"Why?"

"It's nothing. He's odd, that's all."

Ken whispered, "Can you imagine growing up here?"

After a two-mile trek in the blazing sun, the group coalesced at Town Hall. The doors were locked. But white faces peered out the windows. We stood in a semicircle around the steps. Behind us, across the street, white people stood shoulder to shoulder, watching us. Down the street from us, the town square—with its shops, movie theater, and restaurants—looked like any southern town.

Several students, including Bob, spoke about the biblical injunction to act in the face of racism. Reverend Lawson spoke about Dr. King's legacy.

He knocked on the town hall front door and asked to speak to the mayor. But the doors remained locked.

We marched into town, in pairs, black and white, tried to enter a Stonewall Five and Dime, and a nearby restaurant with "White Only" signs on the windows. The doors were closed. Locked. Shades pulled. One proprietor gave us the finger and yelled, "Get out of here, nigger."

Ken said, "They're ready for us. Made it a racist's holiday."

Lawson and Warren conferred.

We marched back to the buses and drove back to Vanderbilt.

Bob asked Ann and me to stay the night. Exhausted, Bob had one drink, excused himself, and went to bed. Ann and I talked about the eyes that glared at us with such vitriol. I stroked her long brown hair. She rubbed my neck. We make love to obliterate the feeling of being reviled, having people call us names. We had trouble letting go of the day until we fell asleep.

~

From October to early November, I paid little attention to the presidential election. After a slow start, Hubert Humphrey had tightened up the race. On election night, the polls looked bad for Democrats. Nixon finally snatched the job he'd always wanted.

At Bob's apartment, we watched a smiling Nixon, arms extended, turn one way and another, his fingers in a "V" for victory.

Bob muttered, "What a jerk."

"Can't believe it." I took another sip of beer. "No one sees he's a fraud."

"Americans like fairy tales," Bob said. "They want someone to patch up divisions and put it back the way it was. They believe 'It's the new Nixon.' They don't get that it's the same old thing and even more divisiveness."

Back in my dorm room, I opened a book by Moltmann on the theology of hope. I thought it might make me feel better.

Nixon later made grandiose statements at his inauguration that I desperately wanted to believe:

The greatest honor history can bestow is the title of peacemaker. This honor now beckons America—the chance to help lead the world at last out of the valley of turmoil, and onto that high ground of peace that man has dreamed of since the dawn of civilization.

Good idea. One I agreed with. But I didn't trust him. People wanted to hear about peace, and he gave them what they wanted.

Advisor

THE FIRST MONTHS OF classes were much more taxing than I expected. I locked myself in my room and read about religion and sociology, New Testament interpretation, systematic theology, and ethics.

My job as a residential advisor in the freshman dorm also required more attention. Several boys came to see me for advice. A mop-haired boy, Michael, a timid, interested young man, became a friend. He'd rifle through my books on theology.

"What does the Good Samaritan story mean?" he asked one night.

I told him that the parables weren't as straightforward as they seemed. The Good Samaritan wasn't about how a "good" Christian should help the poor or downtrodden. If looked at from the point of view of the injured man, for example, it was more about how a helpless person must rely on someone to help him, how he must accept help from someone with whom they'd never associate. It would be like a racist having to receive assistance from a Black man. Once a person admits they're helpless, they become open to the possibility that the source of strength and spiritual nurture may come from an unexpected source, much as, in AA, a recovering person needs to find a sponsor after he admits he is powerless over the substance. Parables, I told him, twisted conventional thinking.

"That's not what my mom says," he said. "She's a minister."

"Maybe your mom doesn't have all the answers," I replied.

"Maybe you don't," he said, putting his hand on his hip.

"Maybe none of us do," I admitted.

I had no idea why I had become a father confessor to many boys, but the boys came in to talk. One boy, Steven, spoke about his father, an alcoholic, who beat up his mother and, when he tried to intercede, would go after him. He often fled and had to stay at a friend's house until his dad sobered up. Another boy struggled with the pressure to be like his father, a magna cum laude graduate of Vanderbilt. The boy disliked studying and preferred to party. His dad and he came to blows if he didn't receive high marks. His dad had already beaten him once so hard that he passed out. I didn't know what to say. How could I change what was happening to them?

I listened to them and worked long hours to keep up with the reading and the assignments.

During Thanksgiving break, I drove home, caught up with my reading, and wrote several overdue papers.

Back at the dorm, I waited for the freshmen to return, checking them off as they came back, making sure no one was missing.

Before I unpacked my clothes and books and settled down to do some intensive reading, several students came in and said that they were worried about Michael, the boy who had spent so much time with me. He hadn't come back from Thanksgiving break. I told them not to worry.

Hours later, they came back, still worried. I knew his parents were strict, born-again Christians, and assured the boys that his family probably had guests. Things ran late. That's all. Not to worry.

But I was worried, too.

Michael lived only three hours from campus. His mother, as the minister, worked on Sundays and holidays. He often hitchhiked rides back to school. On one trip, a man who picked him up found out it was his birthday. As Michael hopped out of the car, the man passed him a bill. "Hey, kid, it's your birthday," he called out. "Have a good day!" Michael stuffed it in his pocket. Later, he looked: a hundred-dollar bill. He showed it to me.

"My parents," he said, "forgot. Big crusade."

At midnight, his friends informed me that he had arrived. But, even when they knocked, he refused to let them in.

I went to his room—I had a master key—and told him I was coming in. "No, no," his voice whined.

I pushed at the door; he blocked my entry with his foot.

I cleared the hallway and told the other boys to let me handle it. He needed privacy.

I told him that I only wanted to come in and sit. That was all. He needn't say anything.

He flipped the lock open.

I waited a minute to give him time and entered.

He was curled up in the bed, the blanket pulled over his head, his knees tucked up under him, sobbing convulsively.

I sat in his desk chair and spoke softly. "It's all right, all right." An hour passed. I kept whispering, "It's all right." And waited.

Eventually, he peeked out from under the blanket and leaned against the wall. The skin on his face, drawn and pale, looked stretched across his frame like a canvas. There were contusions on his right cheek and a bump on his forehead, right below his hairline. He stared at his hands.

The words came out haltingly with intermittent sobs.

He had trouble getting a ride. It was a cold, raw day. Four guys in a van, jocks, loud, drunk, but friendly, offered him a ride to Nashville, no big deal. They seemed pleasant enough. They passed him a Mason jar of moonshine. He drank some. He told them he was a student at Vanderbilt. They said he was "pretty." He drank more. They asked if he was a "fairy boy." They mocked his lisp. The driver turned onto a side road and told him not to worry. "A shortcut." Michael pulled at the door handle. Two guys grabbed him. They told him, "To get out, you need to put out." Fairy boys did that. They parked. They pulled down his pants. After they were done, they left him there with his duffel bag.

He walked fifteen miles, not stopping until he got to his room.

I told him that it was a criminal act. I had to report it. He should get medical attention. I took him to the emergency room. He spoke with the police. His face was ashen. I asked if he wanted something to eat and bought him a hamburger, fries, and a soda. Back at the dorm, I arranged for his best friend, Sam, to stay with him on a mattress on the floor beside his bed overnight.

The next day, he went to a counselor. He told me that he was worried that he was a "sissy boy"—that he'd never be the same. I said that just because they said that about him, it didn't make it true. All he needed to know was that he was a good person and he'd done nothing wrong.

His parents, once they learned of it, were alarmed. They paid a visit, took him out to dinner, talked with the counselor and with me, and, once assured he would be all right, they left. The father had the same lisp as Michael did. His mother, a slight woman with an athletic build, ruled the family. She was pleased that I was a divinity student. If I had any concerns, I was to call.

"Here's my card," she said. Her family ran like a business: if there was a crisis, deal with it, then move on. She called frequently for several weeks to check on him, then, as if the matter was settled, moved on.

❧

Later that winter, after Christmas break, Michael seemed better. He laughed more, dated again, and seemed more secure.

I asked him what caused the change.

Sheepish at first, he said, "The therapy and…"

"What?"

"Drugs."

"Really?" I asked.

"Yeah. You'd like 'em."

Taking psilocybin mushrooms, he believed, kept him sane. "You know, reality is relative." Violence, he went on to explain, could step into your life just as easily as grace. Sometimes it's hard to know the difference: the guy with a hundred bucks and those guys with moonshine. He couldn't change it. He was grateful to be alive. A few nights later, he brought me several tablets—psilocybin—and told me to take them.

"No, I can't be doing that," I said.

His doleful eyes melted my reserve. "Hey, they're good."—the two tablets sat in the palm of his hand—"They give you a different perspective!"

❧

The psilocybin did send me into a new world. Disoriented, I stumbled into my chair, fell over, and stared at the things around me. A chair on its four legs came to life as if I had just discovered how it worked. It seemed alive. It wanted to walk. The bookcase with the shining spines smiled at me.

Michael laughed. "Told you so."

He escorted me around campus, and his arm was tucked into mine. He had me sit under a magnolia. The soft, round leaves quivered above me;

each one of them, caressed by the air, seemed to be breathing. Their green startled me. I stood under a 14-story student housing complex. *Up* as a word came alive. The flat facade went up and up and up. It blotted out the horizon. A building I'd passed hundreds of times became a Stonehenge monolith: huge, otherworldly, and sacred.

With the drug, I was *in* the world, a *part* of it, not just an observer *of* it. I felt the *under*-ness of a tree, its looming *over* me. I was *thrown*, as the philosopher Martin Heidegger called it, into the world. I *dwelt* in it—the sky *above*, the earth *below*, the trees *around*, the wind *through*, the birds *up*, the walls *in*.

⁂

A few days later, when I was on it, a car accident happened right in front of me; it was beautifully orchestrated. One car, a blue sedan, collided with another. Each sequence—the screeching of brakes, the sliding of vehicles, the smoking of tires, the darting of pedestrians to avoid being hit—seemed to happen in slow motion. I viewed it all: the front fender bent, the headlight shattered, the glass splattered, the man's arms behind the wheel thrown up.

I stood, calm and assured, mesmerized as it unfolded. It seemed prearranged. Two lost lovers were being united: one fused for a moment with the other, then ricocheted to the side, and twirled until it stopped ten feet from me. I never flinched and, almost as if preordained, I sensed how the speed of the one car would propel it to a specific spot. I could have pointed to it before it came to a halt on the road.

Two middle-aged men, faces flushed, emerged from their cars and screamed at one another. Like dancers, they strutted, chests out, and stepped back and forth with fingers pointing. Someone called for help.

The dancers were bleeding.

I couldn't help. I could only observe. I was and was not there.

I scampered to a parking lot and retreated to my dorm.

⁂

Over several weeks, I enjoyed the mushrooms, being in the world and not of it. One afternoon, I attended my New Testament class while under the influence of psilocybin. I couldn't follow the discussion. Words made no sense. But the sensual world came alive. The breasts of a girl who tried to adjust her bra without letting on, the finger of the professor who pushed his glasses up on his nose every few minutes, and the hand of a student who cupped his crotch—all caught my attention. I heard the fabric of his jeans move and the slight moan in his throat. Another boy picked up a pencil, sucked it, and I got an erection.

❧

The evening was my favorite time to take it. I liked to peer up at the pretzel-like bend of branches and the vines like snakes crawling up the side of a dorm exterior.

But one evening, someone was watching me. I could feel his gaze on my back. A campus police officer, not twenty feet away, was studying me.

If he had inquired about what I was doing, I would have been incoherent. I stuffed my hands in my pockets, looked straight down the path, and walked in a direction (although I had no idea where I was going) and invented an aphorism: "Always look as if you know where you are going, even if you don't, and people will leave you alone." I kept going in a direction, and the officer thought I knew where I was going.

❧

Michael and his friend Sam came into my room often to talk. Sam, who had dark hair that obscured his eyes, recounted how his mother would go into rages and chase him around the dinner table with a carving knife. Quick and nimble, he outran her. Both got exhausted. He suggested they stop to smoke a cigarette. She put the knife down. He took out his cigarettes. While she puffed on hers, he hid the knives. She forgot about what she'd just been doing, and the next day, she went about her business, never apologizing. She had a reputable job in town as a secretary in a big law firm. No one believed she had such rages—how could such a sweet, loving lady act like that? He had bided his time until he was free from her.

I may have been learning an incredible amount about the New and Old Testaments, about ethics, and the sociology of religion. Still, the dorm opened me up to something far more real than anything that I read and studied in class about how students, even ones who seemed privileged, lived with family violence.

Obligations

BOB CALLED AND asked if I could come over to his apartment. Since his voice sounded odd, I wondered if there was anything wrong.

"No," he said, "but I need to talk." It was early afternoon, not a time we usually met.

He made lunch: some salmon, beans, and a baked potato. He poured us wine and told me it was a special meal for a special friend.

"What's the occasion?" I asked.

"You're the one person whom I can talk to about anything. Do you mind listening?"

"That depends," I said, sipping on the wine.

"Depends on what?"

"If you have another bottle of wine."

"Asshole!"

"Well, what type is this one?"

"A merlot, French; it's different. You like it?"

"I guess."

"Let me tell you something." He tightened his lips. "It goes like this," he explained. "I really love it here. I've never felt more at home than with you and Ann. The girls here are hot. I love the faculty. We can be ourselves without any game-playing. We're equals. We marched in Mississippi. We protested the war. We have the most amazing classes with the most amazing minds." He took a sip of wine. "Good, isn't it?"

"Bitter, but tasty," I said.

"Want another glass?"

"Sure," I said. "And what were you saying?"

"About here, what we have. But that isn't the issue. The more I think about the other guys, the ones who were drafted and who are dying over in Nam, the more I wonder, 'What am I doing here?' I'm on Easy Street. If

I'm against war, if I'm for peaceful resolution to conflict, I should be laying it on the line—you see what I mean?"

"No, not really."

"I should be a conscientious objector, not have a 4-D deferment."

"But what's the difference?"

"If I'm 4-D, that means I want to serve the church, to go into the ministry, right?"

"No. I don't plan to..."

"Exactly," he interrupted. "You don't plan to. If that's the case, then you're using the status quo to avoid recruitment."

"You got it!"

"But that's not right. If you oppose war, especially this war, you should be making a stand and say, 'I will not abide this war, not serve in the military to advance the immoral war efforts,' and not just sit silent and get by," he said, cocking his head to the side.

I cupped my wineglass in my hands. I felt unmoored. He was my anchor. Yet, in an instant, the currents of his moral code were pulling him away from me, from what we had together. Indeed, he had a point: doing nothing was not the right course of action.

I told him that if I was doing something productive to help others that, as a soldier, I could not do, then I was using the 4-D status to do good work.

"What are you doing?" he asked.

"Nothing, but maybe we could find some work in Edgehill, the Black area. Reverend Warren needs help with his summer programs. I've seen notices. You could apply to work for him. I might join you."

"No," he said. "I need to make a stand."

"A one-night stand?"

He slapped his knee and laughed weirdly.

"You all right?"

"Sure, but let me tell you what happened last weekend. You know that older girl, the blonde with that amazing face? Well, you reminded me of my one-night stand. You wanna hear?"

He dated an older woman, in her late twenties, whom he'd met at a party. Tall and model-like, she caught his attention. He was infatuated with her. She biked; they'd gone on day trips. She asked him over, and one thing led to another. They made love. He pulled out before he came and ejaculated on her belly.

"You'll not believe what happened," he said.

"Tell me," I said. I imagined him doing it with me, not with her.

"She screamed and jumped back in bed, waving her hands and asking, 'What's *that*? What's *that*?' pointing frantically at my cum," he said, laughing.

"Why'd she ask you that?"

"This is the incredible part. You will *not* believe this," he said. He could barely stop laughing. "She had never seen cum before and didn't know—this is even more unbelievable—what it was and why it came out of my penis."

"What did you do?"

"I calmed her down, held her, and wiped it up. Then I explained the birds and the bees and how semen played a pretty big role in it all," he said, giggling.

"Did she understand?"

"Sort of. She thought it was gross. She didn't like its smell. Nor how sticky it was."

"Have you seen her since?"

"No, she called me a few days later. Was leaving town—a business trip—and said she would call, but never has."

He served pecan pie and poured us more wine. We finished half the pie. He talked about where he would go and what might happen.

I admitted how hard it would be for me to go on without him.

Time got the best of us. Near midnight, I staggered to the front door. He put his hand on the door. He didn't want me to drive. I had to stay. I could sleep in his double bed.

We undressed, each on one side of the room, and got into bed, each on our own side. Before he fell asleep, he reached over and tapped me on the shoulder. I turned over and he hugged me, his slender body pressing against mine with a tenderness I'd never felt from a man.

"Thanks," he whispered.

"For what?"

"For being my friend." His voice choked back a grief I knew too well. He patted my face and let his hand rest on my cheek. He stared at me; I think he knew how I felt and loved me just the same.

"It'll cost you," I said, trying to make light of the moment.

"Now what?"

"Fifth of Jack."

"Go to sleep."

I turned over on my side and listened to him breathe. "Yes," I thought, "friendship is like this: being together without expecting anything else." His breathing grew still, and I could hear the traffic, slow and intermittent, passing by, heading somewhere even late at night, just as he would be in a few months, or whatever it took for the paperwork to grind out his fate.

Star Light

BY EVENING, AFTER studying my sociology books with language that made my head spin, I was tired and planned to be in bed early, but Michael and his friend Sam came in and asked if I wanted to smoke some good weed.

"No, not tonight," I said.

Sam said, "It's better than weed."

"Don't tempt me," I said.

"It's hash."

❧

Several blocks from campus, an old Victorian house with a wraparound porch stood. Sam opened the stained-glass front door and led us into a study. Floor-to-ceiling bookcases covered the walls, but only one or two books were on the shelves. A small coffee table with two candles sat in front of the couch in the center of the room. Incense burned.

Sam patted the couch. We sat down. He put his finger to his lips, motioning us to be quiet.

Several other people came in—long-haired kids dressed in psychedelic vests and jeans with peace patches. A stout man who wore a gold vest and black leather boots sat with a short-haired girl who could have passed for his daughter. Others arrived as if they knew where to sit. Some sat on scattered pillows on the floor. But everyone faced the wall with a brick fireplace. No one seemed to know anyone. Everyone was as quiet as guests at a funeral.

After fifteen minutes, the door swung open. A tall, skinny Black man with a red bandana around his afro entered the room and bowed to us, his hands clasped in front of him.

"Good evening, my children," he said in a deep voice.

He wore skintight bellbottoms that outlined his ample anatomy. His shirt, open at the top, revealed strings of beads. He wore bracelets and had three rings on each hand, one with an emerald. He bent down and, going from one to another, asked who we were. His quiet, gentle manner reminded me of a dentist who was sizing you up before extracting a tooth. He smiled when we gave him our names and made comments—"Oh, aren't you a cute one," and "An elder has joined us."

In front of the fireplace, he sat in a lotus posture, closed his eyes, and breathed for several minutes. He sang something in a language I didn't recognize—not French, Spanish, or Latin, more likely Hindi.

He pointed at himself. "I'm Star Light. You've come here for what I have to offer. It's a chance for you to explore the invisible world that's here all the time, right in front of you. You'll feel sensations you've never experienced before. I'll take care of you. Just let yourself be open." He tapped his chest. "The key is here to unlock your soul." He fetched a small gold pipe out of a cloth bag that was slung over his shoulder. He pinched some greenish herbs from a small pouch and carefully placed it in the bowl of the pipe.

"Are you ready, my children?" he asked.

There was a murmured assent.

I felt skeptical. Here was some crank who bamboozled Sam. But I nodded and decided to go along. He lit the pipe, took a toke, and passed it to Sam, who passed it to me. I passed it to Michael, who passed it to a blond girl with sunglasses, who passed it to a boy with war paint on his cheeks, who, in turn, passed it to the boy in shorts and a torn T-shirt, who passed it to the gold vest and his girlfriend, then the pipe came back. It went back around until nothing was left. My body tingled as if Tinkerbell had cast her fairy dust on me, and I felt as if I could fly. My skin titillated with any sensation—a wisp of air on my face, the tug of my sleeve on my wrist—anything sent shivers down my body. My hips lifted involuntarily as they did with an orgasm.

Sam leaned and put his face next to mine. It startled me.

"Wild, isn't it?" he said.

His hand was on my leg. I felt as if it had been caressed by the hand of God. I put my hand on his leg. Our two bodies became one. This was wild.

Sam saw that I was aroused, but I wasn't embarrassed since I saw he was too.

I felt a moment of dread. *This wasn't what I should be doing. I needed to get out of here. What's happening? This isn't right.*

Sam whispered, "It's all right. That's what happens."

The hippie girl next to me leaned over to kiss Michael. He kissed her back.

Star Light sat in front of each of us, took us by the back of our heads, and kissed us gently. It seemed to be part of the ritual. This was not a Christian ritual. Yet it didn't feel intrusive. Not at all. It felt almost liturgical.

His lips were soft and yielding. He traced his tongue on our lips, letting us feel the pleasure of the tongue. After the kiss, he drew his hand down our face onto our chest and belly and into our lap. He caressed our thighs and genitals. There were groans. Yet he didn't want to have sex with us. He had a role to play. He was our guide. He wanted us to experience as much sensation as possible. Then he slipped away from the circle and sat in a lotus position, and let us bask in the afterglow radiating over our bodies.

I found myself watching myself watching myself, almost as if my body had stepped outside itself and was now observing what was happening. Two books tilted against one another on the shelf. Everything and everyone were uniting. The candles cast a muted yellow glow on the paneling. The streaks in the windowpanes shivered in the light of passing cars. I wanted to rub my hand on everything. I wish Bob were here to experience it and to let me touch him in a way that would tell him how deeply I felt about him.

Star Light lit another pipe, and we passed it around. He continued with his ministrations, methodically edged us to the point of an orgasm, and then let us slide back.

Time, if there was such a thing, seemed to melt like the wax on the candle. One candle went out. Another was lit. Star Light was standing in the middle of the room, bowing and putting his hands together. "Good night, my darlings." The door closed behind him.

The blonde kissed Michael. He pushed her away and pulled his legs up close to him. She turned to the painted boy, and they fell to the floor, starting to make love. The old man curled up with his young companion. Taboos melted away. Sam began to kiss me. I'd never kissed a man as passionately as I did him. My hand caressed his cheek. I felt the stubble of his whiskers. The simple touch on a lip, a cheek, an arm, or a leg sent off fireworks inside me. I wondered if other men became as soft and gentle as Sam did when they kissed.

❧

Gradually, I came to my senses, panicked, and pulled away from Sam, not wanting to compromise my role as a dorm counselor.

Michael was still wrapped in a tight ball as I had seen him after he was raped, wincing as if he were in pain.

"Something's wrong." I pointed to Michael. I sat up, tucked in my shirt, and crawled across the floor to the divan by the window.

Sam took Michael in his arms. They pressed together, not kissing at first, just exploring. Eventually, they kissed and seemed content in each other's arms. The other couple on the floor had exhausted themselves and had passed out. The old man had left. His girlfriend had curled up in a fetal position. Other members of the group had also fallen asleep.

The last candle went out. Gently, I nudged Michael and Sam and said, "We should get back." Arm in arm, the three of us floated on our respective clouds to the dorm.

❧

The next day, Sam asked what I thought of Star Light.

"He was amazing," I said.

"Good," he said, smiling weakly at me.

"But, I'm sorry I did…"

"It was fine. No big deal."

I said, "No, it wasn't okay. I'm a dorm counselor."

He winced and started to apologize. "It wasn't you. It was me. I shouldn't have brought you there. I shouldn't have…"

"No, no," I assured him, "what we did was nice, real nice. But I'm not sure, you know, I'd do that if…"

"I know what you mean," Sam said. "You're okay with me, though. Right?"

"Sure, sure," I said and tousled his hair and asked, "How's Michael?"

Sam's face lit up. "He's great. Something happened to him. We went off to some new place in our relationship, if you know what I mean, and he let go, and I did too. We're doing great!"

"Good," I said. But I wasn't so sure. Maybe I had encouraged them to get sexually involved by telling Sam to go over to Michael. If Michael's parents found out, he'd pay a price.

Sam and Michael kept hanging out and talking, but we never mentioned the night with Star Light again. I pushed it out of my mind. I'd slipped and had just barely gotten hold of myself before I fell over the edge. I thought of that squirrel outside my room at home and how he could leap with an assurance that he'd land where he should. I wish I had such an assurance. I focused my energy on my classwork, my relationship with Ann, and my concern about what Bob might do once he heard back from his draft board. I also had to figure out what I would do during the summer. I had to get as far from my dad's inquisitive eye as I could. I needed to do something, as Bob had suggested, that justified my having the luxury of a 4-D status.

Quivering Essence

I'D CHECKED OUT THE jobs at Edgehill Methodist Church. But they were all taken. I had to do something to justify my 4-D status. I couldn't have a free pass while others were blown to bits in Nam. I didn't want to spend another summer at the Glen Oak Country Club, among people who thrived on cocktail parties, clandestine affairs, and scrambled golf matches.

I kvetched about my lack of options with Jack Kirk, the loudmouth I'd initially detested at The Plunge. He was more active than I had ever been in the civil rights movement and seemed to share my compassion for the down-and-out. When he wasn't grandstanding, he enjoyed discussing theology and the arts. He lived in a swank apartment off campus on 16th Street, a two-lane residential neighborhood illuminated by round white globes like oversized Christmas ornaments. Jack loved drinking, debating, and engaging in conversation. Mostly talk. He never lost his passion for anthropology. Every argument came down to one ineluctable fact: it had an anthropological explanation.

We discussed the nature of God, since we were both taking Systematic Theology. Our intellectual battles helped me hone my arguments in class and refine papers that were polemics against his ideas.

Jack had noticed that I'd published a short poem in the Divinity School's student journal and admired it. I'd written poems for several years, mostly dabbling with form, learning the tricks of metrics. Leaning back on his chair, Jack read me one of his poems.

I told him it was not bad.

"Not bad? Let me tell you, a few years ago, I had it published in Cincinnati, in a religious journal. So, it's more than 'not bad.' It's good. You like the idea?"

"Yeah, I think so."

"Think so?"

"I'm not sure I get it."

Jack slammed his hand down. "The idea is that a hunter," he said, "is able to give or take life like a God."

"Sure, I get that. But I'm not sure I agree."

"Why?"

"I don't think God hunts, does he?"

"No, but we're hunters and gatherers—that's how mankind started. All our early gods were nature gods: they were associated with the hunt."

"Yes, yes, I see. Good poem, nice, short, and to the point."

"Thanks, you want to read another poem?"

"No, not now. Can I have a beer instead?"

"Sure."

If Jack's argument scraped bottom, he said, "Yeah, but" and raised his voice. One night, he was contending that God was a "quivering essence" that surrounded us like an ether in outer space.

I asked him to clarify what he meant.

He said, "There you go, trying to name it, to fit it in a category, to describe it. That's what I refuse to do. God is a quivering essence. God defies any rational explanation."

"That may be good for you, Jack, but for me, if there is a God, I want some clarity about who or what it is."

"That's not for you to say."

"Why?"

"Because God's essence is ubiquitous, everywhere, all around us! It's quivering! Don't you get it?" He raised his hands in the air and swung them around his head to create a clear visual.

Jamming my hand over my mouth to stop laughing, I wondered if I should give up arguing. Still, I was not willing to embrace his vague generality and flapping of his arms like some hysteric without a counterargument.

"Listen, you may think that. But I don't buy it. You seem to think that I should give up trying to figure out what this term 'God' is. But I don't want to. I think that's part of developing as a religious thinker: being able to question, not consigning God to some 'quivering essence,' which, to be honest, sounds like more like a description of Jell-O than God."

Jack's ears turned red; he scowled and jabbed his finger at me. "Don't insult me."

"I'm not. But it's all relative, Jack. You think what you think. I think what I think. If it works for you, fine. Relativity doesn't just apply to motion and space, but to God, and ethics too."

"You think everything is relative?"

"I didn't say that."

"Yes, you did!"

I threw up my hands, exasperated. "Fine, I did. Let's call it quits. I need to study."

I took the beer and headed out of his apartment.

"Hey, wait," he called after me.

"What?"

"Forget it," he said, patting me on the back.

And I did. I strolled across the block by the wooded campus area that had loomed above me in my altered state months ago. I thought, if there is any God, it would be in these trees. I stopped and gazed up into the trees, the intricate weaves of their branches, and smelled their musty aroma.

II

Although the word is common to all,
most men live as if each had a private wisdom.

—"Four Quartets," T.S. Eliot

It is impossible to be an American in any deep sense without being a visionary and a mystic, without feeling the whole of human history as a mystic presence, and without having a mystic vision of the future.

—Erling Duus, *Danish-American Journey*,
Gauntlet Books, Franklin, Mass., 1971

Encounter

JACK INFORMED ME THAT he had landed a summer job as an interim minister with full pay and benefits and asked what my plans were. I told him my dilemma: I had work that I didn't want to do. My dad wanted me back in his orbit, working at a plant with Commonwealth Edison or the country club.

As another option, Jack offered to introduce me to another student, Erling Duus, whom he knew from taking several classes with him. He had a project in eastern Tennessee that might interest me.

"What's he doing?" I asked.

"He plans to start a school up there, studying Whitman, Emerson, Wolfe, and other American writers—Sandburg and Cather—and learning about the folk traditions in that area. It's where the Hatfields live. You know who I am talking about. I was going to be his assistant director until I landed a real job. Not sure you'd be right for the job," he said. "But it might work out. What do you think?"

"Sure, I'd like to see what he has to say," I replied.

❧

A week later, he barged into my room and called out, "Let's go. I told Erling about you. He wants to meet today!"

We hurried down 16th Street to a house set back from the street, surrounded by magnolias and overarching oaks. It seemed like a faded Southern mansion hinting of lost glory.

At the front steps, Jack held up a finger and said, "Listen, Jason, let me take the lead here. I know him well. Good friend. You know, bright. He respects me. I have his trust, if you know what I mean."

"Sure," I said and stepped back to let him proceed up the stairs.

A screened-in porch ran the length of the building. Its screen door, with a long scar, hung on one hinge. The front door, oak laced with filigrees of beveled glass, opened into a hallway. On the other side of it were two parlors with enormous bookcases. The books were covered with dust, as if whoever had lived there had made a quick escape and left the library to the next occupants.

Seated in a chair at the end of the living room, Erling motioned us to sit by him. He didn't bother to stand up to greet us. A copper lamp shone dimly, making it hard to make out his features.

I'd seen him in the hallways. Or in some class. I wasn't sure.

He held a thick book in his long, delicate fingers.

He seemed to be a man both self-absorbed and rude.

Jack tugged on my shirt sleeve and whispered, "Come along," and stepped in front of me. "I'll take care of this."

Jack's cowboy boots clomped on the floor. His hand held out, he said, "Erling, it's so *good* to see you!"

Erling finished the paragraph that he was reading, inserted a scrap of paper to mark his page, and closed the book. He looked like a watchdog trained to keep still before barking at an intruder. He lifted his eyes, didn't look at Jack, but beyond him toward me. The right side of his mouth lifted slightly, and he winked.

I was not sure what the wink meant. He was dressed in wrinkled pants, an un-ironed white shirt, sleeves rolled up and open at the collar, and unpolished shoes with the leather scraped and frayed. His slight figure reminded me of photographs I'd seen of a young D.H. Lawrence: the narrow face and gaunt, haunted look of an artist who'd seen too much of the world and wanted to speak of its grave truths.

On the way to the meeting, Jack had talked about him: a poet, writer, and mystic of Danish heritage, yet raised in Kansas. An expert on the Transcendentalists and the works of Walt Whitman and Thomas Wolfe, he had a mystical streak, often reciting whole passages from Thoreau and Emerson. Jack had talked about the school that Erling wanted to start in the Cumberland Mountains, where Jack was originally slated to be the assistant director, but had soured on the idea because it didn't pay at all.

"Hello, Jack," Erling said, shaking his hand. "I see that you have brought the first-year student."

I was not sure how to take his calling me "the first-year student." For a moment, I was put off. But that quickly passed. Maybe it was the wink that put me at ease. There was something more to him than met the eye.

Erling extended his hand to me and said, "I hear you're a poet."

"Well, yes, I write some."

"You might be interested in being part of my Folk School?"

I blanched slightly, not willing to commit to something of which I knew very little. But not wanting to act uninterested, I nodded.

His blue eyes behind the wire-rimmed glasses were intense. "Good, have a seat; let's talk."

Jack glowered at me, signaling me to keep back, and set his chair in front of and to the side of me.

Erling pulled up a chair closer to me.

Jack shoved his chair right next to Erling, his feet extended between us and interposed, "Erling, remember what I said earlier. Don't jump too quickly. Jason here is a fine fellow, but I'm sure you need to consider his views on…"

Erling waved Jack off. "I know, I know—come, Jason—let's get to business." He scooted his chair even closer to mine, taking his leg to scoot Jack's legs out of the way.

His brow furrowed, Erling looked at me as if he could see right into my soul. "What makes you interested in the Folk School?" he asked. "We need those who are willing to take serious risks, life-threatening. We need people who can let go of their fragile egos and get involved with people who live very different lives from most Americans."

Risks, I thought. *That's what I want to do.* For my whole life—years of living in the suburbs, playing football, basketball, and golf, years of never worrying about walking the roads at night, never doubting my direction or my fate, because, no matter what I did, my dad had connections and I was always safe—I wanted to break away, to do something bold.

He put his hands together, held them prayer-like next to his lips, and stared at me.

Jack started to say something, but Erling deflected him.

I fumbled out, "I think I'm…"

"You're what?"

I spoke about how I wanted to change my life. Every word I said, every move I made, he observed as if he were examining an actor auditioning for a part in a play. I said I needed to ensure it was a good match. "Tell me what you are doing," I said, "so I can determine if I am the right man for the job."

"Sure. That makes sense. Let me tell you what it will be like." Erling paused to make sure I was listening. "We are going into the heart of Appalachia, the Cumberland Mountains in eastern Tennessee, to start a Folk School. It's Danish in origin, built on folk traditions that are being lost in the rapid-paced, urban, industrial society. The founder, Frederik Severin Grundtig, believed that the best way to spread democracy was to involve all people and ensure that all voices were heard. He set up regional Folk Schools. People learned about each citizen's right to have a voice. People also explored the rich folk traditions in each region. People were empowered to speak up and understand their rightful place in a larger democracy.

"The same usurpation of local ways and the undermining of their way of life that was happening in Denmark is happening right now in Appalachia and, in fact, in small ways and large, all over America," he explained. "Coal companies have bamboozled local people, taken their land, strip-mined their mountains, polluted their streams, sapped their lives, and left them in poverty. Many go to the cities for work. But they don't do well. They aren't familiar with the demands of urban life. I want to help them stay and preserve their folk traditions: their stories, their art, their crafts, their way of life, their way of earning a living. That's what we'll be doing."

He sat back and stoked his pipe, puffing on it, and continued, "It will not be easy. Some people may think we're communists. They may try to drive us out. It's not luxurious. We'll sleep in sleeping bags and wash in wash basins. Not for the faint-hearted. Could you handle it?"

"I think I could," I said.

His arms moved as if he were sweeping something out of the air between us. His eyes combed over me carefully—my Oxford buttoned down shirt, my slacks, and penny loafers with pennies in them.

"You sure?"

"Yes."

"It's not suburbia."

"I know. Well, I don't know. But I would like the chance to prove myself, to find that maybe I can find a place I belong that's not where I call home."

He bowed his head and then lifted it quickly. His voice filled with intensity.

"Before you commit—I must tell you this—a lot of people's lives will depend on you. I have talked with a few families in Rose's Creek," he explained. "Some are interested in the school and getting a better education. They're poor. They've seen strangers come and go. They've been let down. You need to be able to commit fully, not half commit, to being there."

I asked him to give me a history of Rose's Creek.

"There are three ex-nuns from the Glenmary Home Mission Sisters of America who have bought a place in Rose's Creek Hollow and are working to start alternative businesses—ladies making quilts, folk carvings. It hasn't been easy for them. Ninety percent of the locals have migrated north to Chicago to find other jobs. Only ten percent have stayed. They're trying to get them to work so that they can buy back their land. It's largely owned by a British coal company that defrauded local people and acquired all rights to their land. Now that they have strip-mined it, they have little use for it, yet they are asking a high price for anyone trying to repurchase it. As a result of such duplicity, it's no wonder that local people are skeptical.

"But, to their credit, the nuns stayed. Some accuse them of being communist, just as I suspect they'll accuse us. Someone shot at their house at night. It was—and still is—dangerous. That's it," he leaned back in his chair and peered at me over his glasses.

I put my hands between my legs and mulled over my options for the summer—working maintenance on a golf course or at this Folk School. The one option—the one I had done for years and required no thought—was the other. I looked up. "I'm your man. I'll do it."

He smiled, stood up, and shook my hand. "You sure?"

"I'm sure!"

"Then we have a deal," he said, smiling and turning to Jack. "Thanks for bringing him by."

Jack stood up, took Erling by the arm, pulled him aside, and spoke in a hushed tone, one he intended I should hear, "I told you that I have some misgivings. I think you should reconsider and let me..."

Erling shook Jack's arm off and turned toward me. "Care to come to my room, Jason? Let me show you some books I'd like you to read."

Jack's lips tightened. "Erling, I need to talk with you privately, *now*."

"No, not now, Jack. Later, sometime when I'm not busy."

"I just have—"

"Save it."

Erling motioned for me to follow him to his room. "We need to start making plans. I want to go over when it will start," he said, tapping my chest. "When would you be available?"

"When do we start?"

Erling laughed. "Start?! Right now, my friend."

Jack hadn't given up. He stuck out his hand like a patrol guard, waving it. "We need to talk first. Come on, over here. Would you excuse us, Jason?"

Erling glared at Jack's hand. "No, Jack, we don't. Jason is a good match. He was in my New Testament Theology class. I was impressed with his sensitivity and insight. He's a guy who hears something and embraces it. I like that."

That's where I'd seen him, but he was dressed up: a jacket and a scarf flung over his shoulder. He loved to question the professor. A gadfly. His range of knowledge initially intimidated me, but he enjoyed the exchange of ideas and was as good a listener as well as a talker.

"Do you think you could raise some money from your church up in Illinois?" he asked. He slung his arm around my shoulder.

"Sure," I said, "how much?"

"A thousand."

"Probably," I said. "My church wanted to do more service work. Anything you want. Just ask."

"It must be nice," Jack muttered.

Erling looked at him. "Jack, I thought you said you could pull in a bundle when we last talked."

"I may still do it," Jack said, stepping in front of me. "Hey, Jason, don't you think you're being hasty. You just met the guy." He nodded his head toward Erling. "Let's talk before you decide. Let's go back to school. We can make it there for supper. And talk. Give you a chance—"

"No, but thanks," I said. "Catch you later."

His boots drummed across the floor. The screen door opened and slammed shut.

Erling told me about Whitman's and his own vision of America, how it included everyone, particularly those excluded from the American Dream. He lent me several books and spoke with the passion and intensity of someone who knew much and knew it well, and who could be my passport out of the suburbs.

❧

Jack usually met me for breakfast at the Divinity School's cafeteria before our Systematic Theology class. But the next day he didn't show. I saw him later in the hall. He paused long enough to ask, "What do you think of our idea?"

"What idea?"

"The Folk School," he shot back.

"That's not your idea. It's Erling's. He told me about—" I didn't get to finish.

He pushed me against the wall, "*I'm* the one who encouraged him when no one would listen. *I'm* the one who recruited you to join the school. *I'm* the one who brought you over to see him. Don't forget that! Don't think you can barge in because you have Daddy Warbucks for a father. I warned him about you. You think everything is relative. You can do whatever you want because you have it made. Don't think you can get what you want because you—"

I shoved him away. "Save it!"

❧

Erling, full of plans, put together a budget, staff, and housing for the Folk School, showing me on a map where it would be located.

Jack kept visiting Erling. I'd seen him come and go. He volunteered to help with fundraising—or so he said. Erling never mentioned their conversations. Jack had something against me. Whatever it was, I had to prove him wrong.

The Test

EARLY IN MARCH, Erling showed me a map of the Cumberland Mountain region—the town of Clearfork, and Rose's Creek Hollow, where he planned to have the Folk School.

"I'd like you to see it," he said.

"Anytime," I said.

He said, "Let's go!"

He threw together some food, a cooking stove, and a sack with odds and ends. I gathered some notebooks and several textbooks, some clothing, and a towel, and we headed off. He drove five hours from Nashville, all the way across the state, to the Smoky Mountains. He wanted to visit a waterfall that he loved. It was nestled in a hollow, a ribbon of water that fell first down one ledge, then another until it sprayed out and cascaded into a pool where we could swim. Locals skinny dipped. They waited for those already in it to clothe themselves and leave before stripping off their own clothes and slipping into the water. It sounded enchanting.

Late in the afternoon, exasperated with his aborted efforts to find a back road to the falls, he pulled off by a TVA reservoir parking lot.

"We're lost," he said. "We'll camp here."

He heated beans in a can on a burner and said we would sleep in the car, covered with a frayed quilt.

Over beans, he bragged that he was a great boxer and challenged me to a match. The first time I ever fought, I lost terribly. My father bought my brother and me gloves because we fought so much. He laced on the gloves and told us to fight. We could barely lift the gloves, swinging them like a windmill. We flailed, swatted overhanded at one another. A straight-out punch, because of the gloves' weight, caused us to topple forward, missing the other entirely. Bigger than I was, my brother swung a roundhouse, and his glove whapped my head. I was out.

I wasn't so sure I wanted to box. But Erling pulled out his gloves and handed me a pair. He took off his shirt and tightened up the belt on his trousers above his belly button. I took off my shirt and let my jeans ride where they were. Thirty pounds heavier than he was, I was worried I would hurt him.

"You sure you want to do this?" I asked. "I'm much bigger than you are."

"Don't worry," he smiled, flinging a fake punch at me. "I can take care of myself. You're the one who needs to worry."

Once we laced on the gloves, he circled me, peppered jabs at my stomach and face. I cautiously backed up, keeping my gloves in front of my face as I'd seen Muhammad Ali do in his heavyweight fights against Liston. I figured that if I could keep moving, since I had a longer stride, I could make our encounter more of a dance than a real fight.

I soon learned otherwise.

As I was bobbing to the left, Erling's glove smacked my temple. It staggered me. He laughed and gestured with his fist, "Come on, try and hit me."

I backpedaled. He came at me, hit me on the side of my head again, and then slugged me with an uppercut that practically knocked me out. I staggered backward and ended up on one knee. I stared in disbelief at him.

He bounced around me to the right and left. "Come on. Come on!"

My head ringing, the bruise on my face stinging, I stood up but was still woozy. He laced me in the belly with four quick punches. He knocked the wind out of me. I toppled back, nearly fell over, but caught myself with my glove on the ground. I propped myself up and darted away to get some distance from him.

"Come on. Fight. What's wrong with you? Don't be a sissy."

I wasn't a sissy. I was afraid of my rage.

In seventh grade, when I was shooting baskets in the gym to perfect a left-handed layup, a younger boy flung basketballs at me, taunting me. I told him to stop. He thought it was fun. He pelted me again.

"Leave me alone, okay?" I spoke.

He nailed me in the back as I shot a layup.

The next thing I remember was seeing his body recoil, his hands pressed against his face, blood oozing through his fingers, lying on the floor beneath me. The coach raced into the gym and glanced at my clenched fists. He called my name, "Jason. Jason. Stop it! Stop it!"

He pushed me aside. "What the *hell* have you done?"

I couldn't remember what happened. A button was pushed, rage erupted, and my body took over.

The coach told me that I had better watch myself.

I'd been watching myself ever since. I'd nearly lost it several times but always kept my rage at bay and took walks to cool off.

If I could keep the fight just a playful dodge, if I kept breathing, I could keep the rage at arm's length. I paid more attention to it than Erling, the quick moves he made, his punches to my face.

"Come on!"

He came at me, moving in, his hands up and his fists, one after another, jabbing me.

The blows hurt. The bones in my cheeks smarted. My jaw was sore. The thick gloves pummeled my scalp, numbing it. If I pulled my head back to protect it, he'd land a flurry of hits to my stomach. I was fighting for my life.

The son of a bitch, I thought, *wants to knock me out.*

"Hey, I've had enough," I yelled and put my arms up in surrender.

He slugged me right in the face. I fell back, stumbled for several yards, my eyes blurry. All I could see were his eyes and his gloves in front of him. I straightened up and jabbed at him. He ducked down, bobbed to the left, and slammed me in the stomach with a left.

He laughed and circled to my left. I saw an opening and hit him in the jaw, sending him back about 4 feet.

He smiled. "Good. Good," he said, encouraged.

I dodged to the right and left, avoiding his best punches. When I could see an opening in his gloves, I thrust a jab at him. My gloves felt as if someone had poured cement into them. It took more and more effort to hold them up.

I had to act fast, or he'd knock me out. He was crouched down, bobbing to the right and left. For an academic—someone I thought to be non-athletic—he was tough. He skipped to the right, ducked, and then to the left.

I realized that he had a set routine. Move one way, then the other, jab with one fist and then the other. I waited until I was sure of his next move. We had been boxing for fifteen minutes before I saw him move where I knew one glove would be down. I threw a hard punch at his head. He toppled backward, only the whites of his eyes showing. I quickly lunged forward and grabbed him before he slammed into a tree. I held him against me, both of us drenched with sweat.

As he came to, he looked me in the eye. "Good punch."

I asked, "Can we call it quits? I'm exhausted. Come on, the game's over."

"No," he said firmly. "It's *not* over yet."

He jabbed me in the stomach and leapt back three feet. He maneuvered more consciously, his feet not as quick as they had been, but his arms just as powerful. He tossed jabs at me. He wove, bobbed, and ducked lower, forcing me to throw my punches downward. It put more stress on my upper arms. My hands dropped. He hit me four times in the jaw, twice in the forehead. It sent me backpedaling, reeling. I stumbled to one knee.

But he came at me like a bulldog, growling. I stood up and backpedaled.

His eyes bulged. He was looking for a knockout punch.

I dropped both my arms, shaking them to loosen them up and relieve the pressure on my neck. I danced to the right and left, nearly bumping into the car. I was running out of time. He wanted to knock me out. My body moved as if I were dancing with fire. He pursued me, and a few jabs landed on my belly. I still let my arms dangle. My legs were giving my arms a reprieve. He surged at me; I fluttered to the right and left. He didn't let up. He had me on the run.

He walloped me with an uppercut to my jaw. I shook my head: He was trying to kill me. He wanted a knockdown. This was no game, this was for real.

Somewhere in my head, something snapped.

I felt a surge of energy. My left arm landed a punch on his upper chest. He tilted slightly to the right. My right hook landed on his jaw. The impact knocked me off balance. I swirled back to my right and turned around. As my upward gaze caught the scarlet tint of the last light in a maple, I failed to see what happened to Erling.

By the time I turned back, he had toppled, as if he were going downhill, his head gazing upward, his legs wobbly. With the suddenness of a puppet whose strings are snipped, he slumped forward, shoulder first, then his whole body crumbled in a heap. He hit the ground with a thud, then sprawled out. His head thumped on the pavement, and his body bounced and then settled, motionless. His head was turned sideways, his arms at his sides, his legs grotesquely spread out like a frog about to leap.

"Damn," I muttered and ran over to him, knelt, picked up his head, which had lolled to the side. A large black and blue bruise was deepening on his cheek. I held his head in my hands, gently lifting him, cradling him in my arms.

His eyes were open, but unresponsive; his expression was vacant. I called his name, "Erling, Erling," and continued to cradle him for several minutes, then let him down, careful to put his head down gently.

Shaking off my gloves, I went to find the canteen. When I lifted him again, his body was surprisingly heavy. I pulled him onto my lap and splattered water on his face. He looked awful, his skin a pasty white. He wasn't moving. I put him down again, gently, and grabbed the comforter from the back seat and covered him, rocking him back and forth, looking at the car, wondering if I should drive him to the nearest hospital.

I had no idea where we were, where the nearest hospital was. Whatever rage I had unleashed—and this time, I was conscious of it, using it—had dissipated. It was replaced with dread. I may have killed him, or if not killed, since he was breathing erratically, may have damaged his brain. It took about ten minutes for him to come to. First, he twitched, his muscles reflexively tightened, then his eyes focused on me, querulous, uncertain what was going on and who I was. He lifted his left arm to wipe his face and realized that he still had his gloves on. He smiled weakly and shook his head, "Not a good idea: might knock myself out."

He lay back more comfortably, stretching out, supine in my arms. He breathed more intently, taking longer breaths, moving his jaw around, sorting out the effects of the blow and his tumble to the pavement.

"I didn't see it coming, but it was a good one," he said. "Can you get these gloves off me?"

"I thought I'd killed you," I whispered as I unlaced his gloves, not looking him in the face.

"Yeah, I thought you did too!"

"I'm sorry. I really am."

"No, no, don't be. It was a good punch, solid." He shook his head. "Face it, if you had missed me with that one, I would have clobbered you and been damned delighted to have done it."

I laughed. "So we're done?"

"Yep. Done. Good fight. For a country club kid, you're better than I thought you'd be."

We sat down on an embankment and analyzed the fight. First, he thought that he had me when I shuffled back on my heels and tried to avoid him. Then, he was sure he had me when I angrily charged at him. My guard was down. He had a perfect opening but miscalculated. As we talked, I saw his jaw move back and forth as if checking if it still worked after my punch.

I realized the boxing match was a test of my mettle, a measure of my willingness to stand up and fight. One good punch was all it took to win Erling's confidence. I felt proud.

The sun settled in the trees. We drank water from a canteen. Our breathing returned to normal. Torrents of sweat still poured over our bodies. He motioned to the water. We walked down to the reservoir, stripped, and swam into the sunset, sprawling across the water, our arms out, floating and letting the water hold us up.

"Where do we sleep?" I asked after we were toweled off.

He patted his car. "In Mabel."

"Mabel?"

"That's her," he said, rubbing the faded blue finish of his Rambler. She was called Mabel because the 'r's had fallen off the front of the hood. He transposed the 'm' and 'a', leaving her official name: *Mabel.* Her fold-back seat came in handy. We reclined on it, pulled out the quilt and two pillows, and had a comfortable bed. The next morning, we sat over a kerosene stove. The water boiled. Two cups of coffee warmed us. We drove to our next destination, one that he had no problem finding: Rose's Creek Hollow.

Rose's Creek Hollow

AFTER GETTING OFF I-75 north from Knoxville, he exited at Jellico, the last town in Tennessee before the Kentucky State Line, then took Route 9, which joined up with 25W as it rose into the mountains and skirted along the Kentucky border on the Cumberland River. The road wrapped around the mountains, carved snugly against its slopes, then unwound in a valley and meandered along the river. We came to Route 90, which took a serpentine path deeper into the mountains.

At the town of Clearfork, Erling turned left on a rutted dirt road. Dust billowed up. Some homes were set a few feet from the road. Some set back, up on knolls or down by creek beds. I could see the exposed undersides of the ones on risers. Some were painted, many were not, with only gray clapboards.

On a particularly steep incline, Erling pulled up into a yard. The house, set on posts, had an unscreened front porch.

"This is it," he said. "The future home of the Folk School."

"But, look"—I pointed at a boy on the porch—"somebody lives here."

"Right."

"Who lives here?" I asked.

"Peggy Metzler and her family," Erling said. "They have another house up the hollow and want to move back to it. They've agreed to sell us the house and the land."

A teenager with a mop of blond hair waved at him.

"That's Bobby." Erling waved back and called out, "How are you?"

"Can't complain," he said and stepped down the front steps.

Erling introduced us. I shook Bobby's hand, which was soft yet firm. He smiled at me and told me Erling said that I played football.

"Is it true?" he asked.

"Yes," I said.

He raced off, grabbed a football, and tossed it to me. I flung it back at him.

"Go out for a long one," I told him. He sprinted off, and I launched a long one right into his hands.

"Well, you've made a friend," I heard someone say. Standing on the porch was a large woman, her hair pulled back across her forehead. She had a beautiful face—not the beauty of a fashion model, more so the beauty of someone who'd lived a hard life with deep-ridged crow's feet at her eyes, and a sturdy jaw. Her bold, radiant smile, full of warmth and humor, put me at ease.

Bobby trotted back and said, "Nice pass." We walked up the yard, his body inches from mine, his arm brushing against mine.

Erling introduced me to Peggy, who said, "Pleased to meet you," shook my hand, and gestured for us to come in. The front door swung open to a hallway between two front bedrooms. We walked down the hall past two smaller rooms to the kitchen.

Peggy said, "Erling told us a lot about you."

Not sure what to say, I leaned back against the door frame and joked, "I'm not sure what he told you, but none of it is true."

She laughed and pointed to a chair at a kitchen table. "Set yourself there. Get a load off your feet. Bobby's been anxious to meet you. He loves football. You played it?"

"Yes, I did."

Bobby placed three chairs at a long wooden table. I sat down next to him. A wide grin lit up his face, his cheeks lined with freckles, his eyes full of delight.

Peggy asked, "You hungry?"

"No, that's fine."

"I'll not hear it. You've driven a long way. A feller your age needs his food. I'll fix you some vittles. You eat if I fix some?" Her tone led me to believe there was only one right answer.

"Yes, ma'am."

"That's better. Nothing better than a feller with a good appetite."

She carried herself with graceful dignity. Her dress, clinging loosely to her, denoted the plainness of her nature. She pulled out an iron skillet and shoved wood in the stove. I liked her manner: She said what she thought and expected the same from me.

Later, Erling told me that she had twelve children and raised them all, even when her husband, George, had black lung disease. His lungs had become coated with the fine coal dust that, over the years, clogged the lungs just as smoke did, but worse, so that he was out of breath and tired most of the time.

She plopped a dollop of lard in a skillet and threw in large, thick slabs of bacon. After cooking it until it browned, she set it aside and cracked several eggs in the pan. They sizzled in the grease. She flipped one after another onto a plate, put several slices of bread on the stove top to toast, slapped butter on them, poured some applesauce from a canning jar into a bowl, and set plates in front of Erling, Bobby, and me. She filled a cup with black coffee and leaned back to admire her handiwork.

I said, "Best eggs ever."

"I know," she said. "Used to be a short-order cook. I served thirty at a time." Bobby scooted his chair by the window and tossed crumbs outside. He stuck a wad of tobacco in his cheek and spat tobacco juice at the chickens.

They 'baaaked' and skittered away.

He laughed and spat some more.

"Lord sakes, leave them alone, Bobby," Peggy scolded him. "You torment them so."

Bobby's dark eyes sunk deep into his face. With dusty blond hair sticking out at odd angles, he looked as if he'd just woken up. He had the same problem with his hair as I did. He'd comb it, pat it down with water, but it never cooperated, always poked out in all directions. He walked across the room with an easy lope, his hips naturally swaying like a dancer's, carrying his weight lightly on the balls of his feet. As I came to know him, I found that he rarely stood still, forever wanted to be doing something, to show me something he'd found, or to ask me questions about what it was like in the city.

Peggy introduced me to the girls, who'd been playing in the creek. She stood by each, patting them on their shoulders as she told me their names.

"Come on, don't be shy. This is Donna, and that's Katie, and the two young ones, they're twins, Valerie and Joanie," she said.

I shook each of their hands (they giggled) and told them what a delight it was to meet them. Skinny, with long, angular faces, their hair was cut short. They scampered off to the backyard and chased the chickens.

Bobby stood by the door tossing a football up and down. He eyed me so that the minute I'd scooped up the last egg yolk with some toast and cleaned my plate, he could flip me the ball and take off running. We went into the dirt yard with a chicken coop at one end and a large fenced-in garden at the other. Quick on his feet, he darted up and down, snatching my throws with good hands, snaring them high and low.

He treated me like an older brother, and Peggy fed me like her kin.

I felt at home. It wasn't a society circumscribed by social events—parties, golf tournaments, bridge games, cocktail parties—where everyone was obsessed with keeping up appearances. No one had to wear the latest fashion styles. I didn't need to pay attention to how I looked and what impression I was making. I could be who I was without putting on airs. I tossed one pass after another. The ball sailed over the parched red earth to Bobby, who could have played all afternoon if my arm hadn't given out.

Bobby wanted to show me the swimming hole. Erling drove us up the road to where it narrowed to one lane. No guardrail. The side of the road fell off hundreds of feet into a ravine. The tops of pines poked up from a creek bed below.

Bobby yelled, "Pull in there." He hopped out of the car and raced down a rocky path. "Come on!"

In a clearing, a creek flowed off a jut of boulders and pooled in a basin dammed up by rocks. The swimming hole appeared to be fifteen feet deep and fifteen yards wide. Tall poplars and ash surrounded it.

We sat by its rim and tossed pebbles into it. Bobby asked if we wanted to go for a swim. Erling begged off. I stripped off my clothes, stepped my foot into the ice-cold water, and pulled it out.

"No time for wimps!" Erling cried.

Bobby had already stripped and jumped off a rock. He was paddling around. "Come on," he called.

I dove in. My skin felt shrink-wrapped. Every muscle contracted. I took several strokes, and Bobby splashed me. I splashed him back. He leaped at me, trying to dunk me, and I dodged him and pulled him underwater. Wiry, he squirmed away. We spent fifteen minutes playing in the pool.

When we hopped out, Bobby sat on a rock in the sun, and I joined him.

Bobby was self-possessed, comfortable in his skin. It felt natural to be in my body as well. Once dried and dressed, we headed back to Peggy's house. Peggy gave me a big hug and told me how glad she was I was working with Erling. She invited me to come up anytime. Her home was my home.

❧

We waved goodbye and drove off. I asked Erling if she was sincere, if she meant what she said about her home being my home.

"Yes," he said, "that's how she is."

I nearly cried, thinking how easily I'd become family without having to prove myself. This was a very different world. Not at all like my own home, where any outsider, even if he were well-to-do, had to be assessed and meet specific societal standards before anyone would ever say, "Our home is your home."

Before we'd gone too far, he stopped the car and turned off the engine. The evening light clung to the distant high ridges.

"Hey, I've been thinking," he said. "I need an Assistant Director you know, someone to help organize the day programs, to fundraise, and to work closely with me in selecting students."

"That's what I thought Jack was supposed to be."

Erling laughed. "No, no, never. That was *his* idea, never mine."

"Really?"

"Yep," he said. "Even before he got the job at the church that pays him so well, I never wanted him as an assistant."

"That's not what he said."

"Jack has a unique way of seeing the world," he said. He slung his arm on the back of the seat and turned to me. "He seems to think the world revolves around him and his anthropology. I don't think he could ever be anyone's assistant. He has to be the one in charge."

"I've noticed that."

"Well?"

"Well, what?"

"You want to do it?"

The dust behind us had roiled up and swept over the windshield. It settled, and the view was clear again.

"All right," I said.

"Good, then I want you to meet several others. They're important people. We need their cooperation," he said. He started the engine and drove down the hollow.

❧

Erling introduced me to Marie Cirillo, the nun whose work developing jobs and programs for local people he'd told me about. Longtime residents like Peggy found that they could sometimes retain ownership of their homes, but the land around them became wastelands, contaminated with sludge from strip mines. Marie wanted to rebuild the communities, buy back the property, and preserve the land. which had game and fresh-running brooks with fish and crawfish.

Erling supported her efforts and wanted to work with her. He asked her to serve on the Folk School's board. We had a long conversation and stayed for dinner. She wondered what it entailed and what he wanted her to do. After considering it, she agreed to serve as the board chairperson.

With Marie on board, we headed back to Nashville.

On the long drive back, Erling told me what he needed from me in terms of money. He had already lined up three students to attend the Folk School: two college girls and one local girl. He had also purchased a cabin for us to stay in. The other students would be housed at a Methodist lodge near the Kentucky border. Folk School classes would meet at the lodge in the mornings and evenings. We'd have our summer arts and activities in Rose's Creek during the day on Peggy's land and, on Fridays, have a campfire for community gatherings.

Money Matters

IN LATE MARCH, I drove back to Glen Ellyn to raise money. A church trustee, Mr. James Hook, agreed to talk with me about the project.

His house sat in a residential neighborhood across from the Glenbard football field. I walked by the bleachers and stood on the playing field, where I had been a starting fullback; the white 10-yard lines were ribbed in the grass. I remembered how, when the band played, we burst through a large hoop with Glenbard Hilltoppers painted on a large screen. Just on the other side of the hoop, cheerleaders with pompoms screamed at the top of their lungs. Spectators stood and clapped. For an hour or two, we'd give up our bodies for the team, rush for a few yards, be tackled, slammed into the ground, only to get up and go at it again and again. It seemed so long ago. Yet my right knee remembered it every time it rained.

Mr. Hook, a bespectacled man, greeted me and told me to have a seat in his living room. His wife, a white-haired lady with a matronly build yet the graceful movement of a former dancer, offered me a Sprite. We spent an hour discussing the town, the church, and my project. Mr. Hook seemed interested, but wanted to know what my career interests were—"The ministry, perhaps?"

"Not sure," I said.

"What do you mean?" he asked. I was at a loss as to what to say because, if I were to admit to him my primary interest in attending the Divinity School was to avoid the draft, not to become a minister, it might offend him and dissuade him from supporting the Folk School.

His wife, having brought out chocolate chip cookies and more Sprite and noticing my hesitancy to answer his inquiries, interrupted her husband. "I think, whatever your career interests, what you are doing is noble. In my mind, it's very Christian. Serving the poor—isn't that what Christ asked us to do?" She directed her question not to me but to Mr. Hook. It took him a moment to register it. She continued, "Then it only makes perfect sense that the church supports him in his endeavors."

Mr. Hook nodded his head and winked at me. "She has a way of making her point, don't you think?"

She admonished him, "Now, dear, you know I always allow for differences in opinion."

He put his hand to the side of his mouth and whispered, "'Allow' is the key word. 'Permit' is quite another thing."

"Did you say something, dear?" she inquired.

"Nothing, my dear, just confirming our support for his work."

He agreed to do the fundraising. By the end of the holiday, he had a fifteen-hundred-dollar check cut for the Folk School. I drove over to his house, rang the doorbell, and practically hugged him. Nonplused, he invited me in and offered me a Sprite. We discussed the civil rights movement and the anti-war fervor on college campuses. His open-mindedness struck me.

He informed me that the church's one requirement of me was that I keep a journal of my "mission" to Appalachia and that I come by again before I left to go over what the money would be used for.

&

Several days before leaving, my parents took me to dine at the club. I put on my usual uniform for the occasion: blue blazer, tie, and slacks.

When I came downstairs, my father was on the back porch. Still wearing his black pinstriped suit from work, he leaned over the porch, tapping his cigar on the railing and letting the ashes fall to the patio below. His dark hair had streaks of grey at his temples. He patted the railing next to me, noting where he wanted me to stand, and offered me a cigar.

"No, thanks."

He pursed his lips and stated his concerns about the Folk School. "Your mother tells me that you're planning on working in Tennessee, some sort of school, is that right?"

"Yes," I said. I hadn't informed him for fear he might object.

"Well, we're worried about your decision," he said. "Does it pay well?"

"No, not at all. But room and board are free."

He stared at the backyard garden, and, beyond it, to the bank of trees, and, farther, to the faint headlights of cars on Butterfield Road. He paused and puffed on his cigar.

"Sure you don't want one?" He held one out to me.

"No."

"Is this part of your program at the seminary?"

"No. But it's something I want to do, Dad. We're working with the people in Appalachia who are struggling to reclaim their land. They have it pretty hard and—"

"I know all too well," he said and tapped his cigar, knocking off its ash. He took an extended inhalation. I'd forgotten that his father had worked in southern Ohio during the Depression and hated it. His mother had committed suicide there.

His face drawn, his lips tight, he shook his head.

"I think it would be better—your mom worries you know—for you to work here. Mr. Selman has a good job with benefits at his warehouse. I told you earlier it could be arranged. It pays quite well. It's time you started earning a living. And you'd be out by three and could play—"

"I don't want to do that."

"Money, son, is what makes this world go around," he said. "You'll come to—"

"Dad, this is part of *my ministry*," I said.

"Ministry?"

"Yes."

He cocked his head sideways, held his cigar at a distance, and looked at it.

"Ministry?" he repeated, more to himself than to me. He was trying to find his way around the word, to see if he could find a rebuttal, some other word that could trump my word. "Ministry," he said again. "I see." He took a long puff. "This is an excellent brand. Cuban. Sure, you don't want one?"

"I'll take one for the road."

"Here," he said, passing me one. I put it in my jacket pocket. "You sure, son, you know what you're getting into?"

"I've been there. The people are great—"

"I've lived there. And, believe me, they're not as great as you think."

"Dad, I want to give this a shot. I'll earn money at school. I have a job as a dorm advisor during the year."

He furrowed his brow. "Well—"

"Dad, it's what I want to do."

"All right. But keep us informed. Your mom's worried."

"I will."

"Here, take another one of these," he said. He held out a cigar. "They're from Havana. Don't ask how I got them!"

"You're trying to get me addicted," I said.

He laughed. "How did I raise such a puritan?"

"Thanks, Dad."

"Any time," he said. "Look, your mom is waiting for us. Doesn't she look stunning!"

He pushed back my unruly hair, which had begun to grow over my ears and down my neck.

"You should get a haircut before you leave," he said as we entered the living room where Mom was waiting for us.

Mother reached out to take his arm. "Everything all right?"

"Fine," he said.

⁂

I sat in the back seat as my parents sipped their martinis in the front seat. At the club, my father drove under a vaulted canopy. A valet opened the doors of the car. "Good evening, Mrs. Follett and Mr. Follett."

And my door, too. "Good evening, Mr. Follett."

A red doormat led to the main entrance.

Cocktails were served in the Green Room overlooking the 18th green. I had several beers. The conversation—how the course was opened, who shot the best round of golf, who was winning the latest PGA tournament, what the weather was like, or what was forecast to be like, what the dog had done—bounced from topic to topic like a ping-pong ball.

Our dinner guests, the Johnsons, joined us. Mrs. Johnson wore thick makeup, her face like a mask with heavy eye mascara and ruby lipstick. In the caddy shack, she was known as a "ballbuster." If she didn't like where a caddie stood, if his shadow transgressed her line on the putting green, if he moved an inch while she prepared a shot, she'd shriek, "Young man!" and glower at him.

We were paired off at dinner so that each woman had a man by her side. Mrs. Johnson sat beside me and asked what I was doing for the summer. I told her about the Folk School.

She smiled and said, "Why, yes. I remember when I was your age. I worked with the poor in Cleveland. For a summer, I took a bus to a shelter, served meals, and provided day care for some women. Very pathetic. Ignorant people, really. It was such sad work. Those people, I learned, will never amount to much. Born poor, they'll die poor—"

I interrupted. "I'm sorry, but I completely disagree. From what I've seen—and I have only been there once—people want to regain control over their lives. Their homes and land were bought out from under them."

"Such idealism," she spoke over me, her voice pitched higher. "Yes, it is commendable for a person your age, and natural, I suppose."

"I don't consider myself an idealist," I responded. "I see myself more as a person who wants to learn and who—"

She smacked her hand on the table and glared at me. Her mouth tightened, causing the muscles in her cheeks to bulge. "Young man, listen, I don't want to discuss this matter. But let me say that—and mark my words." She pointed a long, pink-tipped index finger at me. "In a year, you'll tire of them and their sad lives and move on, as I did, as we all do." She smacked her lips together and glanced around the table for approval. "You must eventually find work with more reputable people." Pleased with herself and, surely, delighted that others felt the same way she did, she made one last declaration. "Those sorts of people wouldn't get a lick of my money—or anyone else's—if I had my way." She nodded her head, smiled, and asked my father about his plans for the summer.

The waitress brought our salads. My mother shuffled her cucumbers onto my salad plate—she never ate them—and patted my hand. She whispered, "That's just Hilda." She raised her eyebrows, sighed, and added, "Your dad and I are proud of you."

I finished the meal hurriedly and excused myself, careful to thank the Johnsons for the meal and tell them how nice it was to see them. I would just as soon have told Hilda to stuff her damn money up her ample ass.

I walked down the tenth fairway. When I played golf, I could block out anything and think of each shot: how it would fly, land, spin back, and settle on the green.

My parents had finished their coffee and were saying goodbye to the Johnsons when I came back. Hilda sashayed by in her purple dress (She loved purple. "Doesn't everyone love purple?" she was fond of saying.)

I snuck in behind my parents. My father was talking to my mother, who saw me coming before he did. "That's the last time I'll have dinner with that pompous ass!" he said. I didn't let on that I heard him, but I smiled all the way home.

Before I headed back to Vanderbilt, Mr. Hook invited me to come for a chat. Since his wife was out of town, he asked if I'd like a beer. "How about a Bud?" We sat in his living room and talked about the present antiwar demonstrations and how in his youth, before Pearl Harbor, many of his friends were protesting against our entrance into the war. The one beer led to two, and two to three. He spoke about himself and his life, including his work as an accountant and his lifelong passion for painting. He showed me his landscapes; they were gorgeous, rich in texture, and adept at detailing the lake near his house, misted with fog, in different seasons.

A thoughtful man, he was honest about his struggle with finding the truth about his faith, or lack of it. He lived what he called two lives: his work life, the one he had to do to raise his three children—all grown—and the artistic life, the one he kept to himself.

He said, "I've learned some things over the years." He took off his glasses and wiped them with a napkin. "It seems that each generation believes that it has staked a claim on The Truth. Some of my business friends say that the world comes down to money. Money makes the world go round."

"My dad tells me that!"

"He's right in many ways. But as a painter, I work alone. Oh, I have a few artist friends and mentors. We have another perspective on life. We agree it's not about money. It's beauty that's most satisfying. I could be happy with just my paints and a landscape."

"That's how I feel when I write a good poem," I said, although I realized that I had barely written anything in the last year.

"Bet you would. Being an artist is never easy."

"You don't make a living out of it."

"No. I've wrestled with it my whole life. Sometimes I think I've figured myself out. But it's not so. The older I get, Jason, the more I come to see that every time I come across some wonderful revelation that makes me more aware of something in myself—how I always strive to be the best and, say, as a result, overreach and do poorly—I discover that, much as I think that I will not make the same mistake again, I do. Have you noticed that?"

I laughed. "Every time I think I have myself figured out, I discover I'm just beginning to understand how I'm not what I expected. Who I am seems like a vanishing trick, one day this, another day, that."

"Exactly," he said, tapping his bottle against mine. "It seems that as I come to see something is true, I think, 'Yes, this is so,' only to get busy with my life and then forget what it is I saw. Years later, in a different time and a different place, I discover the same truth again. It means just as much to me now as when I first discovered it, because this time I know how to use it better." He took another drink from his beer.

"Do you want something to eat?" he asked.

I did.

He put a frozen pizza in the oven, and we sat in the kitchen. As we ate the pizza, he went back to our conversation.

"The truth, it seems to me," he said, "is more an accumulation of insights, each coming in different ways. The more I can expose myself to different situations—ones that push me out of my comfortable ways of thinking, that shake up the same routines I've grown accustomed to—the better I will be at discovering what my truth is. The real truth comes to me when I'm vulnerable and filled with doubt. At those moments, whatever I have forgotten in my past, the little truths will come together in my heart..." He tapped his chest. "Right here, and I'll know what I only guessed at was there all along, waiting like a stranger, to greet me and say, 'Here, this is your Truth,' and, finally, I will know it too and can accept it."

I'm not sure I entirely understood him, as what he was saying seemed very personal, so I nodded my head. He thanked me for the talk and admitted, "People of my generation generally never talk much about themselves. They're doers. But me, I'm different."

I thanked him. Hilda's words at the country club had left a bitter taste in my mouth, but his words felt sweet. Instead of shaking hands, he hugged me and said that he'd share my reports with the church.

I felt lucky to know him, fortunate to be on my way to some truth that I hoped to find in the mountains.

Goodbyes

ONCE BACK AT Vanderbilt, I checked in with Michael and Sam. I'd miss Michael and Sam hanging out in my room. But I felt good that Michael had endured his trauma and found a friend. Odd how some guys had violated him, and another boy saved him, how men could be so cruel to one another, yet also be so kind.

⁂

Bob's efforts to get a conscientious objector status had failed. He'd have to go into the service. Because of his facility with language, he'd been assigned to a special unit for decoding enemy messages. He had to report for boot camp, but at least he didn't have to be in combat.

He threw a goodbye party. Eight professors and their wives came, along with several students. By the end of the party, his apartment looked like a bomb had exploded. People were strewn on the floor and couches, everyone drunk and maudlin. Like at an Irish wake, one couple after another hugged him and slipped into the night. Ann and I stayed overnight. We sat up until one or two, chatting with Bob and his latest girlfriend.

The next day, after breakfast, I drove him to the airport. I had a knot in my stomach, but I bantered with him about how hungover we were and how Ann and I wouldn't have a place to crash on the weekend.

When he stepped to the curb to wish me goodbye, he looked at the cement, not me.

"Something wrong?" I asked.

He lifted his head, his eyes filled with tears, his face contorted with pain. Without thinking, I opened my arms. We hugged and sobbed helplessly.

He whispered in a raspy voice, "I need to go."

I held him tight. "I know. I know."

"I do need to go, but Goddamn, this is hard." He rubbed his hand across his face.

"I don't want to lose you," I said and pushed him back slightly, staring at his face—angular with high cheekbones, blue eyes, and a mop of curly brown hair. I brushed his hair back like he usually did.

He blinked and grabbed hold of me. "Damn. Damn. Maybe I should have just kept my 4-D. Never thought it would come to this."

"We look pretty pathetic," I said, trying to joke. I noticed that several men who had hopped out of cars were glaring at us, just as they had when Paul and I embraced at the airport months ago.

"Yes, we are." He laughed and looked at the other men. "They must think we're a couple of queers!" He waved at them, kissed me quickly on the lips, and gave them the finger.

"Figure we should give them something to talk about," he said. "They don't know what love is."

He held my hand and said softly, "I do love you. You know that?"

I bit my lower lip. "Yes, yes, I do."

He said he'd write and that I must write to him too. The mindless regimentation of boot camp was going to be hard.

"I'll miss our conversations," he said, "and the…" His voice trailed off. "Being together."

"Yeah."

"Me too."

"No more times like we had," he said.

He stepped back and picked up his bag. I wiped my tears away, my chest torn open. I watched him go through the turnstile. Once inside, he waved, entered a line, and turned away. I got in the car, touched my lips with my hand, looked at him once more, and drove away.

❧

I saw Ann the next day. She asked how it had been. I told her that he said that he loved me, and no guy had ever told me that before. I couldn't get over it. He said it as if it were the most natural thing in the world. Yet, for me, to say it—or even to think it—brought up fears and doubts about my sexual feelings. No matter how deeply I had buried them, they broke through the crust of my denial. I said nothing to Ann of what I felt for Bob, but she knew Bob had cracked my shell so that grief worked its way out.

We went back to my dorm room. She held me most of the night, and although she may not have understood that I'd lost a part of me that I could not name, she did understand that I needed to be held.

Her fingers traced lines down my chest and belly. My fingers glided over her nipples and her soft, round belly and legs. We stopped to kiss and then, almost without thinking, made love.

She left the next day for a summer job in Seattle. I felt choked up as I drove her to the airport, just as I had with Bob. We repeated the same goodbye ritual I had done less than a day ago. She took her two suitcases to the ticket desk and waved. Several planes took off, cleared the hills, and headed into the clouds. Life, I realized, was often a long goodbye, one after another, and how, if I were to go on, I would ever escape the losses, I was not sure. I was sure, though, that those I lost would continue to linger inside of me. I could hold on to them my memory, which became fuller and fuller with each loss.

❧

I drove home and worked at the Glen Oak Country Club pro shop for a few weeks. The pro, Al Huske, taught me most of what I knew about golf—how to swing and make tricky shots. He liked me and put me in charge of starting times. I mowed the yard at home, weeded Mom's garden, went out with my friend Jerry. Jerry liked to try to pick up girls, but liked even more to drink too much, driving home at an ungodly hour with a sizable bar bill for our ill-fated efforts.

In June, I packed my bags, including my journal and writing paper, and consulted a map of Eastern Tennessee to find Clearfork, ensuring I knew exactly where to meet Erling.

Too Old

A FEW DAYS BEFORE I left for the Folk School, my mother said, "Before you go, dear, your father and I want to take you to the club for dinner."

I was standing at the kitchen window, looking out at the daisies alongside the driveway, and replied absently, "Thanks. That would be nice."

The tone of her voice changed. "Good, then you need to get a haircut."

I ran my fingers through my scruffy, dense hair, now covering my ears. "No. I don't want one."

She pressed her hands on the counter, turned away, and began to weep, her hand over her eyes.

"What is the problem, Mom?" I asked, still standing halfway across the room.

"You can't go looking like that. It's embarrassing. You know what that does to us. People—"

"Talk," I completed her sentence.

"Yes."

"Let them."

"I can't. It's much more difficult than you know," she explained. "Not only do they talk, but they also gossip, they say things, and it hurts your father and his relationships with important people—"

"Is that all you care about?"

"Yes, dear, it is. Friends are very important. We cannot change that."

I stared at her. "Why?"

She looked directly at me—but, as I later realized, not at me but at who she wanted me to be—and said, "We're too old to change."

"Too old?" I scoffed.

"Well, will you?" she asked.

Not knowing what else to do, I said, "I'll think about it."

The more I thought about it, the angrier I felt. I determined I would hold my ground. No haircut for me. I put my bags in my car, called my friend Dick, who had offered to let me crash at his apartment, and said I was coming early, and left a note on the kitchen table. "Needed to leave early."

Confession

I PULLED UP A narrow driveway, pinched between two apartment complexes. Scorching heat hit me when I opened the car door. My shirt was drenched with sweat before I took the ten steps to enter the apartment.

Pam welcomed me with a hug and said, "Just in time." She waved her hand toward the kitchen table, which was filled with a big pot roast, a bowl of mashed potatoes, and a mixed fruit salad.

I put my suitcase on the floor, hugged Dick, and sat down.

We talked about John Lennon and Yoko Ono doing a 'bed-in' in protest of the war. Dick mentioned Midnight Cowboy, a movie he'd seen, and I'd seen in Chicago. It scared me, especially the scene when Joe Buck couldn't make money hustling women, offers himself to men, and after sex, beats them up.

"What did you think of it?" Dick asked.

"It was okay," I said.

"Okay?"

"Well, I must admit that scene when Joe beat up that old man, and when he beat up that young kid and took his watch was disgusting."

"The homosexual scenes bothered you?"

"Not that. It was just that I felt sorry for those guys, you know," I said and turned to Pam, asking what seasoning she used in the pot roast.

She told me that it was an old-fashioned recipe from her mom, some mix of savory herbs. Trying to change the subject and keep from discussing the movie, I asked if they'd watched the Apollo 10 launch. Dick didn't take the bait and pursued his questions about *Midnight Cowboy.*

"You felt sorry?"

"Yes, I—"

Pam, sensing my discomfort, intervened. "How were your parents, Jason?"

I was about to reply when Dick said. "Linda, you changed the subject."

"Dick," she shot back, her tone decisive, "can't you see he's bothered by it?"

"Sorry, honey. I just—"

"Just nothing," she said emphatically. "Now, Jason, do you like chocolate or vanilla ice cream?"

"Both," I said.

"Oh, a gourmand," she said, "I suspected it," and winked at me.

After dinner, we lounged in the living room. After an apéritif, Pam excused herself and kissed Dick and me goodnight.

Dick discussed the course he was taking on liturgy for the Episcopal Church.

"You wouldn't believe how sophisticated they are. The whole Eucharist, for example, must be staged carefully; the bread is held up just so (he mimicked the move), and the wine is poured (he mimicked the move). Each is sequenced. I've seen it done a thousand times, it seems, but I always bungle it. I need to review my crib notes. I feel like an idiot," he said. "You're lucky. Many Protestants don't even use wine."

"You forget I'm not going to be a minister."

"Right," he said and lowered his voice. "Sorry, I pressed you about Joe Buck."

"It's okay."

"It's just—I don't know why I'm telling you this—but back in college, I had a crush on another guy. Very intense. I couldn't get him out of my mind. Obsessed. Head over heels in love. I wanted to be with him all the time. It disturbed me. I saw a counselor. I didn't want to be...you know, a..."

I added the word, "Homosexual."

He wanted me to say more, to tell him that I, too, had the same feelings and found him attractive. I wondered if he knew about me. It would have been easy for me to say something. He was married. I didn't have to worry. But I flinched. Facing my feelings was too much. I stood up, shoved my hands in my pockets, and told him, "That must be rough."

Like Judas, I turned my back on him.

"It was," he said. "You want another drink?"

"No, thanks."

"That's just between you and me, right?" he said.

"Sure."

"It gets better," he said. "Pam is great."

He sat on the couch, his head down. "Thanks for listening," he said in a small voice. He wiped something off his shoe. I got up, sat next to him, and put my arm over his shoulder.

"Hey, it's all right. No big deal. I…"

He tilted his head toward me. The sadness in his eyes seemed immeasurable. The left side of his mouth lifted in a half-smile. He waited for me to go on.

"I…I understand."

He nodded his head.

❧

In the morning, Dick seemed distant, and Pam took me aside and asked if something was wrong. I told her, "No, everything's fine."

Dick walked me to the car and said, "Sorry about last night."

"Hey, as I said, no big deal."

He shook his head. "Still friends?"

"You bet."

I reached over to hug him. He grabbed hold of me and held me tight. "Have a good summer, and write, will ya?"

"You bet."

III

What might have been and what has been point to one end, which is always present.

—"The Four Quartets," T.S. Eliot

Road to Clearfork

DRIVING WAS TORTUROUS from Nashville to the Cumberland Mountains. Rain ricocheted off the windshield and flooded the highway. In the mountains, the pelting rain made it impossible to know how sharp the turns were. In Jellico—the foothills of the Cumberland Mountains—the rain slackened, yet driving was still slow. Road signs jumped out at sharp curves. One pointed one way; another pointed in the opposite direction. My foot rarely left the brake pedal. A large boulder appeared with yellow lettering and a jagged cross painted beneath the words, "Jesus Saves."

I wondered if he could save me from careening off some cliff.

Erling had told me to turn at "Jesus Saves." By then, the road was clear. No rain. Another twenty miles to go. I downshifted up the steep rises and braked on the way down. Some curves were so severe I wondered if I'd meet myself coming from the other side.

I was going to meet Erling at one o'clock. The last twenty miles put me behind schedule. I gunned it down a straightaway to the small, pitted sign "Clearfork," and took the first right before another hill on a side road ribbed like corduroy.

I pulled up to the Clearfork Post Office. Five minutes early. I stood on the front porch. Yellowish-white dust rose from the road, caked the trees, shrubs, plants, and stairs. Just off the porch, under a large maple, its leaves whitened with dust, a man in bib overalls stood beside a green rocking chair with his rifle in the crook of his arm, staring at me.

"What you doing?" he asked.

He had several badges on his overalls. His black hair, unkempt, was shoved under his blue cap.

"I asked you, mister—what's your business?"

The front door squeaked; I turned around to see who was there. A husky lady with gray hair stood behind the screen door. She peered at me.

"Can I help?"

"Yes, ma'am, you can," I said, "but first—" I nodded toward the sheriff.

She stepped out the door, noticed him, and gave a big guffaw.

"Oh, Brady, put that away. This man means no harm. Get off now," she scolded him. He bowed his head and sat down under the maple, the gun in his lap.

"It's not loaded," she said, smiling. "Now what's it you need?"

"I'm to meet Erling Duus," I said.

"Why didn't you say so? He's expecting you. You're at the right place. I'm Ida Handford, Postmistress," she said, extending her hand. "Y'all come on in. I'll get you something to drink. You thirsty?"

"Sure am."

She looked at me closely, "You look it. Lemonade—will it do?"

"Yes. Thank you, ma'am."

"Land's sake, call me Ida."

"Okay, Miss Ida."

"It's so damn hot, likely to kill a man. Fan keeps me going these days." The post office was more like a home than an office of the United States government. There was a small booth with a counter, just like other post offices, but to the right was another screen door that opened into a living room with a couch, a chair, a desk, and a huge fan.

"Make yourself at home." She aimed the fan at me.

"Mr. Duus is hunting for you, too," she said. "Been here twice. He's at the Community Center just up the road a piece. He's got the girls with him." She handed me the lemonade—cool in my hand, dripping with condensation. "Should be back soon."

I wondered, What should I say? Tell her about myself? Where I came from, how I knew Erling?

I didn't have to worry. Words poured from her. She told me about the community, the excitement about the Folk School, and how folks liked Mr. Duus.

"He's just regular folks," Ida said.

There was a knock at the door. Erling came in, put his hands on his hips, "Well, well, here's my golf buddy!"

My outfit: golf shorts, golf shirt, and golf hat. I replied, "You wanna play nine or eighteen?"

"I wanna just shake your hand," he said. "You made it."

"Yes."

"You met Mrs. Handford?"

"Ida, please," she chastised Erling.

"Of course."

"She's been gracious," I acknowledged, "and she's told me a lot about the community too."

"As Postmistress, she knows pretty much everything about everyone in Clearfork. And she has the biggest, kindest heart of anyone I know."

Ida smiled. "You're too kind."

"It's true."

"Darn right," she grinned. "Make it my business."

Erling chatted with her and thanked her for taking care of me.

"Drop by any time," she said. "Gets pretty lonesome here."

We squatted on the porch steps and surveyed the road. Erling wore a white shirt, rolled up at the sleeves, and beige slacks, which made him seem too well-dressed for the setting. The thick cloud from his car had not settled. He pointed to a parking spot in front of the post office.

He said, "That's the center of town." Dust swept over the porch. I coughed. "You get used to it," he said.

I leaned close to him and pointed at the sheriff in the chair with a gun. "What's with him?"

Erling signaled me to follow him.

"Brady," he said, five feet from the man, "this is my friend Jason. Listen up: you need to take care of him. He's a good man. You understand?"

Brady nodded.

I stepped forward to put my hand out. Erling blocked it. "Not a good idea," he said. We walked a few yards away.

"Brady is—well—limited," Erling explained. "The local sheriff deputized him years ago. He gave him that rifle. It can't shoot. Brady watches out for Ida. He lives out back in a little two-room cabin. He wouldn't do any harm. At least not yet. He can fly off the handle. Especially if he doesn't know you, getting too close can be a problem. He's a little edgy. He's at all the big town events. He stands guard. He delivers papers, too, to those who live nearby."

He pointed at his car. "Mabel's doing fine." It looked the same: a faded, powdery blue, shaped like a shoebox.

"Would you like to see our accommodations?" he asked. "They're five-star. A golf course is right down the road. But I'll tell you right off I'm not caddying for you!"

At the head of the road, a tall, rusted metal structure on iron stilts loomed. It looked like an enormous canister with its bottom gouged open. Erling noticed my quizzical look and explained.

"It was used to load coal into train cars. They'd pull under it, fill up, and go west." He pointed past the tracks to a road that swung up a hillside. "That's where they mined, stripped off that whole ridge."

Three mountains triangulated around us, each sloped upward like a green pyramid. Beneath our feet, the dust puffed like gun smoke with each step.

"What do you think?" he asked.

"Don't know. Not like Illinois. Never been in any place like it."

"I'll show you the digs. And then we'll meet the girls. They'd like to swim." "I could use one." I tugged the shirt off my chest, damp from perspiration.

He moved gracefully around his car, stopped at the front grill, and brushed off some dust. He dipped his head down and regarded over the rims of his glasses. He sucked his lower lip in and pointed at my outfit. "Well, you do look comfortable. But," he inhaled sharply through his teeth, "there aren't too many golf clubs in these parts."

I followed as he drove up the main road to a narrow road carved precariously from the shale hillsides. It dipped down and twisted around several hills and curves. He parked along a wire fence. Our cars teetered on an embankment that sloped off at a thirty-degree angle down to a log cabin. Gravity flung my door open, and I nearly slammed it against a fence.

"Watch your step there, bub," Erling said. "Can't afford to lose you this early." He opened a gate and escorted me to the two-room cabin. It rested on the slope of the steep pasture, overlooking a farm with a white house. Honeysuckle vines climbed on one side of it. Knee-deep grass crowded around the cabin. Further on, Route 90 snaked along the valley, winding by a creek, and disappeared around a bend in the road.

"That's the golf course," Erling joked. "Deep rough. Nothing you can't handle." He stood in front of the cabin. It was pale brown, aged, and had a green front door. To the left, an old tool shed sat under the shade of two sycamore trees. On the right, a gnarled apple tree sagged slightly to one side as if it were drunk. The front room was ten by twelve, with windows on each side. Two chairs in it—wooden chairs with frayed wicker seats. Erling's sleeping bag was rumpled in one corner, and his brown suitcase lay open next to it. A side door opened onto a narrow stoop.

The next room—behind the first—was down three steps. It was small, had one window that faced the pasture, and a back door to the right. Peeling wallpaper had come loose and hung in long strips, the color of rust. A musty smell pervaded the interior. Out back, down a grassy path, was the outhouse with a quarter-moon window on the door, which sagged on its hinges.

"The lady who owns it—hers is the white house down the hill—says there's a well in the back by the creek, but I can't find it. We'll need to locate it. It's our water source," he said.

"How do we wash up?" I asked.

"Oh, here's the bathroom," he said. He stepped out of the side door on the first floor.

"I have a washbasin on the side stoop. Do your daily ablutions here," he chuckled. "Not exactly Triple-A-approved!"

I unloaded my sleeping bag and suitcase from the car and set them on the other side of the room.

❧

Another car pulled up. Erling took me lightly by the arm. "Come meet the girls," he said.

Girls? I thought. He called them girls.

He swung open the gate and tapped on the roof of a yellow Mustang. A woman let down the window. He leaned in the window and pointed to a young woman in the front seat. She had straight black hair and a dark complexion. "That's Lois—you may remember Peggy mentioned her."

I peeked through the window and said, "Hi." I wasn't sure I remembered her, but she looked familiar.

Before I could ask her a question, he pointed to another woman sitting in the back.

"That's Lorraine."

She waved at me. Finally, he tapped a woman in the driver's seat and said, "This is Emily." A petite woman with a ponytail reached out to shake my hand. She had a firm grip.

"My pleasure," she said, her mouth in a tentative smile. Her eyes had the steely acuity of a police inspector.

I pulled my hand back. "Nice to meet you." I'd lost some circulation in my hand.

Erling declared, "Hey, girls, let's take him for the scenic view."

Lorraine chimed in, "Good, we love it there."

Emily winced but pasted on a smile.

The Dead

As Erling backed up Mabel, dust billowed into a white cloud. He waited for it to settle, then drove down for a mile before turning onto a road with more ruts and washouts than pavement. It was more like a creek bed than a road, and his car hiccupped down it carefully.

He pulled up the embankment and parked. I was baffled as to why he stopped. The surrounding were much the same as they had been for the last few miles: nothing but a few trees and shrubs. I hadn't paid too much attention to the road because I was busily trying to remember the names of the new Folk School students.

He hopped out of the car and headed down a path, the three women following behind him.

He called back to me, "Come along. Be careful. There's lots of poison ivy." I stopped in my tracks and looked for the plant. What did that jingle say?

"Leaves of three, let it be." That didn't help. What did the leaves look like? Bending over, shielding my eyes from the sun, I couldn't find a three-leaved one, but was careful to stay on the worn path. I was highly allergic to poison ivy, and had shorts on.

I hurried after them. We trekked a quarter of a mile up a steep embankment. At its steepest point, a stone stairway led to an iron gate. Each stepping stone, carved precariously from the shale hillsides, was a different size. I watched each step to make sure I didn't trip.

"Where're we going?" I called out, out of breath.

"To a cemetery," Lois replied, turning her head slightly to answer.

"A cemetery?"

No sooner do I get here, I thought, than he takes me to a cemetery. I'd never been in one. Never had a need. No one had died that I knew. I'd seen them from the road—particularly that huge one by the East-West Tollway in Illinois. As a kid, I'd avert my eyes when I passed it. If I looked too long, I'd be the next headstone on the lot.

The cemetery was enclosed by a raised picket fence. It occupied about half a football field, small by Chicago standards, with forty or so granite and sandstone headstones nestled under gnarly pin oaks. Their wide branches overshadowed the cemetery.

The headstones were cracked. Weeds overgrew them. Vines fingered up and obscured the inscriptions. Blanched plastic flowers drooped by them. "Gone but Not Forgotten," etched on two stones.

I laughed out loud and said, "These graves are long forgotten!"

Erling glared at me.

Lois looked away.

"This is a place," Erling hesitated to gauge his words, "where your bourgeois cynicism needs to take a break." He motioned for me to button my lip. "Why don't you quietly look around?" He pointed to the distant mountains. "Give some thought to Lois. She happens to live here. Her relatives are buried here."

Lois bent over a grave and cleared away some weeds. She was trying to read the names on it.

The sunlight stippled the ground with the gravestones. Off in the distance, dark splotches lay on mountainsides where clouds hid the sunlight. Gray-blue mountain ranges were visible through openings in the trees. Below, a truck wound along a road. Dust rolled up behind it, lifted skyward, then dispersed in brownish smoke.

I felt embarrassed that I'd made a fool of myself.

Erling placed his hand on my shoulder. "It'll take a while. It's not suburbia."

He went over to Lois and discussed the lettering on the gravestone. I examined the dates on the tombstones. Many had died in their teens, most in their thirties and forties.

On the way back to the car, Lois asked me a series of questions, one right after another. Do you believe in God? Why did you come here? Why is your hair so long? Do you always wear shorts? Is blue your favorite color?

I held up my hand and told her to slow down. We had plenty of time to get acquainted. I wondered why she was so interested in knowing so much about me. She acted as if she had the right to find out.

Erling called out, "Let's head to the lake."

I trotted to Erling's car for the ride to the lodge, fifteen miles away, near to the Kentucky border.

Nestled in tall pines on a ridge overlooking a lake, the lodge was where we'd meet in the mornings to discuss "The American Experience."

The lodge's cook, an attractive guy with a winsome smile, introduced himself. "I'm Will. I'll make your breakfast, lunch, and dinner," he said and extended his hand.

"You any good?" I asked.

"The best!" he said. "I aim to please." His hand, soft, lingered in my hand.

Erling headed toward the bathroom to change into his swimsuit.

Will asked if he could join us.

"Hurry up," Erling said. "I want to beat the girls to the beach."

Will and I went into the bathroom, the size of a broom closet. Will shed his clothes quickly. He leaned against the door, his trunks in one hand as he yanked off his pants. He had a wiry, athletic frame with a dark, furry chest. I almost said—"beautiful"—out loud. I hadn't yet undressed.

"Something wrong?" he asked.

"Not really," I lied. Unnerved being only a few feet away from him, I was aroused and tugged on my sweaty shirt, which stuck to my back.

"Here, let me help you," he said. He grabbed the shirt and pulled it off.

A narrow fringe of pubic hair formed a line to his belly button. His penis had stiffened slightly. He was chewing gum. Spearmint. "Hurry," he said. "Erling doesn't wait." He pulled on his trunks.

Off came my shorts and underwear; I hopped into my suit.

Erling rapped at the door. "What's keeping you?" he asked.

Will pushed the door open. "Ta-da, we're ready!"

❧

The road to the lake, fringed by pines and hickory, opened on a sandy beach packed with families, some in the water, others stretched out on towels.

Will flung out his towel to join them.

Lorraine called out, "Over here!"

Erling slapped his thigh and muttered, "Figures."

The three women and I waded into the water and swam out toward an island in the middle of the lake. We treaded water and chatted. Loraine attended Wheaton College in Maryland. She wanted to be a doctor. Lois, the elder daughter of Peggy Metzler (that's why she looked so familiar!), had graduated from high school. She planned to go to Bethel College. She wanted to teach. Emily majored in philosophy and also wanted to teach it. Her father, an English professor at Indiana University, had taught with Erling for a semester at a small college in the Midwest.

Lois, short with piercing eyes, still peppered me with questions. "Do you believe in God?"

"No."

"No?" She was startled.

"No, I don't."

"But you're in a seminary, aren't you?"

"Yes."

"What do you believe in?"

"Not much. I suppose I believe there's good and evil. We must try our best to do good, although even with that, it's likely we'll fail."

"I don't get why you don't believe in God."

"It's easy. Who needs Him?"

"God?"

"Yeah."

"You some sort of nut?"

We waded to shore as we talked. I asked her about her mom, Peggy, and her brother Bobby. It turned out Bobby had cut his foot badly playing chicken with a knife; Tommy, his older brother, had tossed the blade a little too close, and it pierced his foot.

"Were they barefoot?"

"Of course," she giggled. "Silly boys!"

She joined Lorraine on a blanket. I spread a towel next to Emily. Lois muttered to herself, but loud enough for me to hear, "I can't believe he doesn't believe in God."

Emily overheard our conversation. A lanky woman, nearly as tall as I was, she spoke quietly and asked how I had met Erling. She wondered why he hadn't recruited more women from Vanderbilt.

"There were only two women in my class," I told her.

"Figures," she said.

"What do you mean?"

"Sexist," she explained.

"Why do you say that?"

She furrowed her brow and said, "Can you count?

"Yes."

"How many students are in your class?"

"Thirty or so," I said.

"And only two women." She shrugged her shoulders. "I rest my case."

She had a good case. Only one woman, Penny, had been in my New Testament class, and she was bright and asked more questions than any other men.

Emily leaned close to me. "Do me a favor," she whispered. "Call us women, not girls."

Will beckoned for me to move my towel beside him. "Catch some rays," he said. His body needed some sun. Milky white except for brown rings around his neck and on his lower arms, he looked like a monk. He offered to rub some suntan lotion on my back.

"You're tense," he said after massaging the lotion down the back.

"I've driven hundreds of miles," I said.

"Time to let go," he said and patted me. I crawled onto the towel, careful to keep my feet from soiling it, and closed my eyes.

Water splashed my face.

I shot up. "What the—"

Lois stood over me with a bucket in her hand. "Hey, sleepyhead, wake up!"

Will offered his towel, so I could dry off. "It wasn't my idea," he said on the way to the car.

"Whose was it?"

He whispered, "The dark-haired one."

"Lois?"

"That's it. Think she has a crush on you," he said. "You should see the way she looks at you."

"Not sure it's a crush," I said, "or a curse."

⁂

After dinner, Erling read Walt Whitman's "A Cradle Endlessly Rocking." There were yawns and a desultory discussion. A fan whirred in a corner. The kitchen lights went off. As did others down the hallway. Will said, "Good night." The door closed. The women headed to their rooms. Erling and I drove to the cabin.

⁂

The next morning, we looked for the well so we could shave and wash. With a plastic bucket in hand, we walked to the bottom of a path where a wetland with tall grass and several dung heaps was located, as well as a metal pipe about four inches in diameter protruding from the ground. But no well.

Erling decided to ask Peggy where the well was located. Bobby took me to the side yard, a bucket in hand. He walked over to a cylindrical pipe, like the one we had seen protruding from the ground at our place, and said, "This is it."

"But how do you get water out of it?" I inquired. The pipe had a lid, but, unless it worked on suction, it didn't seem possible to get water from a pipe.

He demonstrated how another cylindrical contraption, approximately three feet long, was inserted into the pipe and lowered down by rope until it submerged into the water reservoir. He pulled a string, and a lever closed, trapping the water inside the cylinder. He hauled it up, dumped it into a bucket, and lugged it inside.

We went to the Tibbitt's General Store and purchased a cylinder, some rope, and some string. We filled several buckets in our cabin, washed, brushed our teeth, and left the rest for drinking water.

Erling and I spent mornings and evenings at the lodge during the first week. With a kitchen, meeting rooms, and dorm rooms, it was the safest place for the women. The cook, Will, told us that he'd fix anything we liked.

I asked if he knew how to make waffles.

"For you, *mon cher*, they'll be the best you have ever tasted," he said. "Come, let me show you the kitchen."

The kitchen, a small room lined with ceiling-high cupboards, had a substantial black iron stove with burners on top. He pulled out a cast-iron waffle iron. "This will do," he said.

He had long, sturdy fingers with perfectly trimmed nails. Aqua blue, his eyes were mesmerizing. His hair draped across his forehead. His lips, moist and full, were inviting.

"Something wrong?" he asked.

"No, no, sorry," I said. "Just got lost for a second."

He pushed out his lips. "Anywhere I've been?" he asked.

I blushed.

Every morning, he prepared a cup of tea for me. Once a week, he'd fix different types of waffles—Belgian, Liege, rolled—telling me how the Dutch made the first waffles back in the 16th century. During breaks after lunch, we went for swims with the women—or, as Erling said, "the girls." Will's compact body moved through the water with effortless grace. He'd lounge on his blanket, me beside him, turn on his side and talk about life in New York City, how he didn't own a car, never drove one, since he could get anywhere he wanted by the subway.

❧

Our daily routines were jam-packed. In the morning, Erling led us in Danish folk songs, and then he would read from Whitman, Wolfe, or McLeish and discuss the readings. After breakfast, we drove to Rose's Creek Hollow. The women set up tables to do arts and crafts. Children arrived on foot and by car. I'd play touch football with the older boys. Most days, after the women left, Erling and I explored the hollow. Roads wove like arteries into the mountains. We'd drive up a side road, mostly one lane, and discover narrower roads like capillaries going up a creek bed.

The deeper we drove into the hollow, the more the roads were scarcely stitched to the sides of mountains. We abandoned Mabel and climbed up the slopes to talk with residents. Erling explained the history of the Folk School, who was involved in it in Denmark, and how, as a core principle, the history of the area was central to the school. He talked about the kids' program, the bonfire on Fridays, and the upcoming potluck cookout.

Long periods of silence punctuated our conversations. On one ridge, an elderly man in bib overalls and a white shirt rocked in his rocking chair. "Let me," he said, "give you some history." A family feud. His brother had been shot while working just down the road. The following week, his folks shot the culprit who did it. There had been bad blood ever since.

His ire was so intense that I worried we were in the middle of a feud.

Erling asked, "When did it happen?"

The old man rocked for three minutes, not uttering a word, and then said, "Well, I'm supposing it was '38 or '39."

❧

By Friday, we had met most of the families in the hollow and planned for the Saturday cookout to be at the old one-room schoolhouse. The food would arrive at about noon. Everyone would gather and celebrate the start of the Folk School.

Jack called to announce that he planned to attend the big event. Erling drove to Jellico to have dinner with him and told me to relax and enjoy myself.

After Erling left, a blue pickup pulled up. Bobby hopped out of it with his older brother Tommy. They sat on our cabin porch.

Tommy, taller and stockier than Bobby, worked as a mechanic in a nearby town. He told me that Bobby said I was a good man and asked, "So what's up?"

"Not much doing here," I replied. "Erling's off to Jellico."

"You like to drink?" Tommy asked.

"That would be an affirmative," I replied.

"What does that mean?" he asked.

"Yes." I laughed at my pretentiousness. "I like a drink."

"Ever had moonshine?" he inquired, raising one of his eyebrows and giving me an impish smile.

"Nope."

"Well, then it's time for you to give it a try. Let's get drunk and be somebody!" I had misgivings, but I liked his enthusiasm.

"Come on," he said. He brushed his dark brown hair back from his forehead, but it didn't stay and fell over his brow.

He tapped his knuckles on my shin. "Come on. No harm in it."

Bobby gazed up at me, quizzically, as if something was wrong.

"You coming, too?" I asked him.

Tommy interjected, "He comes with me all the time."

"Really?"

Bobby said, "Yeah," and shrugged his shoulders.

"I'll drive," Tommy said. "Come on."

❧

We drove to Rose's Creek, turned in a drive, and walked across a plank bridge to a rundown house in a yard with foot-high grass.

Tommy said he'd do the talking. I gave him twenty dollars.

A man with a gray shirt peered out the front door. He asked Tommy several questions. He looked at Bobby and me. He said, "No." As he started to close the door, Tommy flashed him the money. He looked at it and closed the door. Tommy gave us a thumbs-up.

With a mason jar of moonshine—the best you could buy according to Tommy—secure in Bobby's lap, we drove to a strip mine pit at the end of a red scarred lane. We sat beside a small pond with surprisingly clear water and passed the jar back and forth.

The moon dipped its milky face in the pond. The trees cast three dark shadows.

Bobby had been drunk once before. By his third swig, he yelped and staggered to his feet, fell over, got up, and fell again like a doll whose battery had run out.

Tommy told him to stay by us, not wander off. By our fourth swig, we were no better than he was and stripped off our clothes—it was warm—and plunged into the water. We howled at the moon, leapt on all fours, and chased each other from the shallow to the deep end. Midway into a chase, Bobby crumbled to his knees.

"I feel sick," he said.

I took him in my arms and carried him to the shore. He vomited in violent waves until his body became slack. We dressed him and brought him to the truck.

Tommy wanted to drink some more. "Come on." But I could barely stand upright, so he drove me back to the cabin.

I aimed my feet at the front door and missed it by four feet to the right. With my hands on the wall, I edged my way into the cabin and down to my sleeping bag on the lower level.

❧

In the morning, I heard voices speaking in the upper room. I squinted out of one eye. Jack, perched on a chair, was talking with Erling, who was pacing back and forth.

"I told you that he was not reliable," Jack warned. "He's a relativist. He doesn't have a moral center. He'll do what he wants when he wants to do it. He's like a fraternity brat. Get rid of him."

"Why do you say he's a relativist?" Erling asked.

"It's easy. When he and I were discussing what someone would do if faced with the decision of supporting a friend who had violated the law or obeying the law and reporting them, he said that 'it all depends.' In some cases, he might support the friend, and in others, he might back law enforcement," Jack explained. "No firm moral compass."

"But he's right. In many cases, it is relative," Erling countered.

"You're not getting the point," Jack insisted. "He thinks that he's the one who decides what is wrong or right based on what pleases him. Not God. Not the Bible. Don't trust him. He'll bring down the school. What fool would get an underage boy drunk? Tell me that. How do you think he can justify that?"

"I get it. He messed up, that's for sure. He has some serious explaining to do," Erling admitted. He stood by the window and looked out into the field. "Our program may be in jeopardy."

I must have moaned because Jack startled and jerked his head toward me. Erling walked over to Jack and whispered something. Jack, not happy with what Erling requested, left, stood on the front porch, his eyes on me like an inquisitor.

Erling sat on one of the steps, expressionless. "Not feeling too well?" he asked.

"No, bad hangover," I said, propping myself on my elbow.

"The word got around the hollow quickly about your escapade last night. Everyone could hear the three of you for miles."

"Shit."

"Yep, that sums it up."

"I'm sorry. That was really dumb of me. I just didn't—"

"Not sure what to do about it. You may have cooked your goose and ours," Erling said. He went to the back door and gazed at the ash tree by the side of the house. "Some tell me that I should dump you. Not trustworthy. Too self-centered. Even immoral. What you did is egregious. You're a liability."

I stood up, tucked in my shirt, and brushed back my hair. "I wouldn't blame you. I fucked up." I walked over to the doorway and stood beside him.

"This is not easily resolved," he said, glancing sideways.

"It's not on you. It's on me."

Erling's voice became strident. "You don't get it. It's all on me. This is my idea, my dream."

"Fuck," I said.

"Exactly. What do you have to say?"

There were two clouds in the sky, and then blue went on forever.

I took a deep breath. "I know it seems I'm untrustworthy. But I don't think I am. I learn from my mistakes. I swear this is the last one I'll make, if you'll give me a second chance." My words, however, carried as little weight as the clouds.

Erling stared off for quite a while. The wind tickled the leaves. Two clouds moved on.

He turned to face me, put his hand under his chin, and squinted his eyes, asking several questions about the night before. I answered them. He nodded and turned away from me to look out the window. "Some say you are out for yourself—," he took out his pipe and knocked the old tobacco out of the bowl, and then took out a pouch, unlaced it, and poured fresh tobacco in the pipe bowl. He lit a match, put it to the bowl, and sucked in smoke. "Is it true?"

"What?"

"No moral center."

I stepped back. "It may seem that way. But, Erling, I gave up a job that my dad said paid well and had benefits. I raised the money you needed to fund the school. I've never asked for a salary. My parents were supportive but not entirely happy with my decision. I came up here because I believe in what you are doing and want to help. If that means I have no moral center, well, so be it." I turned from him and slammed my fist into the cabinet.

"Hey, calm down," he said, turning me around to face him. "Listen, I get it. You made sacrifices. But we're in a quandary now. We're just getting started. This will cause problems."

"I know."

"Well, if you were me, what would you do?" he asked.

"Me?"

"Yes, you."

"Well, I guess I'd apologize to Peggy and admit I made a mistake."

"Okay, fine. But what would you do if you were me?"

"I'd tell me that I needed to step up and take leadership and see the implications of what I did and not act like I was some stupid fraternity bozo."

My last statement amused Erling. He put his hand to his chin again and paced back and forth. As he paced, he noticed Jack standing in the front doorway, shaking his head, staring at us. Completing his ruminations, he pivoted and looked me directly in the eye.

"Well," he began, "I guess you better shave and put on clean clothes and get yourself up to the picnic, because you have apologies to make and fences to mend."

I rushed over to him and shook his hand. "You will not regret this!" Changing quickly into a fresh shirt and a pair of jeans, I took out our washbasin, filled it with water, and shaved. I refilled the basin, splashed my face, and combed my hair. Finally, I checked with Erling to make sure I looked okay. He gave me the thumbs-up.

As I headed to my car, Erling was sitting on the front porch. Jack was speaking, pointing at me and pulling his chair close to Erling. He was about to make a long speech, and I was his subject.

On the way to the picnic, I parked by a stream and hopped out. I made notes in a journal and worked out what I should say. I shouldn't blame anyone. I had to admit my mistake, convince them that I would do better, and also figure out why I hadn't seen how my actions could harm our program.

Jack was right in a way. For me, getting smashed was perfectly okay; it was something I did to connect with other guys. That had to change.

Jack always knew what was right and did it. He would have said, "No." Tommy would have stayed and drunk a soda if I had said no. But I did as I had done a hundred times before, caved in, and got drunk.

Jack might have my number. Maybe I wasn't worthy of Erling's trust.

❧

At noon, I drove to the picnic and arrived well ahead of Erling and Jack. Twenty people were clustered around picnic tables nestled under the trees. Near the back of the tables under a large maple, I spotted Peggy. Clad in a bright red and yellow dress, she was mixing something in a bowl with a wooden spoon. She focused intently on the bowl as she poured something from a jar into it.

My stomach growled. My head throbbed. My scalp sweated.

She seemed surprised to see me and raised an eyebrow. "Morning, Jason."

"Morning, Peggy."

"Just added the final touch. You want some potato salad?" she said. She spooned a large portion onto a paper plate.

"That'd be fine."

"Get yourself more grub. There are some mighty fine hot dogs and sausages there on the grill." She pointed to a tall, thin man named Shady John.

"Peggy," I whispered, not looking at her but gazing down at my potato salad, "I need to say I'm sorry. I made a mistake. I should have known—"

"You need to speak up," she said. "I'm deaf in the right ear."

I repeated myself.

She leaned over, picked up my chin with her hand, and motioned for me to look her in the eye. "I always tell my boys to look me in the eye when they talk to me. I know what they say by their eyes."

I looked at her. I couldn't tell from her expression what she might be thinking. She flipped the potatoes up with a spoon and folded them back into the bowl, then licked a finger to make sure it tasted right.

I repeated what I had said, keeping my eyes on her. As I told her this time, my eyes welled up. I brushed the tears away.

She shook her head. "You like it?" she asked, pointing at my plate.

"Yes."

"Worried it had too much mustard."

"It's fine. It's terrific."

She didn't seem to have heard me. Her hands on her hips, she nodded, "Good."

"I'm sorry," I repeated. "I feel awful."

"You should," she said.

"Well, I really messed up…"

She nodded her head and looked over at the man at the grill. "Them dogs done? I got a hungry man here."

I started to repeat myself.

She shushed me. "Now, my dear, it's not that bad. Hell, I'd be damn proud if I were you," she said. "It takes a lot for a man to admit he's done wrong. And, hey, my boys, they know they done wrong too. I think all of you paid mightily for your shenanigans. I can see you don't look so hot. My Bobby, oh my, he's got a head full of thorns. If your stomach is up to it, get yourself something more to eat." She pointed the spoon at me. "And, Jason, hold your head up. You have a nice-looking face. You should let others see it." She was smiling. Pointing at the plate, she said, "Tell me what you think of my potato salad. Some claim it's the best in the county."

I took another bite. The potatoes had a sweet-sour tang. The sauce was creamy. "No, I think you're wrong," I said. "It's the best in the world!"

I ate several hot dogs, a second helping of potato salad, and baked beans. I chatted with fifteen or twenty people. Bobby was leaning against a tree trunk. He was shading his eyes with his hand. I squatted next to him.

"Not doing so hot?"

"Nope."

"How's Tommy?"

"He's at work," he said. "I'm sorry. We shouldn't—"

"Don't be," I said. "I'm the one who should apologize."

"Mom's okay, you know," he said. "She's mostly mad at us."

"I know. You should get some of her potato salad. It's good."

"I know."

Jack and Erling were enjoying the food, too, making the rounds of all the tables. At first, Jack wouldn't look at me. I greeted him, however, with a handshake. He offered a weak, "Hello." Then, abruptly, he turned, his face inches from Erling, and whispered something to him. Erling nodded several times.

I felt lightheaded and sat at a picnic table, my head in my hands.

I heard a booming voice. Jack announced that he was headed back to Nashville and must prepare for Sunday services, but he had enjoyed meeting everyone. He shook hands with Emily, Lorraine, Lois, and numerous others. He scowled at me, shook his head, and trudged down the hill to his blue Oldsmobile, leaving a trail of dust behind him.

Erling took me aside and asked, "How did it go?"

I told him that it was fine. She wanted to get a good meal in my stomach.

"We dodged a bullet," he said. "They like you and seem to have grown to trust you. Remember," he tapped my chest, "you're no longer a student out for a good time. You stand for more than that. You have to be a bigger person. Trust is perishable."

"Thanks." Tears welled up in my eyes again.

"Hey, no tears," he said.

"Heaven forbid."

"You have a sense of humor, I like that," he said. "That's why I chose you." He hugged me around the neck, slapped me on the back, and said, "Now, why don't you go back to the cabin. You don't look so hot."

I started to walk away, but caught myself, intent on leaving yet drawn back to have him answer one question.

"Erling, I need to know something."

"Okay."

"You did choose me. But I don't get it. I really messed up. Lord knows Jack opposed me from the start and told me that he wanted to be the assistant director. He would be far more experienced and a better choice than I am. He managed a large company, is ordained, and leads a major church. Why didn't you choose him? Why didn't you take his advice?"

"You overheard us talking this morning."

"I thought my goose was cooked."

"I thought you heard," Erling mused, then asked me pointedly, "So are you a 'relativist'?"

I bowed my head, not knowing what to say. But I admitted, "To be honest, I don't know what that is. It sounds bad."

"I don't have the faintest idea either," he said, laughing. "I was hoping you did."

He put his hands on his hips and shrugged. "Suppose it's relative!"

We laughed together. I put my hand on his arm and pulled him close to me.

I wanted one other question answered.

"I still can't figure out why, with all Jack said, you stood by me. Why?"

He slapped his hand on the side of his head. "Oh, Jason, that's a no-brainer. Jack's bright, earnest, and has tons of experience, but to be frank, he's a pompous ass, full of himself. He promised to get money for the school to help us get started, yet all he does is give me advice and tell me that he knows Dean so and so from some big university, and a president of a bank—but it comes to nothing. He has an opinion about everyone and a doctorate in self-righteousness. But his word is no good. You, my friend, have kept your word every time I've asked you."

Startled, I winced and felt dizzy, losing my balance.

Erling grabbed me by the sleeve. "You all right?"

"Dizzy."

"Sit over here." He sat by me at a picnic table. "Listen," he said, "you have your flaws. But you don't need, as Jack does, someone worshiping your grand ideas and someone patting you on the back, saying how wonderful and bright you are. You listen to others. You care about them. I'm much more interested in having someone who can learn than having someone who already knows it all. Now, sit tight, let me get you something to drink." He went over to a cooler and pulled out a Coke.

"Drink this," he said. "And go back to the cabin. Your breath stinks. I mean, outhouse, lid left up, stink. If you stay here much longer, your breath will kill someone. Besides, you look like hell. I need to check in with the girls."

He went over to them. They were sitting under a beech tree, plates in their lap, and five teenage boys with plates in their hands stood by them.

I said goodbye to Peggy, Bobby, and the women, as they preferred to be called, and drove back to the cabin. I stripped to my underwear and slipped into my sleeping bag, its cool skin like a soothing bandage.

I made notes in my journal. I remembered the words of the theologian Dietrich Bonhoeffer. In times of great upheaval and even greater evil, a man must 'come of age' (that was his term). A man cannot rely on old palliatives to resolve his moral questions. Instead, he must determine what is right for himself. He had to act and trust in what he thought was in the best interest of everyone. As an assistant director, I had to put aside my own needs for the larger good of the Folk School. I must come of age.

I thought of Mr. Hook's words, how he had to learn time and again the same lesson.

The apple tree leaves whispered outside, and I nestled in my sleeping bag, letting the leaves converse with the air.

The Classes

Monday morning, I shaved on the porch, my razor in the cool water. No mirror, so I rubbed my cheek and neck to discern where the whiskers stuck out, then dressed and waited for Erling to perform his morning ablutions.

He didn't drive toward the Methodist Lodge but instead took an unfamiliar road on a side trip, a mile or so up another hollow, and pulled over, parked, hopped out, and said, "Follow me."

"Where are we going?" I asked.

He motioned for me to keep up with him. We trekked up a narrow path between a dense grove of hemlocks that nearly blocked out the light, climbed a cliff with good footholds, and, at the top, followed another route around the side of the mountain. On the far side, east, where the sun had nestled in the sky, a deep ravine cut through two cliffs, only forty feet wide, and dropped straight down at the bottom of a stream. He picked up a rock and told me to count when he dropped it. Ten seconds, hundreds of feet. "Think about the animals—I've often seen tracks here—that frequent this trail in the dark," he said. "They never fall in. They sense the danger. We're not as adept." He peered over the rim of his glasses at me.

I looked down.

He added, "One false step and it'd swallow you up. No one would be the wiser."

"What's it called?" I asked.

"The Grand Abyss," he said, a smile in the corner of his mouth.

A chill went through my body. I shuffled closer to the edge, the dark ledges along the effacement.

"Is there any way down there?" I asked.

"I'm sure there is. I've never seen it. That stream starts at that large mountain and dips down and, over the years, has cut this cavern. Something, isn't it?"

"Hmm," I responded, woozier than I liked to feel.

"We'll head back," he said.

ᘛ

At the Methodist Center, several missionaries had gathered in prayer at the end of the conference room where we usually met. Erling waited for them to finish. He went over to the lead minister to chat with him. A plain-looking woman in her forties introduced herself to me.

"Now, who are you?" she asked in a singsong voice.

"Why, I'm Jason. Who are you?"

A huge smile lit up her face. "I'm Joan. I'm a missionary. I leave for Africa in several days. I've never been to Africa. Have you been to Africa?"

"Not recently," I said.

"So you've been there. That's nice. Did you like it there?"

Holy shit, I thought, she speaks like a Dick and Pam primer.

"No, not ever."

"What, may I ask, do you do?"

"I'm a revolutionary."

"Oh, isn't that nice," she said.

"Yes, it is. We plan to overthrow the government."

"That must be a lot of work."

I asked, "May I ask what you used to do?"

"You certainly can," she said. "I was a first-grade teacher for twenty-eight years."

"Twenty-eight years," I said. "Amazing."

"I loved every minute of it."

"I'm sure you did."

Will had overheard her as he picked up dishes. His eyebrows raised, he shook his head back and forth and stuck his tongue out. I laughed.

"Are you all right?" she asked.

"Yes, yes,"—I frowned at Will—"I just remembered a funny joke that someone told me."

"Really, do tell."

"It's a little off color."

"Well, then you should keep that to yourself."

She invited me to tell her more about the revolution; I said to her that I had to "take a pee-pee really bad" and excused myself.

"By all means," she said. I half expected her to take me by the hand and escort me there.

Erling had started the class. He read a poem by Philip Larkin called "Church Going." It was about someone in an abandoned church. It ended:

A serious house on serious earth it is,
In whose blent air all our compulsions meet,
Are recognized, and robed as destinies.
And that much never can be obsolete,
Since someone will forever be surprising
A hunger in himself to be more serious,
And gravitating with it to this ground,
Which, he once heard, was proper to grow wise in,
If only that so many dead lie round.

Based on the poem, we discussed the usefulness of religion. As a Jew, Lorraine believed religion was central to her sense of self. Not just the rituals and the Old Testament history, but also being part of a larger community. Emily didn't have much use for religion. She agreed with the poet: maybe it once served a purpose, but for her, philosophy—Bertrand Russell and Ludwig Wittgenstein, who believed the world had an underlying structure that could be discerned mathematically—was preferable.

Erling puffed intently on his pipe.

"Well, young lady," Erling interrupted her. "If your Mr. Russell is so right about his arguments, then, I suppose you'd agree about his being a profligate—having extramarital affairs and flaunting it."

Emily's cheeks flushed. "I don't know about his personal life," she countered. "But I have great respect for his ideas."

"A person's personal life doesn't matter?"

"I didn't say that. I said I didn't know about it."

With her on the defensive, Erling wanted to prove her wrong, as he had once tried to outmatch me in our boxing match.

"Well, once you find out, will that change your opinion?" he inquired.

I jumped into the conversation. "Erling, I for one wouldn't change my opinion. I know Paul Tillich, whose theology I admire, was also a man of his time. He grabbed any graduate student he could get his hands on. But his writing is beautiful, and his ideas make sense to me."

Erling recounted a story about one of Tillich's female students who said that Tillich might have a big mind but wasn't well-endowed in other parts.

Everyone laughed.

Lois had been quiet. Erling asked her what she thought about the poem.

She gripped the seat of her chair tightly. "I don't understand it," she said.

"What part?" Erling asked.

"What does 'blent' mean?"

Her honesty allowed us to have a more casual discussion of religion, its good and bad sides, until Will called, "Lunch time."

For the remainder of the week, we followed the same routine: breakfast, class, lunch at the lodge, and, in the afternoon, arts and crafts at the hollow. On Friday night, we had a campfire with food, football games, storytelling, banjo, folk music, and dancing.

On very hot days, we broke the morning with a swim. I enjoyed undressing with Will in the tiny bathroom where he'd sit naked on the lip of the bathroom sink. His penis, uncircumcised with a hood like a sweatshirt, caught my eye. He noticed. "Never seen one?"

"A couple of times. What's it like?"

"Works the same as yours," he said. "Want to see?"

"No, no, that's okay."

But I wondered what happened to the hood when it was erect.

"If you ever do," Will said, grabbing it. "I'll show you."

"Thanks," I said. He sensed something about me, something that I tried to hide from him, from everyone, including myself.

Snipers

BY THE SECOND WEEK, we were in the public eye. The afternoon folk arts and crafts activities attracted children up and down Rose's Creek, and beyond. Children wove lanyards, made baskets, and painted watercolors. Everyone played football or softball.

On the periphery of the property, men would stop in their cars with the windows down to check out what we were doing. Erling engaged them in conversation and invited them to play baseball. Some joined us, but mostly they watched from a distance.

Erling felt sure we'd made it over the hump. We'd been seen around town. Parents gave us positive reports. We went to Tibbets' Store—where anyone who needed something had to go—to buy snacks and soda for the day program.

An off-kilter screen door banged shut when we entered the store. A few flies rose from the windowsills to herald our entrance. The clerk, a wisp of a fellow with a mop of muddy brown hair, took great interest in us the minute we came into the store, straightening up like a watchdog.

"What do you want today?" he asked and shook the hair from his face.

"The usual," we said. We picked up a case of soda, chips, pretzels, and assorted candy bars. He sized us up, craning his neck over the counter to see what we were doing down the two aisles of the store. The black-and-white-keyed cash register tallied our items.

One day, he leaned over as if he wanted to make sure no one noticed him and whispered, "Where are you boys from?"

Erling told him that we came from Rose's Creek Folk School. "Come up some time," he said. "It's lots of fun."

The clerk said, "Yeah, sure it is, but, honest now, where you from?"

When I told him Illinois, Erling shot an angry look.

Erling asked him, not unkindly but with an edge, "What's it to you?"

"We don't take too kindly to outsiders," he said. "You with the feds?"

"Not on your life."

"Well, that's good," the clerk said and went back to ringing up our total. I sensed that the "good" he said was more a mockery than a sincere reply. I was about to say something when Erling squeezed my arm hard. I turned to see what the matter was. He shook his head as I picked up the cartons of soda and headed to the car.

Later that night, after coming back to the cabin from the lodge, I got into a T-shirt and gym shorts, prepared for bed, and asked Erling, "Why shouldn't I tell people where I'm from?"

"We're outsiders and we're dangerous. Some outsiders, like the Drug Enforcement Agency, try to nab moonshiners. Years ago, union operatives tried to unionize mines. They ended up getting men fired and families kicked off their land. Your telling him that you came from Illinois is asking for trouble," he said. "Keep the focus on what we're doing here."

On a moonless night, I slept soundly because, when I woke up and gazed around the room in the morning light, I noticed that Erling wasn't there. His sleeping bag was gone. One of his sneakers was by my sleeping bag.

Why would he go out without one shoe?

I pulled on my pants, one leg at a time, tossed off my T-shirt, pulled on a shirt, grabbed my socks, and, skipping to the front door, slipped on my socks and shoes. Mabel was parked by the gate. I called his name, circled the cabin, and walked to the outhouse. I checked by the well, called his name again, louder, then trotted to the road to look for footprints. A cluster of prints was by our gate. He might have gone to a ridge to watch the sun rise. I sprinted to the hill.

He wasn't there. This was not like him. He kept to a schedule: up by six; out on the porch for his morning ablutions; over to nudge me awake; then to the chair on the front porch to read, all done in sequence, never varied, no matter how late we were up the night before.

There were different tire tracks on the road, larger than ours, on either side. It might be from the family living down the hollow.

I stood on the road, stuffing my hands in my pockets.

What could have happened to him?

At the gate, on a whim, I glanced into his car.

There he was, snuggled in his sleeping bag.

I tapped on the window. He stirred, stretched, his arms emerging from the bag, his head lifted. He pulled on the door handle, unlocking it.

"What's going on?" I asked in a tone that, once I spoke, I realized was severe.

"Hey, calm down," he said. He scrunched up and sat upright, rubbing his eyes. "Where are my glasses?"

I picked them off the front console. "Here."

He put them on. "Didn't you hear them?" he asked.

"Hear what?"

"The gunshots," he said.

"Holy shit!"

"Two or three blasts."

"When?" I asked.

He tugged on the steering wheel and scooted his legs down so he could pull on his trousers. He patted the seat next to him. "Sit."

"Last night," he said, "midnight, maybe later, I heard noises. There were voices. I got up and looked out the window." He shook his head. "There were four or five guys. And shotguns. I couldn't make out how many."

"No way."

"Yes. And I tried, I honestly did, to wake you up. I mean, I even threw my shoe at you. You didn't stir." He sat upright and turned to look up the road, his neck craned.

"What'd they do?"

"You didn't hear?"

"No."

"They shot at us. Two or three times. It splattered against the outside wall. I called your name. Told you to keep down. I thought we were done for. I saw other guns, too. Shots hit the door hard. It cracked open. Some shots hit the window, and the glass shattered. I slammed the door shut. I yelled, 'I know who you are.' There was a scuffle. Car doors slammed. They were gone."

"You knew who they were?"

"Have no idea. It scared them."

"Holy shit!"

"Yeah," he said and shook his head. "You slept right through it. Never flinched. For a while, after the shots, I thought you were dead. I crawled across the floor and poked you. You muttered something. I told you we had to get out. But you never woke, even when I called your name."

"Really?"

"Slept like a baby."

"Why'd you go to the car?"

"Figured it was safer. If they came back, you know, they wouldn't think to look in the car."

"And left me there."

"Well, you were like a corpse," he laughed. "I thought they'd never notice you're there in the corner."

"You left me?"

"I gave it my best. You didn't budge. If they shot you, you'd die in peace." He shrugged. "And, well, if you must know, I was scared to death!"

~

We told Peggy about the encounter. She said there were rumors we were communists, outside agitators, and some talk about trying to scare us off. They were not Rose's Creek folks, but from another hollow up the road. She knew who they were and planned to give them a piece of her mind, telling them to let us be.

For the next few days, I barely slept.

Erling said we should have a sentry. I stayed up well into the night, posted by the door, listening to any car sounds, the grinding of gravel, the hum of a motor. I heard every groan of the wood in the cabin. Every susurration of a branch startled me. After a few nights, we gave up sitting on sentry duty. If they were going to get us, at least we'd die with a good night's sleep; but sleep was hard to come by.

Peggy told us, "There's nothing more to worry about," but the cabin door and walls had peppered indentations, and buckshot would fall out and tinkle on the floor as a reminder.

I dreamed of falling off a ledge like the one Erling showed me, with no one to save me when I called out. Erling heard me several times and nudged me awake. Despite the cracked windowpanes, I tried to convince myself everything was fine; but once back to sleep, I fell off the ledge again.

When I asked Erling about it, he said, "It's the abyss. You've come to face it. We all have to sometime or other."

The dream came less often, but it never left. Some mornings, I woke in a sweat, hands aching from grasping at something that wasn't there.

Grace

ONE AFTERNOON, I was lounging on the front porch when I spied two children, a mop-haired boy and a younger girl with pigtails, standing by the slats in our fence. I waved at them. The boy perched on his tiptoes and waved. "Come in," I called. But they stood by the fence, either frightened by the sight of me or hampered by something. I put down my journal and walked toward them.

They scurried off down the hill, their feet kicking up puffs of dust. I went back to the porch to write a long letter to Mr. Hook as I had promised, and a shorter one to my parents to let them know our progress, without mentioning the shotgun blasts.

Every evening at about six, the boy and girl would creep up to the fence. If I stood to greet them, they'd run off. At sunset, I'd hear a woman singing "Amazing Grace." Her voice would well up and fill the air with the passion of the old spiritual.

> Amazing Grace, how sweet the sound
> That saved a wretch like me
> I once was lost but now I'm found…

I'd sing along with the mysterious voice, wondering who she was.

One evening, after the serenade, Erling and I walked down the hill to introduce ourselves to her and to tell her how wonderful she sounded.

The house, with its gray shingled structure, had cardboard in some of its windowpanes. A wire fence surrounded it. On the front porch an older man, perhaps in his seventies, sat in a large chair, and next to him, an older woman in a smaller chair. Right next to them on a railing, a smoldering rag hung and nearly blotted out our view of a younger woman with a gaunt face and shoulder-length dark hair. She smiled at us. Several of her front teeth were missing, and her right cheek was bruised and swollen.

We asked if we could join them. The man invited us up with a wave of his hand.

"Hi, I'm Erling."

"Pleased to meet ya," the man replied.

"Your names?"

"This here's the Missus. I'm Jack. That there is Melinda. She's the mother of them two rapscallions."

Erling stepped forward to shake his hand and introduce himself. I shook each of their hands, too. They stared at their hands for a second, seeming bothered by the formality.

"Sit a spell," Jack said.

"That'll be fine," Erling said. He motioned for me to sit on the stoop while he stood, looking very much like a politician on a campaign. He talked about how dusty the road was. The smoking rag caused me to cough and squint my eyes. They laughed at me.

"That keeps the mosquitoes away," Jack said. "Smoke does the trick."

We discussed how little rain we had and their garden, with its two rows of corn barely waist-high.

The boy and girl came out of the cabin and sat on their haunches in the yard. Melinda called them over. With one on either side of her, she introduced them: Travis and Alice. Proud of them, she brushed back the boy's hair and tugged on his shirt to straighten it out.

Jack was taciturn, but Melinda loved to talk and told how she became pregnant with Travis. His father was long gone north to Chicago, hadn't heard from him since. Alice was by another man. Got sick—black lung—died. She clerked at Tibbets' Store.

By and by, the boy edged his way over to me and sat in my lap. The girl scrunched up, nestling beside me. I reached over and held her under my arm.

Melinda seemed pleased. To hear her tell, not many men were in their lives except Pa, but "He weren't much for little ones."

I asked who sang. Jack spoke up and told us Melinda had a mighty fine voice and sang in the church choir. But stingy with compliments, he complained that he never had much luck keeping her quiet.

She agreed, grimaced, and stated that was the way she was.

As we were leaving, Melinda rose to walk us to the gate. Her left leg, atrophied and stunted, dragged as she leaned sideways to compensate for the shorter leg. Polio, we learned later, was the cause.

Travis and Alice raced ahead of us like two pups as we trod up the road. They opened our gate and followed us to the front door. Inside, we sat with them for several minutes and asked about their school—Travis was in second grade, and Alice was in Head Start. We asked what they liked to do. (Read for Travis. Dolls for Alice.) Then we heard a voice calling them—their mother—and they traipsed down the road.

One afternoon, when I was writing in my journal, the two of them came to the fence. I waved them in. They sat on the stoop while I continued to write. Alice was telling a story to a little doll with a white, frilly dress and blonde hair, adorned with a red bow. It was quite an interesting story, about a fairy and a witch.

Travis sat beside me.

"What you writin'?" he asked.

I told him that I was writing about last week: what I did, how I felt. He studied the page.

"You don't have very good writin'," he noted. "Them looks like chicken scratches."

I laughed.

He leaned over my shoulder, ran his fingers in my hair, and put his arm around my back. "What if everything cost only a penny?" he mused.

What a wonderful question, I thought. "That would be something. What if everything cost a penny?"

His face brightened. He came around in front of me and sat, cross-legged at my feet, and put a finger to his lips.

"Let me see," he pondered, frowning. "Everyone'd be happy since everyone would have what they want."

"That's true."

Excited now, he stood up and squirmed between my legs, sat on my lap, face to face with me.

"You could have a boat and sail to Paris, France. You could own a plane and fly to Florida. See them alligators. I've seen 'em in books. And you'd never have to worry or work," he said. Tapping on my chest, he asked, "What do you think?"

"If everything costs a penny," I said, thinking for a second, "the poor would be rich and the rich wouldn't know what to do because money wouldn't matter."

Travis added, "If you had a lot of money, you wouldn't know what to do with it, so you'd give it away."

I was impressed with his imagination, how he loved to toss out ideas. I folded my hands around his waist. We thought of all the things that cost a lot of money—mansions, boats, fancy cars, exotic food, and even wild animals like a giraffe—and considered how anyone might have them for practically nothing.

I had a strange feeling with him there in my lap. I couldn't name it entirely, but it was a fatherly love that one might have for a child, and it felt good and true and was altogether different from anything I'd felt before. It overwhelmed me. Eventually, his mom called. He hugged me, as his sister did, and they ran off, pulling open the gate and letting it slam shut. His sister trailed behind him, and the dust swirled up behind them.

I checked my watch. Late for dinner.

The Abyss

AFTER BREAKFAST, Erling began each session with a Danish song. His favorite was Jakob Knudsen's psalm "Behold the Sun is Rising."

See the golden sun from the ocean rise,
Glitter on the waves and the flaming skies!
Silent happy moment when night is o'er
And the dawn is landing upon our shore.

Once we sang and discussed the previous day's events—what some kids had done, how the day camp was working—Erling introduced us to Walt Whitman's "Passage to India." The poem's repetitive lines and shifts in tone and mood, along with Erling's deep baritone voice, rendered it in a rising cadence, making it spellbinding.

Passage, O soul, to India!
Eclaircise the myths Asiatic, the primitive fables…
The far-darting beams of the spirit, the unloos'd dreams,
The deep-diving bibles and legends
The daring plots of the poets, the elder religions;
O you temples fairer than lilies pour'd over by the rising sun!
O you fables, spurning the known,
eluding the hold of the known, mounting to heaven!
You lofty and dazzling towers, pinnacled, red as rose,
burnished with gold!
Towers of fables immortal fashion'd from mortal dreams!
You too I welcome and fully the same as the rest!
You too with joy I sing!

After his recitation, he asked what life passages we were making.

"Look at your own soul and find what it's calling you to be," he said. "Find ones closest to your heart. Don't just look through the eyes of materialism and of social expectations. Don't imagine what you can have. What is calling to you that is outside the world you know?"

We went off to be by ourselves, to write, take walks, and ponder his question. As I sat on the porch, looking out toward the lake, my wish to become an artist resurfaced. I wanted to find myself if I could—apart from my home, and my identity as the son of a successful father. I had no inclination about how to achieve that, but it was something, however elusive, that appealed to me.

A few days later, Erling gave a presentation on "The Abyss." To him, "The Abyss" was real, existing within each of us, not just a geographic aberration. To make his point, he read several poems, including Dylan Thomas's "Do Not Go Gentle into That Goodnight" and William Stafford's "Traveling Through the Dark."

In Thomas's poem, a son pleads with his father not to go into the dark.

In Stafford's, a man must decide whether to dispose of a dead doe with a fawn in her womb or to let the fawn live.

In each poem, the narrator had to face the abyss, which, as Erling contended, we also have to do in our own lives.

None of us had much to say. Maybe it was the heat. Maybe we didn't want to look at the darkness. Maybe it was Will's pancakes that lay in our stomachs like a blessing.

Our silence riled Erling. He took off his glasses, held them by the bridge, and launched into a tirade about how each of us had to face The Abyss, couldn't avoid it, and that someday we'd have to decide whether to push the doe off the cliff, let it suffer, or face the good night of death.

"What is your abyss? What will you do?" he shouted, pointing his finger at Lois, who, more frightened by his ire than rational, said she wouldn't want to kill the fawn.

"That's not the point," he said. "Those are only metaphors, analogies for a deeper, more personal abyss you live with every day."

She dropped her eyes. "I don't know what you're talking about."

"You don't?"

He sat back down, pressing his arms between his legs, rocking back and forth, staring at the floor, and muttering to himself.

I stared at my shoes. Dusty. Needed to be shined. I had no idea what to say. Maybe it was my attraction to Will. Perhaps that's what he meant. Those magnetic feelings that came out of nowhere that drew me towards him, feelings that I wanted to ignore but that persisted, kept pulling me like an obsession, a fantasy that, before I went to sleep, was there, hovering in my imagination, telling me that I couldn't ignore Will no matter how hard I tried. Despite my attempts to keep him at arm's length, he was grabbing ahold of me and dragging me into the abyss of my desires.

Erling told us to write in our journals. "Maybe you'll come to see that the abyss does exist. Find a place where life and death truly matter. A place where a need or a want can't be fulfilled by a pretty dress or—" He glared at me. "A new set of golf sticks."

Picking up his books, he stomped off.

I was irritated that he picked on me, but amused that he didn't even know what to call golf clubs. I wrote about the abyss I'd experienced just a few weeks before when my happy-go-lucky party-self clashed with my obligations as a leader of the Folk School. But I couldn't, or didn't want to find anything more than that, or didn't want in a journal something about Will, something someone could see and expose me.

In early July, Erling suggested that I read James Agee's *Let Us Now Praise Famous Men.* Not familiar with Agee or Walker Evans, the photographer, I became entranced with the tenant farmers portrayed in the book. Agee and Evans' mission was to expose how landowners exploited tenant farmers during the depression. Agee wrote about a woman's daily work with such clarity that I could feel his utter helplessness in trying to do justice to what she faced daily, living in poverty.

> *...how is it possible to be made clear enough...the many processes of wearying effort which make the shape of each one of her living days...the accumulated weight of these actions upon her; and what this cumulation has made of her body; and what it has made of her mind and of her heart and of her being.*

His words made me appreciate what Peggy did in raising her children. Agee saw beyond appearances into people's souls.

❧

When I was reading Agee one afternoon, Erling pulled up, parked by the gate, and practically leapt over the fence, bubbling with excitement.

"We're going to get national news coverage!" he exclaimed.

"From whom?"

"From none other than Walter Cronkite, CBS News," he shouted. "CBS wants to do a series of stories about Appalachia. They want to meet with Marie to discuss her efforts to promote economic development. She told them about the Folk School. A woman correspondent is flying to Knoxville with a crew. Marie and I will meet them in Jellico and drive them to Rose's Creek."

We discussed what he could say, who they should interview—certainly Peggy, her neighbor Bonnie, and some of the kids, maybe Lorraine, since she would be enthusiastic.

The day of the meeting, Erling made sure his clothes were washed and pressed. He even polished his shoes. With a national news story, he could promote the Folk School not only in Appalachia but across the country—in the Dakotas, in his home state, Nebraska, and even in North Carolina. We washed Mabel.

At midday, he headed off.

❧

Erling was as enthused as I had ever seen him after he had met the correspondent. He said she was gorgeous, just plain beautiful—tall, with brown hair, and sexy in a reserved way—and they had hit it off, gone out for drinks, several of them. She liked him. She listened to him and flirted with him—yes, he was sure of it—flirted with him and, yes, he would gladly have gone back to her room. Might be love. He was not sure. But, no, he needed to be professional. She was working on a story about this region. That would not be right. But, oh God, she was something, never met a woman like her: powerful, bright, confident, and he couldn't help himself, beautiful, too. He could fall for her, no doubt. They had so much in common. Her father had been a minister, and she was well-versed in the latest theological thinkers—Bultmann and Tillich—and loved Whitman.

His face glowed. Unable to sit down, he paced back and forth and talked for an hour or more, basking in the pleasure of knowing her. After he settled down, he said that he was to meet her the next day at Marie Cirillo's house. They would give her and her film crew of four a tour of the area.

He rubbed his hands together and kept saying, "This is it. This is the break I've been waiting for. Man, I could fall for her." He looked over at me. "You like Agee?"

"What?"

"Agee."

"I love him."

"You'll love her, too. I'll bring her by. Let me know what you think," he said. "What a classy girl. Never met one like her."

"Can't wait."

❧

Neither of us slept. Erling said I should be interviewed. I should call my parents and tell them—impress them—that I'd be on the nightly news.

In the morning, I pulled out my best shirt, smoothed out the wrinkles, and made sure my jeans were clean. I shaved twice, pressed down my cowlick, and dabbed on some Old Spice.

❧

I set up the afternoon program with Emily, Lois, and Loraine. They had planned to make leather purses. When the kids arrived, we told them that CBS News would be coming. Bobby agreed to be interviewed; Tommy drove him home to put on his Sunday clothes.

❧

The afternoon dragged on because we kept anticipating the crew driving up in their big white van. But they didn't come.

We sent the kids home.

I drove back to the cabin. Erling was reading on the porch.

"What happened?" I asked. "Where were you? We waited all afternoon."

"Hold your horses," he said.

"But—"

"Calm down," he said. He set Whitman's Leaves of Grass down and told how, once the crew arrived, the bubble burst. The whole plan fizzled.

He smirked. "Oh, you know, what you would expect from New York."

I sat on the edge of the porch. "Tell me."

The crew with cameras and lights had arrived at Marie's house. The lead correspondent, a dazzling woman, wanted to rewrite the story she was working on.

Marie interceded. "What do you mean by 'story '?"

The correspondent told her that Mr. Cronkite wanted to do a story about poverty, how people struggled against it, and their desperate situation.

Marie explained that she wouldn't do a story about poverty. She would tell how the people, against all odds, lived in a land they loved and were rich in many ways.

The correspondent told her that it may be the case, but what was their annual income? Wasn't it below the poverty line?

Marie said yes, but she wouldn't allow these people to be stereotyped. The mining companies had taken their land and abused it. The residents were fighting back. They were very touchy about the use of the term "poor."

The correspondent told her that she had a storyline approved, and that was what she was going to do. She'd gone over it with the front office; they agreed to run it. Wouldn't you cooperate? It would be great coverage. It could benefit their programs.

Erling said that he hadn't come to Appalachia to work with "the poor." He'd come to promote their folk traditions.

The correspondent tried to change the topic. She didn't want to do a story on his program or mining companies—it wouldn't sell.

Erling jumped on the word "sell" and asked her what she meant. She told him that he knew damn well what it meant: certain stories weren't appropriate. Mining companies were too controversial.

"Walter Cronkite would give them five minutes. That is a lot of time," she said. "He wants to do, as I said, about poverty. Get support for helping the people in Appalachia. I'll make it a good story."

Marie told her that she wasn't interested. Erling, despite his attraction to her, concurred with Marie—no poverty stories. The broadcaster said she didn't have all day to haggle. She had other stories to tell. Marie offered a compromise. They could talk with some of the people in Rose's Creek, but the story couldn't be just about poverty.

The correspondent shook her head. "Look around," she said, "just look at the rundown shacks, the pathetic state of the roads. Poverty is everywhere. Don't you see what is in front of you?"

Marie and Erling refused. She needed to change the storyline.

The correspondent made several calls to New York. A "no-go." She had other leads and left.

"My moment of fame," he concluded, "up in smoke. Lost in the abyss. Too bad. Had she not been a robot, it'd been nice to know her."

The CBS News wasn't, as Cronkite said, "That's the way it was," but was more, "That's the way we'll sell it." Anyone, it seemed, who dared to tell a story different from what he wanted to hear was ignored, silenced.

One after the other, we brushed our teeth, took a leak off the back stoop, and read until the dark fell, and crickets offered the news of the day.

Night Dip

ONE EVENING, after discussing Thomas Wolfe's vision of America, Erling suggested we go for a drive. With Lois gone back up the hollow, Will, Lorraine, Emily, and I crammed into his Rambler as Erling drove by the Clearfork Post Office, and from there, across the tracks to the western side of the mountains, a region I'd never seen.

A narrow mining road climbed up a ridge. At the top, in the twilight, far in the distance lay another deep blue mountain range that spread as far as the eye could see. To our right, a quarry with steep rock escarpments dropped into a pool of water. As the last light slipped away, darkness swept over the hillside.

Erling suggested we skinny dip. Will stripped off his shirt. "Hey, I'm game."

Erling chided the girls, "Come on. No one can see you. Get a little daring!"

The girls refused and perched on a rock outcrop overlooking the quarry. They called back, "You can if you want. We wouldn't look."

We stripped off our clothes and piled them on a rock. Erling went down a pathway toward the quarry. Will followed him. At one point, Will stopped and looked back at me. "Cool, huh?"

"Sure."

We crept forward. Erling muttered, "Those girls will end up just like every other bourgeois girl. They'll marry a rich guy, move to the suburbs, and watch the nightly news, their brains turned off, their souls dried up."

Will whispered to me, "I kinda like them as they are."

"What'd you say?" Erling called back.

Will responded, "How far are we?"

"Not far."

But it was far from the water. Diving into jet black water from twenty feet worried me. What about rocks?

Erling assured us, "It's safe."

Along a slate path, two feet wide, he sidestepped, tapping where we should put our feet. He stopped on a ledge that jutted out from the cliff. A thin reflection of the moon spread on the water. The night air caused me to shiver.

Will put his arm around me. "Hey, it's okay. Trust him."

I felt his thigh against mine.

My hands over my groin, I said to myself. "Down, down."

He looked over at me. "You all right?"

"Sure."

He was aroused too. But he didn't seem to mind.

Erling stepped out on a rock, smooth and rounded like a tooth. "You scared?" Erling asked.

"Some," I admitted.

"Not me." Will flapped his arms as if he were about to fly.

"Follow me," Erling called.

Erling went to the edge of the rock. "Ready?" he asked. "No worries."

"Uh-huh," Will said.

Erling leaned out and disappeared into the darkness. A sploosh. Seconds later, "It's great!"

I rested my hand on the rock outcropping behind me. I couldn't do it.

Will put his hand on my shoulder and squeeze it. "Come on, hold my hand," he said, extending his hand to mine.

Although I felt as foolish as a child, I took his hand. We walked side by side to the edge of the rock. Ripples moved in the water below, wrinkles of white on ink.

"Count to three with me," Will said.

"One. Two. Three." We were off. At the last moment, I let go of Will and raised my arms. Just as I wondered where I was, since I could see nothing in the dark, I felt the water smack my feet. Legs submerged, my shoulders hit the surface. Stretching my legs as I entered the water, I knifed downward, then twisted upward to avoid hitting bottom. My eyes opened, and I could see nothing. I kicked my legs like a frog, reached up and pulled my arms back like a blind man with only instinct to guide him, yet felt a blissful serenity in the black void and stopped, treading water beneath the surface. I blew out bubbles that caught the faint moonlight and pushed upward to the surface, following them. Except for little glints of light in the bubbles, there was nothing except water around me, my naked body inside it like a hand in a glove. I ducked underwater again, diving down, blowing out more bubbles. No sound. My arms strained to keep me underwater. I swam on. Then, when my breath gave out, I surfaced and heard Will call out in a soft voice, "Jason, Jason. You there? You there?"

"Yes," I whispered back.

"Thank God," he whispered back. "You all right?"

"Yeah."

"You let go."

"I did!"

He swam over to me and dunked me. I pushed away from him, but he grabbed on, his body clung to mine, his genitals pressed to mine. Both aroused, but no one could see us, I let him hold me, pressed my lips to his neck.

From the shore, Erling called out, "Where are you guys?"

"Over here," Will called out.

"Come on, let's do it again." We swam to him. Once we got to shore, we whispered, not wanting to disturb the quiet.

We pulled ourselves onto a rock ledge, crept on hands and knees up a slope, then stood and, foot over foot, inched toward the top. We sat down and called the girls. We told them that no one could see anything and urged them to try it. "Besides, we'll get out and let you do it by yourselves."

They giggled and called back, "No, thank you. We're fine."

We jumped and dove several more times. Landing feet first proved more exciting, since the water, once it smacked against your feet, caused a momentary resistance, and then, as if someone pulled a plug, sucked us into a tube, and our bodies darted down into the void. I learned to leap with my arms up on either side of my head like I was diving, so that I shot like an arrow to the bottom, where I treaded and resisted coming up for a few seconds. Deep as it was, there was nothing but blackness, like swimming in ink. After each jump, Will swam over and splashed me. I swam away, but he grabbed my foot, pulled me toward him, laughing, and we embraced, our secret hidden in the night.

Finally, we dried off, pulled on our clothes, and Erling drove us back to the lodge. He told Lorraine and Emily that someday they needed to loosen up, let go of their bourgeois mentality, and just be. They would never experience freedom until they dared to let go of their inhibitions.

Will got out at the driveway to his cabin.

As he scooted out of the back seat next to me, he slid his hand down my arm to my leg and squeezed it. "See," he said. "Listen to Erling. You can do it. Just let go."

"That's what I keep telling him," Erling said.

I said, "Let go. Let go. Where's caution in this world?"

"Hey, get in the front seat," Erling said. "It's late."

Erling complained about the uptight rich girls, their complacency, and their not considering what life was like for the poor. By the way he spoke about them, I knew he was also talking to me by inference, about what might lie ahead if I wasn't honest with myself.

My thoughts drifted back to Will, to leaping with him off the cliff, and to having him hold me. I was afraid of what it might lead to, what might happen if I wasn't more cautious. I didn't want to step into another abyss. Not make the same mistake I did with Bobby and Tommy. I opened the car window and took in the cool night air, remembering being underwater, how it enveloped me and carried me into the dark, into an underworld I craved but only faintly understood and feared. After the swim, I feared that it would swallow me whole.

⁂

By the fifth week, our program drew even more people. As an alternative to going out to a bar on Friday nights, we had campfires for them to attend. In late afternoon, the whole community gathered on the ridge by Peggy's house. The men constructed a large circle with large rocks to contain the bonfire. When sunset blinked out, Cecil, a tall man with a moonshine business, tossed an ignited newspaper on the gasoline-drenched wood, and whoosh, the fire started!

Bud Terry, who sang despite his asthma, played the fiddle. A few clogged on an old tabletop set in the dusty perimeter of the fire, while everyone clapped, whooped, and tapped their toes. I told Appalachian folk tales, stories I'd memorized. The kids' favorite was "The Twins and the Dark Evil Witch."

It went like this: Twins, poor children, heard about a mysterious land with fabulous riches.

They traveled toward the enchanted land and encountered a fox caught in a trap, which they released. He gave them several of his teeth. They came across a fallen pine tree and straightened it. The tree gave them one of its cones. They found a stream that was stopped up. They rolled rocks away until it flowed freely. It gave them a cup of water.

Finally, they arrived in a magical land where gold and silver shimmered on the hillsides. They stuffed their pockets and satchels with enough to be rich for a lifetime. But an evil witch caught them and cast a spell over them, locking them in a room where they smelled flesh burning in a stove, heard the cries of other victims.

One night, a tiny mouse showed them a trap door, and they escaped, running as fast as they could. But that wasn't the end of the story. (This was the part where the children pretended they were the twins because I'd given some children pinecones, some buckets of water, and some chalk (as teeth). The evil witch took off on her broom to capture them.)

The children cheered, "Hurry, hurry!"

The witch cackled, "I'm going to get you, little ones, hee, hee, hee," and flew after the boy and girl, but the children tossed the teeth. An enormous, toothed fence blocked her way.

But she smashed through the fence. Children cried, "Hurry. Hurry," and tossed the pinecones, which sprouted a gigantic forest. But she swerved around the trees. Finally, the children called, "Hurry. Hurry," and threw a bucket of water at her (and me). An ocean rose that swallowed the witch. As in all fairy tales, good won over evil.

The story concluded that evening. Several men lingered and helped extinguish the fire. Then the staff, Erling, and I drove back to our sleeping quarters.

❧

The program became so all-consuming that we rarely read a newspaper, and it wasn't until Lorraine told us that Nixon had pledged to withdraw

25,000 troops from Vietnam that we took notice.

Will and I had several conversations about the war (he opposed it) and civil rights (he'd been in several marches). One night, he wanted to tell me something important and asked if we could take a walk.

"There's been a riot," he said on the path toward the lake below the lodge. "Where?"

"Right down the street from where I live," he said. "You might be interested in it."

"How so?"

He spoke in a hushed tone. "The gays in Greenwich Village rebelled. The police harass them all the time. Arrests. Beatings. Finally, some drag queens at a bar called Stonewall had enough and fought back. It's big. It made national news."

I pulled back from him. For weeks, I'd seen him hiking the roads. Rain, sun, day, night, he walked ten miles home and back. His endurance amazed me. Always upbeat, he made me smile. We'd gone swimming every week, changing in the same room. He was easy to look at. And I did look. He told me his family, strict Catholics, wanted nothing to do with him—too radical. But he never said what "radical" meant. There was a part of me that hoped he wasn't gay, and another part that wanted him to be. When I got aroused in the close quarters, I justified my feelings by thinking that maybe he was just lonely or starved for affection, and horny as I was. That's how I rationalized my relationship with him, how I kept him at bay, yet I could never entirely get him out of my mind. Caught in my fantasy about his body next to mine that night at the quarry, I dreamed of letting go, just accepting what I felt and embracing him. It seemed as natural a thing to do as holding hands. Yet I resented feeling as I did. I felt as if I was violating who I was, or at least who I thought I was.

Now he was telling me about some gays in New York.

"Why tell me?" I blurted out.

"Just thought—"

"Thought what?"

"Thought you'd like to know," he said. "That's all." He shrugged.

"Thanks," I said, and excused myself. My heart was beating so fast that I felt dizzy and nearly fell over, but I kept moving toward the lodge, increasing my pace as I neared the veranda, where several staff members were seated. Still, I didn't stop chatting and kept moving to the back parking lot and stood there looking at the moon. I was sure, if I could have flown away at that moment, I would have been happier there than I was on the earth.

My head was aswarm with questions. What was it that tipped him off? I didn't flirt with him. Or at least not consciously. I was curious about his being uncircumcised, but that was only natural. I never said a word about being attracted to him. True, I found him attractive. He wore a Speedo. His body, like finely carved marble, with a hairy chest and chiseled muscles, made him statuesque. I couldn't keep my eyes off him. Somehow, he did know. My eyes gave me away.

My body seemed to have an intelligence of its own. Despite my telling it no, it always responded yes. I kept thinking of that night in the quarry and how I gave in, willingly, happily. I had tested the limits. But I wasn't sure if I could give in to those feelings again, and if I did, what it would mean about me, him, and our relationship.

I kept my distance from Will after that. I didn't want Erling to suspect my interest in him. That would be a big problem for the Folk School. And me.

A week or so later, Lorraine was in tears because Ted Kennedy had nearly drowned. But worse, one of his aides had drowned. His car toppled off a bridge at Chappaquiddick. Lorraine's family, close to the Kennedys, had gone to school with one of them. She asked if she could spend the day at the lodge listening to reports on the radio and making telephone calls. Erling let her yet whispered to me, "Those Kennedys are always out to get laid. Looks like he got screwed this time instead."

By late July, the lodge was abuzz about the moon landing. With one TV in the lodge, many people who frequented the lodge, including several ministers and their wives, pulled up chairs. Bobby, Tommy, and some of the other kids from the Folk School joined us, and we watched the lunar capsule touch down, dust swirling out across the rock-strewn landscape.

Bobby, who was sitting next to me, said, "Looks like the road from our place."

Tommy asked, "You think it's real?"

"I'm sure it is," I said. "I've seen the rockets take off from the Cape."

"Looks like some movie to me," he said.

Two astronauts climbed down the ladder and pranced on the surface in their inflated spacesuits. President Nixon got into the act:

I just can't tell you how proud we all are of what you have done. For every American, this has to be the proudest day of our lives, and for people all over the world, I am sure that they, too, join with Americans in recognizing what an immense feat this is. Because of what you have done, the heavens have become a part of man's world, and as you talk to us from the Sea of Tranquility, it inspires us to redouble our efforts to bring peace and tranquility to earth. For one priceless moment in the whole history of man, all the people on this earth are truly one…

A minister countered, "I think the president forgot another priceless moment in history."

"What's that?" I asked. "It's pretty darn big if you ask me."

He tilted his head to one side and said, "How about Christ?"

"Oh, yeah," I said. "Can't forget him."

The minister glanced at me and muttered something to his wife.

Will had walked out of the room and was looking up at the moon. With the atmosphere in the room more heated than I liked, I joined him.

"Pretty amazing, isn't it?" he said.

"Right out there," I pointed at the moon. "They're on it, hundreds of thousands of miles from here. "I often feel that way, and yet I'm right here on the earth."

"Hey, don't get down on yourself. You can be ballsy. I liked the way you called out that minister."

"Really? I thought I overdid it."

"Nope. Ministers seem bent on pushing their beliefs on everyone."

We stood side by side, a few feet apart, looking up. I glimpsed him staring at me, and turned, and he blushed, bowing his head.

"Is something wrong?" I asked.

He put his hand on my shoulder. "Hey," he said. "I didn't mean to scare you the other night. You've been distant. I thought we had something special. That's all."

"It's fine," I said and stepped away.

"I just thought—"

"You thought wrong," I said, more abruptly than I meant to.

He was silent. I kept looking at the moon. I turned to say something else to him, to let him know, much as I wanted to put my feelings aside, I couldn't do it, and did like him, and wanted, if he was willing, to go slowly because I couldn't risk getting the Folk School in trouble.

But he was gone.

I went back into the room, thinking he might have gone back to watch the landing. He wasn't there. Not in the main room. Not in the kitchen. I stopped, standing in the hallway, and watched Walter Cronkite interview a scientist, then drove Tommy and Bobby back home.

On the way back to the cabin, I stopped by the road and walked by the creek. Sadness had come over me. I remembered Bob, when I saw him leaving at the airport and felt as if someone had torn my heart from my chest. Water cascaded over the rocks, slipped downward, and the moonlight shimmered on its surface. I remembered Will's face before he left, his gentle expression, his head tilted as if all he needed was a sign, a straightforward acknowledgement, and all I could give him was "You thought wrong." I didn't mean to hurt him. I wanted to hug him and ask for his forgiveness. Maybe I would have said something if he had stayed. I could be such a creep, I thought. I'd tell him the next time I see him. I had some things to figure out first. I wasn't sure what they were, but maybe what got in my way was the feeling I didn't want to admit, the one I felt all along, was not just attraction, but a word that frightened me more than any other: love.

❧

At our next class, I learned that Will had returned to Greenwich Village. His friend had been beaten and arrested. He told Erling he'd write.

After the morning meeting, Erling pulled me aside. He was puzzled by the abruptness of Will's departure.

"Did something happen between you two?" he asked.

"No, why do you ask?" I shot back.

"Hey, calm down. I just thought you were close, that's all," he said.

"We were," I said. By the look in Erling's eyes, I could tell that he knew more than he was saying. He chewed on his cheek, waiting.

I broke the silence. "It might have been something I said. I don't know."

"I'm sorry," Erling offered.

"I said some things—"

"We all do at times," he said, pressing his hand against my arm.

I tried to be casual and act in control. "It's fine."

"Well, they have another cook," Erling said, trying to be light. "It doesn't matter, as long as he knows how to cook!"

But it did matter. I missed Will terribly. He was as far away as those men on the moon, orbiting two hundred and thirty thousand miles from the Earth.

Here I was on Earth watching them in their spacesuits that looked impossible to move in. They seemed just like me, with the full weight and gravity of my fears dragging me down. There was nothing I could do to change it, go back in time and make it different. The abyss I'd feared was of only of my own making, based on my own mixed-up feelings. It had become real, but not in any way I wanted or expected. The abyss was something I'd done to myself, the way I'd cut someone out of my life. What I said to him, "You're wrong," turned out to be something I should have told myself.

Erling looked at me and asked, "Is there anything I can do?"

"Fuck, I don't know. I guess it's just…" My voice trailed off. I was crying.

"Hey," he said. "Take the rest of the day off. You need it."

I drove back to the cabin, pulled out my journal, and wrote about what happened, reconstructed what he'd said, what I'd said. I tried to make sense of it. But no matter how many words were scattered across the page, nothing changed. Words have their limits. They couldn't assuage the fears that stood in my way. I'd made an irreparable mistake.

Two days before the Folk School closed for the summer, Erling and I drove through the Smoky Mountains to see Thomas Wolfe's boarding house, the site of his famous novels Look Homeward, Angel and You Can't Go Home Again. The boarding house, situated in an old residential area, was a three-story building with a wide porch and expansive façade.

Erling made such pilgrimages to his literary heroes. He wanted to see how Wolfe shaped his stories from what he'd experienced and witnessed. Words became rooms we walked through—the stairs where Wolfe's dad, Gant, had raged, staggered drunk and hemorrhaged; rooms where his mother Eliza had cleaned for her guests; the bed where Ben lay with his failing lungs and died. His descriptions of the rooms—the dining room where guests ate, the porch where he gazed at the hills—had, by the magic of his pen, stopped time. I could imagine him coming out of the kitchen, his enormous hand around a sandwich, telling us of his life, of what he dreamed.

Erling read passages from the book and told me that if I read well and trusted the voices of those I read, I would soon—maybe not in a year or even in a decade—find that their voices would meld with mine. He said, too, that if I followed my heart, as Eugene did in the novels, I would discover I couldn't go home again and realize, as Eugene did:

You can't go back home to your family, back home to your childhood … back home to a young man's dreams of glory and of fame … back home to places in the country, back home to the old forms and systems of things which once seemed everlasting but which are changing all the time – back home to the escapes of Time and Memory.

I wondered if that was to be my fate, too. Each time I went home, I felt more like a stranger, yet I felt that, to leave my home, I had to have some place and some people I could claim as my new home. Until I had such a place, I was a wanderer on a voyage to a new continent of my heart, without any clear destination or final place to settle. It was as if, deep inside, I knew that I had to have a place to say hello to before I could say goodbye. I yearned to open a door and look out and see the face of someone who loved me as dearly as I loved them. Right now, when I opened doors, some people cared deeply for me, as deeply as I cared for them. But they weren't my lovers, and they didn't know me any more than I knew myself. I knew I was still a long way from finding a home and being true to myself. I thought, too, of Will and how in an instant he had left my life because I'd denied his love for me. I wasn't ready for his passion, and he knew it; however, what I was prepared for remained a question.

Erling and I drove back through the Smoky Mountains and slept in Mabel under the dog-eared comforter. We hiked deep into the forest to the headland of a stunning waterfall. We sat quietly, each of us taking in the view down the valley, where the stream dove and darted through pines, its spine visible for miles as it bent along the forest floor.

Suddenly, a mother, father, and their young son charged up the path to us. The mother had a camera around her neck; the father, a trail map in his hand; the boy, a miserable look on his face.

The father stepped in front of us and shouted orders to his son, "Stand here, Jerry," and to his wife, "Alice, get his picture."

The heavyset wife stood in front of us, straddling our legs, and took several photographs, never once saying, "Excuse me," as if she owned the place. Once she snapped the picture, the father brought the boy to the precipice and said, "Take a good look."

"Got the pictures?" he asked his wife.

She nodded. He said, "Let's go." They hurried down the trail, the entire encounter lasting only three minutes.

"What is it about the American need to capture everything on camera?" Erling asked. "Nothing seems real to them unless they have it in a snapshot. Trouble is, they never stay long enough to experience what they see."

We waited until the family had gone far down the trail. Once they were out of sight, we followed them back to the parking lot and drove to Clearfork, where, the next day, we'd meet the girls, as Erling called them, to say goodbye.

On our trip east, I'd bought several newspapers and a *Time* magazine. I wanted to find out what had happened in the world. The news was bizarre:

Muhammad Ali was convicted of evading the draft and had his boxing title stripped. Nixon was getting tough on anti-war activists. Charles Manson and his "family" in California had brutally killed an actress, Sharon Tate, and others. In upstate New York, 400,000 naked people at a music festival splashed in the rain, uninhibited.

We parked and ran under the covered front porch of the Clearfork Post Office. Torrential rain battered the roof. Silver curtains of rain charged down the road and were whipped by a deafening sound. The flooded road became a giant, coffee-colored mud puddle; tire tracks filled with a murky pudding.

We had arranged a rendezvous there to bid the girls farewell.

"This is no place to say goodbye!" I shouted.

"No, it isn't. Horrible weather," Erling agreed.

Loraine's yellow Mustang drove up to the post office. Lorraine and Emily bolted out of the car to join us on the porch. They looked as if Christian Dior himself had dressed them. With a white blouse, tight blue and green pants, and pink sneakers, Lorraine looked regal. Emily had a red blouse with a matching skirt and white loafers. They had abandoned the jeans and work shirts that Erling insisted they wear.

They shook hands with Erling and told him that it meant a great deal to them to be part of the Folk School.

Not wanting to miss this last opportunity to warn them of the societal trap that they would fall into, and he hoped someday they'd break out of, he lectured them about their bourgeois society and concluded, "I wish you girls well."

"Erling," Loraine said in a calm yet stern voice, "I used to be a girl, but since you have known me, I have always been a woman. So please call me a woman."

Nonplussed, Erling said, "Well, of course."

"Good."

Erling took a deep breath. "Glad you came here. I hope it was a good experience."

"It was."

"I wish we could have done more, and I do hope that someday you can find the gumption to be fully yourselves."

Lorraine asked, "What do you mean by that?" She seemed intolerant of his patronizing manner.

He explained that they were still uptight, not willing to let go, but that was expected given their background.

"Let go, be less uptight?" she asked.

"Yes," Erling said, "and, well, stop worrying about appearances. How you look." He motioned at their outfits and turned down his mouth. "You always look as if you were about to go to a swank Boston cocktail party."

Loraine blushed and started to thank him, to concede his point, and then caught herself and repeated Erling's phrase, "Let go, huh? Is that what I need to do?"

"Yes," he affirmed. "I hope you can do that someday."

She mimicked him, "Someday."

Grabbing Emily by the hand, Lorraine shouted to Emily, "Someday is today," and sprinted off the porch, right into the rain and into the quagmire that once had been a road. The two girls stomped and leapt, the rain lashing at them, their outfits splattered with mud. They yelped and splashed back and forth. Their hair splattered across their faces. Lorraine's blouse was soaked, the clear curve of her breasts and her nipples visible. She was, indeed, a woman.

They raised their arms and whooped and hollered so much that the postmistress, Ida, came out to see what the commotion was about. She stood, her hands on her hips, and said, "Well, I'll be."

It reminded me of the photographs from Woodstock, naked hippies flopping in the mud, free of all restraints.

Erling seemed genuinely befuddled, yet he couldn't help but smile and gaze with admiration at the wild beasts they'd become.

"What the hell?" he gasped.

I laughed, took off my shirt, and joined them. The girls screeched and grabbed my hands, and we swung around in circles. We didn't expect it, but Erling came out too, after he took off his shoes, socks, and shirt, piling everything neatly on a chair. We raced back and forth. We threw mud at one another. The postmistress laughed and called out, "It's better than *Hee-Haw*!"

When we finished, we stood once again on the porch.

The women asked Erling, "Like that?"

He smiled, "Yes, like that."

IV

Neither flesh nor fleshless;
Neither from nor towards; at the still point, the dance is.

—"Four Quartets," T.S. Eliot

In the Devil's Hands

WHILE ERLING DROVE BACK to Nashville to complete paperwork for his degree, I drove northwest out of the mountains, across Ohio and Indiana, back to Illinois. The patchwork cornfields broken by railroad tracks, and the vast expanse of sky from horizon to horizon, made me feel at home.

My parents had gone to bed, although my dad, a light sleeper, had heard me come in and came out, saying groggily, "Good to have you home, son."

With two weeks to go before the new semester, I typed up my letters to Mr. Hook, who had arranged for me to meet with some parishioners to discuss my experience and gain support for another summer at the Folk School.

I fell into familiar routines: playing golf, going to the club, going out with Jerry to find girls, and catching up with Bob, Ann, and Paul to talk about their lives.

Bob, excited about decoding enemy messages, couldn't tell me much for security reasons. However, he lived on the East Coast and played golf with a few senior officers, whom I imagined came to his place for parties, much as the professors at Vanderbilt did.

After the presidential campaign, Paul moved out west and joined a commune. He met a woman, some hippie who didn't believe in history, only the living present. Nixon, he thought, would tear the country apart even more than it already was. His interest in politics ended with the election. He advised me to drop out as well.

Ann wrote a lovely letter and looked forward to seeing me. She planned to move out of the dorm and wondered if I wanted to get an apartment with her. I told her no because I was still a residential advisor.

Several nights, I went to Old Town, the upscale neighborhood near Chicago's Lincoln Park, to drink and, later, to haunt The Hidden Treasure, an adult bookstore. Wandering down the magazine rack with photographs of men, randy and beautiful, my forbidden urges came back to me. I bought several magazines, hid them in my room, and fantasized about being with one of the men who looked like Will. He'd take me back to his place. We'd slowly undress. I'd fall into his arms.

In the morning, I'd hear my mom call me from downstairs. "Time to get up. You have a tee-off time with your dad." I'd splash water on my face, slip on my golf shirt, shorts, and shoes, and head off to play. Pars. Bogeys. Birdies. Numbers. Missed putts. The Oak Room. Drinks. Shower. Change. Dinner. Coat and tie. Stand when others come to the table—seat mother. Smile. Make small talk. And thus, August ended.

In September, I left home on the day the Chicago Tribune condemned the "Chicago 8" who were indicted based on charges against them at the Democratic Convention. My father claimed they were unpatriotic. Sure, I thought, as patriotic as a president who promises peace but expands the war.

⁂

A long day's drive. New dorm room. New students. Books. Schedule. Classes. A call from Ann. A visit to her new apartment with another girl, Jenny. A long overnight. "I love you." One of us said it: every weekend, some time with her. We wanted the old magic back. But without Bob, it wasn't the same. We knew it. No one said anything. Parties lasted late into the night. We slept together—something missing. I couldn't say. Perhaps, I didn't want to know. Her roommate told Ann I wasn't good for her. Maybe she was right. I went back to my room to study Kierkegaard, a man as troubled as I was about a relationship.

⁂

In October, Tom Winters, a fellow second-year divinity student and dorm advisor who took several of the same classes, came to my room to study Phenomenology of Religion, which confounded both of us.

Skinny and awkward, not an athlete, he carried himself like an adolescent, flinging his arms around as if they were in free flight from his body.

We discussed the difference between "world-view" and "lived-world," two concepts that the professor kept mentioning in his hour-long lectures. In college, Tom majored in English but minored in philosophy and was familiar with recent trends in literary criticism that had their roots in phenomenology.

One evening, after we completed an exam, he brought a bottle of Jack Daniels to celebrate. He poured shots of it—one for every question we answered correctly in the last class. We studied the textbook, read and re-read the pages, and deciphered their meaning to ensure we understood them correctly. Bracketing. Lifeworld. Intentionality. Noesis.

When our scholarly conversation waned, we reverted to storytelling with me on my bunk, propped up against the wall by the window, and Tom at bedside, in a chair, pouring Jack into my glass.

I said, "You're a good bartender."

"I'm tending to you."

"You've fucked up."

He pulled back, offended. "How so?"

"You're getting me very drunk!"

"Oh, no," he said. "You don't get it. That's my intentionality, to use a phenomenological term."

"Aren't you the brilliant one!"

His hand was on my thigh—a casual gesture. I hardly noticed it since it was also holding out a full glass of whiskey. He asked if he could sit on the bunk. We could drink from the bottle instead of the glasses. I motioned to a spot. He leaned back and looked at me.

"I like to look at someone when I talk to them," he said.

"That's fine."

We talked about dating, and how frustrating it was. He put his hand on my stomach. I let it be. It sat there. It wasn't doing anything. It felt comfortable, a good place for a hand. But I soon felt a pressure increase, as if it were trying to get me to sit up. I scooched up more. He looked at me. He wasn't talking anymore.

My penis bulged in my pants. I twisted my hips to the side to cover it up.

He could see what I saw—no use hiding.

"That excites me," I said. I pointed to his hand.

"Oh, I'm sorry!" Tom apologized, lifting his hand high in the air.

"Oh, it's okay. Feels good." I half-realized what I said and wanted to disown it. I leaned back and closed my eyes. I let myself go. That is what Erling told me I needed to do. And Will, he wanted me to be more open. I found myself giving myself a pep talk. To hell with it; I'm drunk, very drunk. This is bad, I know. But I don't care.

Tom caressed my stomach. It felt good. If it feels good, do it. His fingers were on my cock.

I'll lie here, I said to myself, and pretend it's Ann. I don't know what he's going to do next. If I'm still, he can do what he wants. He likes it, fine, but I'll have no part of it.

Tom asked, "Are you awake?"

I opened my eyes. "Somewhat."

He unzipped my pants, unbuttoned my shirt—I leaned up—his hand around my neck, supporting me. I unbuttoned his shirt. Undressed, I lay on Tom and kissed him, felt the bristle of his beard, and thought how different it was from Ann's face. Tom's cock was larger than mine. I wondered why he was queer because, in my mind, men were gay because they didn't measure up to other guys. But clearly, he did. I rubbed his dick. How odd another man's penis felt—like rubber, no life in it. I wondered what I was doing; it seemed so perfunctory.

This is sick, I thought. But I couldn't figure out how to get away since I was plastered. I lay back, hoping the dizziness would end, and looked up at the ceiling.

Tom took me in his mouth. I closed my eyes and soon, too soon, it was over.

After wiping me off with a towel, he sat up and said, "Nice."

I reached for my underpants in a vain attempt to cover up. I felt embarrassed. Too little, too late. I knew Tom was probably expecting me to do the same favor for him. But I didn't want to. I felt disgusted. Tom had a mouth like a giant fish, a narrow-looking, starved minnow. Gaunt. That was the word: gaunt. How was it that I just noticed that? He put his hand on my cheek and said, "Lovely."

What was I doing here with him in my bed? It wasn't right. I lay back, drifted off, and awoke with Tom by my side, caressing me again, and I let myself go. He kissed me, dressed, and left the bottle behind. "Good night."

The door closed behind him.

After that encounter, I couldn't face him and stayed on the opposite side of the seminar table. I had given in to temptation. It was the whiskey, I thought. I let down my guard. I wrote in my journal: "I WAS IN THE HANDS AND MOUTH OF THE DEVIL!!" Ashamed and angry at myself for stepping over the line, I wanted to hide, to disappear. Even when looking in a mirror, I avoided eye contact, pretending that the person I was looking at was not looking at me, but he was, and I disliked him. I wanted to bash the mirror and tell him to go away.

Late one evening, when I was standing in jockey shorts preparing for bed, Tom knocked. Before I could refuse him, he entered. He was drunk and held a bottle in his hand and cradled two glasses in the crook of his arm. He staggered toward the chair and said, "Oh, I'm sorry."

"Can't you…"

I pulled on my pants, looked at him, and said flatly, "Don't think you're—"

"No, no, this is just a social call."

"I don't need one."

"Look, sorry, man."

I said sternly. "I have to study."

Tom sat in the chair. "You hate me," he said. He set the glasses on the floor, poured the liquor in the glasses, and held up one, kneeling, pleading, "Come on, have a drink. Come on. It'll do ya' good—Here. Here."

I looked out the window, turned back to see his pathetic, penitent eyes, trying to make up for a mistake of nights before. I hoped if I avoided him, pretended he wasn't here, he would leave. Still, when I turned to face him, he was going about being a bartender as if he hadn't heard me.

He mixed the drinks, poured in soda, and talked as he poured, not looking up. "Come on, let's drink, just one for old time's sake."

As he held the glass up to me, it slipped from his grasp and shattered on the tile floor.

"Oh god. Oh god, I'm so sorry. I'm sorry. I'm such a fool." He bent over and muttered to himself, "Asshole. Asshole," scraping the glass together with his hand. Liquor ran in quick rivulets in all directions, and soon enough, ran with blood from his hand.

"Listen," I burst out, "forget it. I'll clean it up. Just get out! I'm not innocent anymore. Just get outta here. I don't want to. I made a mistake. Do you understand? No more. Do you hear me? I'm not like that. So don't try it again. Just go."

He didn't seem to hear me and continued to pick up glass shards. Both hands were bleeding, the blood dripping on the floor, down his sleeve, his hands coated with it while he picked up the shards, inspecting them, and put them in his glass, mixing with the alcohol.

"Do me a favor. Get the hell outta here, now!"

Deaf to my commands, he kept picking up the shards, looking at them, muttering, "They're blood. Look, they're bloody."

I leaned over, grabbed him under his arms, picked him up, and shoved him against the wall. He gasped and cowered, looking as if he were going to faint. Glass shards fell from his hand.

"Forget it," I said, softening my tone. I grabbed a T-shirt from my dresser, wrapped it around his hand, placed the bottle in his other hand, and put the remaining glass in the crook of his arm.

Tom repeated, "Let me clean it up. I'm so sorry. I'm such an asshole. I'll get a towel. I'm sorry. Let me…"

I opened the door. "Forget it. It's okay. Just get out of here."

Gently, I pushed him out the door.

The puddle of Jack Daniels covered the floor, seeping under the bed, the desk. The splotches of blood blended with the alcohol, as if to tell me, "This is what happens when you stray." I bent over, a towel in hand and mopped up the floor, cutting my hand in the process, my mind going over again questions that troubled me.

How could I have been involved with him?

He wasn't the asshole. I was—a disgusting asshole.

I could hear him stumbling down the hall, bumping into the wall, muttering to himself, and thought that he would probably go out and pick up some other guy, and would, as he did with me, succeed. I went back to my desk, but the cuts in my fingers bled on the page, and even when I wrapped them in a cloth, they kept bleeding. I could hardly focus on the book. I had a strange urge to kill him. I hated him, hated what he made me feel, what he made me be, what he made me do. I felt embarrassed, as I had with Will just months ago, and I was shocked that I should be as aroused as I was with Tom, whom I wasn't attracted to as I had been with Will. Tom unmasked my disguise, stripped me of my clothes and my exposed urges. I didn't like it. I had to see Ann. I had to make it right. But how could I when, based on what had happened, I was wrong? Or at least, my feelings were not what I wanted them to be.

❧

The next day, I asked Ann over to my room. We studied together. After a few hours, I put music on my stereo and we lay down together. We made unhurried love that, for the moment, dispelled my doubts, gave me a sense that whatever happened with Tom, was just an aberration, nothing more, nothing to worry about. I liked her perfume, her breasts, firm and sweet, and how, as we made love, she moaned and kept pace with me, holding onto my back, whispering, "Yes, yes, yes," as we settled, kissed, and fell asleep.

She came over regularly, lounged on the bed, read her books, and made notes in a journal as we listened to the radio. One night, after we opened a bottle of Merlot, President Nixon had a special broadcast and said in faux-sincere voice, "My fellow citizens,"

Honest and patriotic Americans, he said, "*have reached different conclusions as to how peace should be achieved. In San Francisco a few weeks ago, I saw demonstrators carrying signs reading, 'Lose the war in Vietnam. Bring the boys home…'*

He made it seem that any of us who disagreed with him were not only letting him down but were also letting the nation and the peace process down. Ann, cuddled in my arms, glanced at me, her expression deeply troubled.

And I want to end the war for another reason, he continued. *I want to endit so that the energy and dedication of you, our young people, now too often directed into bitter hatred against those responsible for the war, can be turned to the great challenges of peace, a better life for all Americans, a better life for all people on this earth… So tonight, to you, the great silent majority of my fellow Americans, I ask for your support. I pledged in my campaign for the Presidency to end the war in a way that we could win the peace. I have initiated a plan of action which will enable me to keep that pledge. The more support I can have from the American people, the sooner that pledge can be redeemed. For the more divided we are at home, the less likely the enemy is to negotiate in Paris.*

Ann jumped out of bed, jabbing her finger at the radio. She pointed as if I hadn't noticed it. "He's threatening us."

"I know," I said, motioning to her. "Sit down. Let's see what he says next."

He concluded,

Let us be united for peace. Let us also be united against defeat. Because let us understand: North Vietnam cannot defeat or humiliate the United States. Only Americans can do that…

Ann bolted upright again. "He's not ending the war! He's going to expand it."

I loved her outrage. She had a strong conscience, and as the days pressed on into months, she was right. Nixon justified "Vietnamization" to expand the war. His "Silent Majority" raved about his speech. Yet antiwar protests increased. Ann and I didn't make love that night. We just held onto one another because we sensed something awful was about to happen, and we couldn't make it right.

❧

Several days later, Tom came back, sober this time, to apologize. He sat in the same chair he had the other night. With his arms and hands caught between his legs, hiding his hands, both covered with bandages, he asked what I meant about having "a loss of innocence." I told him that I learned that sex had to be more than just getting someone off. It had to include commitment. And I couldn't see commitment between two guys. It just wouldn't work. It wasn't right.

Tom explained how what happened to me also happened to him when he was younger, and at the time, he felt the same way. An English professor had been attracted to him in college. One afternoon, the professor asked Tom to come to his apartment. They talked and drank, and before he knew it, the professor had him undressed.

Before that, Tom had been "innocent" too. He had never had sex with anyone. A few days passed. Enraged at what the professor had done to him, he confronted the professor. The professor invited Tom over to his house to straighten it out. The professor told him that he knew Tom was queer: he could see it in his eyes. Tom denied it. That couldn't be. How can you see it in someone's eyes? But a few weeks later, as if drawn by a magnet, he came back to the professor's house.

"I tried to deny it," Tom said, "but I found myself attracted to him and ended up there one night, then a week, a month. I couldn't help it, although I tried. I even dated a girl after that with some success. I believed that I had turned the corner and defied his prediction. I could be straight."

He went on to explain. "One night at a party where I was supposed to meet my girlfriend—we had a lot of friends in common—I met a lawyer who told me my girlfriend was really hot. And she was. We'd been getting it on for months. He pointed to a young girl who looked like Twiggy and told me that they'd hooked up. The four of us drank together.

"After the party, he invited me to go to his apartment. The girls had left early (they were both in college and had to study for an exam). When we got there, one thing led to another, and you can imagine what happened. I stopped dating the girl. That's the way it's been for me. I tried to deny him, tried to reject him, to tell him no more, but I couldn't. The lawyer pursued every young man he met, but I didn't care. For a while, it was me. That's all that mattered." He shrugged his shoulders and offered a sour smile. "I've never found someone, as you say, someone to be with who feels the same as I do. It's just sex, and goodbye." He glanced around the room and fidgeted with his hands. Two Band-Aids came loose, and he tried to put them back, pressing on them with his good fingers.

I didn't want to say anything, but I had one question. "When you came over here that first night," I asked. "Did you see something in my eyes?"

He blinked several times. "I don't know. Maybe I did. Maybe I just had the hots for you. Not sure."

"It's different for each of us, the knowing," I said, gazing at him. "I'm not like you, I can tell you that."

"Well, at least you see how it's been for me," he said. He straightened up and was ready to leave.

He was right, I thought. There are some things that are in you. But I wasn't sure that was the case with me.

I said, "I'm sorry."

"Oh, don't be. I've accepted it, and, if the gay revolution actually gets some steam behind it, I'll be okay."

"What do you mean by 'revolution?'" I asked.

He laughed and said, surprised, "You don't know, do you?" He told me about the riots in New York City, the ones Will mentioned.

"Wasn't it the one near Christopher Street in Greenwich Village?" I asked. "You know about it?"

"A friend told me," I said. "I want to go to Greenwich Village, 19 Perry Street, to visit Father Flye whom I was corresponding—"

"Is he gay?"

"No."

"He may be: That's right in the middle of the gay district."

"No, I don't think he's gay. He's a priest and a friend of a writer I like, James Agee. But go on. Tell me what happened."

"Well, it was pretty common for the New York cops to raid any gay bar. They would beat, harass, and arrest people. However, on Saturday, June 28th, things were different. Judy Garland had died. Her funeral was to be held on June 27th in Manhattan. It brought out all the 'friends of Judy,' you know, guys in tight trousers, like me." He pointed to his revealing pants. "20,000 came out to mourn her death. The next night, when the police raided a bar—I went there several times—no one was in the mood to put up with the bullshit. It was like Judy's rainbow died. The drag queens and patrons revolted and threw lighters, beer cans, pennies, and even parking meters at the pigs. The cops retreated into the bar until reinforcements came. But tourists and other gays, hundreds of them, joined in and crowded the street, blocking traffic. They called for 'Gay Power.' It was amazing. I wish I'd been there. Cops took one boy, cute too, and beat him. That's when the 'queens' attacked, calling out 'Save our Sister' and reclaimed him. Eventually, the crowd dispersed. But the word got around. Now, at least for some of us, it's a new reality." He smiled. "That's your history lesson."

I wondered if that boy who'd been beaten up was Will's friend. No wonder Will left. Maybe to take care of him in ways I never could have taken care of Will.

Tom reached out for me to hug him. I did, but I angled my body sideways to his. His lips kissed my neck. He stepped back, smiling weakly, his right cheek quivering slightly. I opened the door. Once he was gone, I closed and locked it.

I had coffee with him several times, going over our class notes. He spoke about his battles with depression and how he wanted to find someone. I couldn't make it right for him any more than I could make it right for me, and had no idea how it would turn out for either of us.

Internship

FOR MY INTERNSHIP, I decided to work at the Edgehill Methodist Church.

The minister, Jim Warren, a leader in the civil rights movement, championed the revival of a once-thriving black community that had been cut in two by Interstate 24, severing the heart of the community. Stores, restaurants, and homes were bulldozed to create a barrier, dividing the southern side near the river from the northern side near Vanderbilt.

Reverend Warren was a short, stocky man with the build of a middle linebacker. He explained that, for years, the only place Blacks were permitted to move to was by the river, susceptible to spring floods. "That's how it works for Blacks. They get together, and the white establishment divides them, strips them of their homes and community. It's all very intentional and racist."

He showed me around the church, which, compared to other Methodist churches I'd seen, was small. Three tiny classrooms, a large kitchen, a meeting room in the basement, and a small sanctuary with a simple wooden cross at the front. No fancy windows. Only pennants children had made of cloth, with Love, Justice, and Forgiveness written in bold colors on them.

My job was to drive their bus, take kids to parks and on hikes out of the city, and supervise the youth group. I hated Sunday services, having never attended one since high school, but Jim insisted that I come every Sunday.

In my blue double-breasted jacket and red tie, I sat in the front row at the first service. An attractive woman sat next to me and introduced herself as Julie, and pointed to the pulpit. "I'm his wife," pointing to the minister.

Her two children, a boy with an impish smile and a girl with pigtails, giggled as I shook their hands. During the service, which ran relatively smoothly, Julie occasionally let out long sighs when her husband explained about the next march in Memphis, one in solidarity with Reverend James Lawson. After the service, I asked her what bothered her. She confided in me that Jim spent more time on the streets than at home. His kids barely knew him.

She asked about me.

I told her I was a poet.

Her ears perked up. "That's nice. I'd love to see your work," she said.

"What do you do?" I asked.

"I'm an artist, too," she smiled. "Mostly pen and pencil drawings."

I told her that I'd love to see her work as well.

We agreed to meet next week at my dorm room. In the morning, when her children would be at school or daycare.

❧

There was a tentative knock on my dorm room door. I opened the door to her radiant smile, greeting me. She carried a bag of goodies.

Once inside, she surveyed the space, asked if she could set out some food, and cleared part of my desk, placing a loaf of French bread, a chunk of cheese, and a bottle of wine with two wine glasses, each wrapped in a napkin. She sliced the bread and put it on a plate. She used a short knife to cut the cheese, which smelled like Boursin.

"Here," she said, and held a piece of bread with cheese. "Good, isn't it?" she said, nodding her head. She poured the wine.

"I don't normally do this," she explained. "Most days I'm busy with the kids, getting everyone off to work, doing laundry, and, you know, groceries, cleaning up. It seems I never have time to draw or do the things I want to do. I hope you don't mind, but when I met you, I felt an immediate connection like a kindred spirit, another artist."

"Hey, this is great. I'm glad you feel so comfortable."

She leaned over and kissed me on the cheek. "You're sweet, really. Quite sweet."

She told me how she met Jim. Involved in the Nashville sit-in movement, she had sat with Black people at department store lunch counters alongside other Nashville seminarians, including Jim. They both spent a night in jail and then started to date. Married. Before long, the son and daughter. He had the movement, day and night, meeting with local officials, coordinating with the Southern Christian Leadership Conference,

Dr. King's organization, and planning rallies. Wonderful work. Important work. She knew it and she believed in it. But they'd drifted apart.

She asked to read my poems. I gave her several. She read them, looking up at me as she did. After several glasses of wine, she asked if I ever thought of modeling.

"What do you mean?" I asked.

"Well, you have amazing shoulders—I can see their definition through your shirt—and I would love to draw you, if you're willing to sit."

"I'm not sure if I can sit still that long."

"I can draw very quickly. Here, take off your shirt and let me have a sheet of paper and a pencil. There. Now, time me," she said, sitting back on the bed as I stripped off my shirt.

Embarrassed, I'd never had anyone look so intensely at me. Her eyes took in every muscle, seemed to slide up my chest, over my neck, back and forth, following the contours. Not a word spoken.

I looked at her. With soft, light brown hair and a peaceful countenance, she radiated warmth. Her voice, mellifluous and deep for a woman, conveyed a quiet confidence. She finished and handed me the gift: my head, partial and in profile, my neck, and then the shoulders, each striation of muscle and curve of flesh on bone.

As she left, she thanked me and asked if she could kiss me. I put my hands on her hips and kissed. I felt guilty about two-timing Ann and getting involved with a married woman, but she intrigued me with her take-charge attitude and a devil-may-care wildness.

We met often, sometimes in the mornings, sometimes in the afternoons, all depending on her schedule. Several times we came close to making love, but were restrained—or I was—because I was working with her husband.

One afternoon, when we'd drunk half a bottle of Merlot, as my hips pressed against hers, I pulled back slightly, and she grimaced. She knew I was aroused, but I'd withdrawn, limiting what we did to kissing until our tongues grew tired.

She leaned back, put her arms around my neck, and asked, "Are you gay?"

I paused. "Why do you ask?"

"I've been coming here for months and, today, as several other days, I knew you were aroused and yet you did nothing."

My face flushed. "It's just awkward, you know, being with you and working with Jim."

She looked at me and held my hands, rubbing them to ease my distress.

"It's okay. I didn't mean anything by it," she said. "Relax. I'll be going," she said, picked up her purse, and left.

ஃ

Julie became fascinated with the long-haired students who hung around my room and asked me if I smoked pot.

"Of course," I said.

"What's it like?" she asked.

I explained that time seemed to slow down, and you had a heightened sensuality.

She wanted to try it and arranged for me to come over to her house when Jim was off to Memphis with Reverend Lawson.

Her children put to bed, she called to say the coast was clear and welcomed me with a gentle hug, but one less uninhibited than the ones in my room. She scooted me through the door and glanced out to make sure that no one saw me.

I offered her a bottle of wine.

She promptly handed me a corkscrew.

"Voila!" I said and poured her a glass.

Although neither of us admitted it, we knew that I was playing the role of the young Casanova, and she was the seductress. Dressed in a loose blouse with no bra (I could see her nipples under the overhead light), she meant business.

The sweet-sour taste of wine, the perfume of marijuana joints in my shirt pocket, we moved to her living room. The room had a photograph of King—the March on Washington—and another painting with vivid reds, oranges, and blues. It depicted African women dressed in long, one-piece dresses carrying large water jugs on their heads. They were her work.

Tension mounted with every gesture: every touch, every word spoken. I pulled out two joints and put them on the coffee table. We sipped wine and chatted. Her hand caressed my thigh. I stroked the back of her neck.

"Shall we?" she asked, glancing at the joints. She got up and opened a window, turned on the fan.

"Just in case," she said.

I lit the joint, showed her how to hold it pinched between her fingers, and to inhale it, and to keep the smoke in her lungs as long as she could. The effect was instantaneous. She asked me to take off my shirt. Her hand traced an S pattern on my chest and stomach.

"You're quite beautiful," she said. Her fingers, cool from the glass of wine, made my chest twitch from her feathery touch.

"It tickles," I said.

She pinched my nipples and traced her tongue around each of them. Her fingers tiptoed down my abdomen and tugged on my belt, unhooking my belt buckle. My cock strained against the fabric of my shorts.

"My, my," she said, smiling. "You're a normal boy after all."

I groaned, pleased with myself. "Here," I said, "take another hit," and passed her the joint. Thin strands of smoke swirled around her head and wove through her hair.

"What do you think?" I asked.

"Nice." She kept her one hand on me, gently stroking me. I scooted down on the couch. She loosened her blouse. My hand traced across her breasts, mimicking what she'd done to me. She took a deep breath and shook her head.

"You all right?" I asked.

Her mouth open, her eyes glazed, she appeared terrified. Both her hands flung to her mouth. She raced from the room.

I quickly pulled on my shirt. Had she seen the children?

I hurried after her.

The bathroom door was ajar. On her knees, vomiting, her whole body retched violently.

I asked, "Can I help?"

She shook her head. The sight of her heaving, her shoulders jerking, her belly torqued, frightened me.

"Should I call a doctor?" I asked.

She waved a hand at me as if brushing away a fly.

"Should I go?" I asked.

She paused, turned, her face wan, angry. "Yeah. Go. Now!"

I didn't stop to pick up the last joint or the bottle. I don't know why. I felt sick, too. I left one of my poems—one I'd written for her, a short one about the eyes of a painter being her fingers—and placed it on the coffee table.

⁂

The next day, she didn't call or come by my room. I attended classes, then drove to Edgehill Methodist to meet three teenage girls and two boys to plan a spring break picnic for the younger children.

Jim saw me when I came out of the group and asked how it went. We talked about the park with the lake and how I'd need to drive the old school bus—mostly practical things.

"You're doing good work," he said. He patted me on the shoulder.

I was about to thank him when his face hardened, his jaw tensed. "Julie's okay. She had a bad time of it."

My mouth must have dropped open because he grinned at the sight of me. "Hey, kid, no blame here. She gave me the scoop."

"I'm—"

"I know. I know." I had shoved my hands in my pockets. My face felt as if it were roasting.

"Relax." He took me by the arm and walked outside to the side yard. "Someday you'll have a marriage, kids, and all. Believe me, it's not Father Knows Best. There are rough spots. But you get through them."

All I could focus on in my mind was her blouse, unbuttoned. I bleated, "I'm sorry."

"No need for sorry. Just know she's okay. She wanted you to know that," he said. "And, kid, I'm okay too. Some things can't be helped."

When I got back to the dorm, I pulled out the drawing she'd done of me. For her, drawing was lovemaking: hands penciled the line across the page, also caressing my face, chest, and belly. She saw and gave herself over to it. The drawing, pinned to my bookshelf, reminded me of the face and eyes of a young man who didn't believe in himself, but who someone had seen as real. It was through her eyes that I had come in a small way to see myself.

⁂

One afternoon, a month later, she called and told me she'd gone away, the whole family had—Jim and the kids—spent time at the ocean, walked the New Jersey beaches, and built sandcastles. She drew and read. She saw Jim as the man he once was—vital and passionate—and realized how much she was like him in so many ways, and how much she missed him. But now he had returned. They were happy. A lovely reincarnation of what had drawn them to one another. She couldn't see me again. She knew that now. She hoped I'd understand.

"You'll find another woman," she said.

"Not like you," I said.

"I thank you for that," she said.

Divided

WITH JULIE GONE AND Ann busy with school, I met another woman, Cheryl, who advertised on the Divinity School bulletin board as a typist. As a receptionist for the Upper Room, a religious group that offered training and workshops, she typed my papers for the Kierkegaard and Sociology of Change seminars. She was fascinated by my thinking and that I wanted, more than anything, to be a poet. I'd written a poem about Dietrich Bonhoeffer waiting in his cell to be hanged. She liked it.

We exchanged books. I gave her Eliot's *Collected Poems*, and she gave me D.H. Lawrence's *Selected Poems*. That led to her invitation for dinner. Braised chicken with mustard and wine sauce, beans with buttered almonds, and twice-baked potatoes with cheddar cheese. And merlots and pinot grigios.

We read from T.S. Eliot's "Four Quartets" out loud because for me it had become almost a field guide to understanding the contraries inside of me, how I had to be still and still moving, how time present and time past were one, and how the journey never ending—and his words—kept resonating in my mind, challenging me to reconfigure my view of the world and myself. She asked me what one passage meant:

> In that open field
> If you do not come too close, if you do not come too close
> On the Summer midnight, you can hear the music

To me, it reflected the need to keep my distance, to be an observer, to be free from obligations. To her, it meant letting what you loved be as it is, to be one with the music.

We argued about Eliot's "still point of the turning world." Why did he say, "neither flesh nor fleshless, neither from nor towards"? To me, it meant that we could separate ourselves from our experience and merely observe it. To her, it had to do with the dance, how two bodies could become one.

She grabbed me and we danced across the room, her body pressed to mine.

I remembered what had happened with Julie, and there was my commitment to Ann to consider. I couldn't take another affair. I stopped. But we talked well into the night about one of D.H. Lawrence's poems, "The Snake." She wanted to know why Lawrence had thrown a log at the snake, trying to kill it. I told her to look at the preceding stanza that went.

> And as he put his head into that dreadful hole,
> And as he slowly drew up, snake-easing his shoulders,
> and entered farther,
> A sort of horror, a sort of protest against his withdrawing into
> that horrid black hole,
> Deliberately going into the blackness, and slowly drawing
> himself after,
> Overcame me now his back was turned.

"Look at the terror in these lines," I said. "He sees it as almost demonic. He's afraid of the dark place inside himself, the horror of withdrawal into the unknown."

She felt that the dark was sexy and that he was afraid of sex. We couldn't agree, but enjoyed the debate knowing that a poem, by its nature, could mean whatever we found in it and that, in the end, she was probably as right as I was.

❧

Cheryl knew how to invite the erotic into our relationship whenever I came over. She showed me how to tear open pomegranates, peel their skins and pick the dark purple fruit, our hands stained with sweetness as she sucked the juice off my hand, and I off hers. My fingers in her mouth aroused me. She could tell and, seeing an opening, leaned in to kiss me. I pushed her away.

Here I was again, caught between wanting—as I had with Tom and as I had with Julie—and feeling out of control. How could I balance my allure with my commitments, my urges with my need to set limits? My yearning to be close with my fear of being too close and being taken over by Cheryl's needs?

As we parted that night, she asked for a kiss. I shrugged, compromised, and complied. But she stuck her tongue in my mouth.

I pulled away. "Please, give me some time," I said.

She bowed her head. "So sorry. I'll be good."

A short time later, with Ann consumed with her work, studying night and day, and only available for a quick lunch, with my feeling lonely, only talking to Erling once a week as we schemed how to get more students and money to run the Folk School, I found myself willing to be with Cheryl as long as she kept her distance.

Food was her aphrodisiac. Salmon with balsamic vinaigrette, tomatoes with pesto, and a fruit salad, followed by a pecan pie. Italian wines. Blissfully intoxicated. Conversations about James Agee. Her next to me. More wine.

She asked, "Stay the night?"

"Friends, that's all I want," I said.

She pouted, "Why must it stop at that?"

"Look, I love our talks. But I need distance. Independence, space to write and think." I told her that there was another woman in my life, and I had told her the same thing. I poured more wine for myself.

She clinked the glass. "Hey, I love that you're an intellect, that you love to read. But what does that have to do with us?"

"It's simple. If I'm involved with someone, I give myself to them as much as I do to my work. I invest all the emotional energy I have. If we get involved, I'm going to give myself to you entirely, and I don't want to do that."

"I would," she said.

I pinched her cheek. "I know you would."

"Well?"

"I'm serious. I don't want to be dependent on you or have to worry about you. I want to be my own self," I said, pushing her back. "That's not an easy thing to be. I put up fences. But they have gates. As long as you and I know where they are, we can be as close as we choose to be."

She pulled her knees up under her and straightened up on the couch. She took a folder from the coffee table. and pulled out a sheet of paper.

"Let me read this to you. It's from Rilke's Letters to a Young Poet. You recommended it:

And if we only arrange our life according to that principle which counsels us that we must always hold to the difficult…then that which now seems to us most alien will become what we most trust and find most faithful…

She finished reading, sipped her wine, and asked, "Maybe we might find that we trust each other: you trust me, I trust you?"

"Yes, but what he's talking about is those aspects of ourselves, our inner voices, that we must trust. He wasn't talking about relationships."

"But what if he was? What if you're wrong?"

I picked up the bottle of wine.

She had a point. He might have been talking about both.

"You may be right. But for me, at least now, the freedom not to worry about others and to explore what is in me is the ultimate freedom. I need boundaries. Can't I have them?"

She flung her arm around my neck and kissed me on the cheek. "I've never met a man so certain about relationships."

"I have to be."

"How so?"

She was making me think about myself. I liked that, but I was intimidated, too, unsure if I could explain what I only partially understood. "If I don't, I'll get lost and, if I get lost in what I want to do as a writer, given the demands of time on me already—working on a degree, getting the Folk School started up for another year, doing my internship—I'll forsake my writing."

"Your major concern is your writing."

"Yeah. Why shouldn't it be?"

She poured herself another glass of wine and stood up. She wandered around the room, her hair draping over her face, only one eye peeking out. She stopped across from me, swaying slightly, her face squinted in pain.

"What the hell can you give me?"

I set my wine glass down and stared at her; an inexplicable rage burned in my chest.

She continued to sway, slightly out of focus.

I said, "When you stop asking that question, then you'll have something," and walked to the door. She flung herself on me, turned me around, and kissed me hard on the mouth.

I recoiled, pressed my hands on her arms, and pushed her away. "Let's call it an evening."

As I walked back to the dorm, I noticed that the clock on the bell tower read 2 AM. A few cars drove down the street. The streetlamps were like stage lights, one after another, illuminating me and my long shadow after me. I felt as if somehow, I had lost part of myself, a part I could only half articulate.

Weeks later, Cheryl gave me a long letter, filled with quotes from her favorite poets, and some from mine, while speaking throughout the document about how, when she first met me, she sensed a mystery and danger; that I was like a wild animal, untamed and beautiful, free and powerful.

I wasn't sure I was all that dangerous. Something in me wanted to be tamed. But I wrote her back that I feared she'd possess me, and I would lose the freedom to live alone, to be as solitary as I wanted to be.

If I wanted to make love with her, I could have. It would have been nice, as it was with Ann and Julie, to have a woman who wanted to give herself to me. But I couldn't shake what I was feeling. Mostly alone, afraid, and misunderstood.

In some ways, I wanted intimacy from them. I could feel it because their adulation of me made me feel more like a man, more certain of my masculinity. I liked how they touched me, how their hands lingered on my shoulder, face, or waist. Reassured—that was it, how that was what it was to be a man: to have women want you and need you. Or at least that's how I'd come to see it.

But maybe it was like that saying of Jesus about the city on the hill. Perhaps I was only seeing part of the city of love—the part I'd been raised in, the part others, especially my father, had told me I needed to live in, to find a woman, to settle down, like my brother had, with a wife and child. And yet there were other parts of the city, hidden ones that Will and Tom showed me, parts that I was afraid to enter. Parts like those sections of Nashville where I was warned not to go. Parts I might someday need to enter not because I wanted to, but because something inside of me demanded I should go. Something was holding me back, something pulling me away from them, and, as yet, I wasn't too sure I could face what it was.

Relief

AS AN ESCAPE FROM WOMEN, on weekends, I would drive to Rose's Creek and stay with Peggy and her kids. Once I reached the other side of the state, the mountain roads rewound against themselves, reflecting how I felt inside: drawn in one direction, seeming fated to arrive at a specific place, and then twisted backward, heading off in another direction.

They welcomed me like a member of the family. After dinner, we gathered around a cook stove and sipped coffee. Peggy told a story of how she nearly drowned—her lungs full of fluids—from pneumonia. Tommy drove her forty miles to the emergency room. Bobby told a story of how he cracked his skull diving into the creek, and his ma had to sew him up with her needle and thread.

The bedtime routine was the same every night. If someone started to undress, others averted their eyes until they were in a nightgown or pajamas. In Bobby's room, two beds accommodated anyone who slept there: Tommy the one on the left, Bobby and I on the one on the right. It seemed strange to sleep with Bobby. But he loved it. He tickled me once I got into bed. Once he quieted down, he snuggled next to me and fell asleep, his arm across my chest.

The moonlight cast a milky glow on Bobby. With his hair over his forehead and his eyelids closed, he never budged. It felt nice to be where affection between men came as naturally as affection between a man and a woman.

In the morning, we'd work in the garden, nudge the potatoes from the ground, pull up six-inch carrots, and tote pumpkins to the back porch. We'd feed the chickens and toss leftovers to the pig. The labor dictated the pace. If I wanted to sit on the porch and write, that would be fine. No one bothered me. If Bobby wanted to toss the football, I'd jump off the porch, and we'd throw it back and forth. By the time I got back to Nashville, I felt as though Peggy and her kids had stitched whatever loose ends I had back together.

Baxter

WHEN I RETURNED TO Nashville, the university students were outraged that the Pancake House refused to serve "long-haired, hippie-type" students. Since the restaurant was located across the street from the campus, many students would go there for meals.

The long-haired student who was refused service tried to reason with the owner, who became enraged, called the student "un-American," and threatened to call the police.

Reverend Baxter Bryant, the longtime leader of the civil rights protests in Nashville, called a meeting at a small coffee house for anyone interested in protesting. My hair was long, so I went.

Dressed in bib overalls, Baxter strutted back and forth, anxious to see if enough people would show up for a protest. He had an infectious laugh that made anyone near him smile.

Fifty students packed the house. He called for a peaceful demonstration. If it were done well and lasted long enough, he argued, it would dissuade the regular customers from going to the restaurant.

The next day, a Sunday, we picketed, carrying signs that said, "End Discrimination Now," "Jesus Had Long Hair," and "Pancakes for Everyone." For a week, we demonstrated in shifts with pickets marching in a circle around the front of the restaurant.

Instead of this discouraging business, customers lined up and waited for a seat. The customers, well-dressed and enjoying the spectacle of slovenly long-hairs, came to see it as a circus.

One day after church, I carried a sign with the other long-haired individuals, worried that my father, if I were arrested, would be outraged and cut off my tuition payments. However, I resolved that at some point in my life, I had to take a stand.

Baxter chided the customers who waited in line, read selections from the Bible that addressed civil rights, and led us in songs. Well-dressed for this protest, with his black jacket, heavy leather boots, and holiday red scarf, he was a spectacle. He had a long white beard that framed his wrinkled, ruddy face. His large shoulders and enormous chest made him an imposing figure. He was no fool. He knew how to chafe and irritate the clientele by craning his head back and blaring questions at them as they tried to avert his eyes and scurry into the restaurant. He preached without hesitation, but also engaged people, smiled at them, and greeted them as if he worked for the restaurant. He he was on stage, doing what he did best, standing like God's advocate, castigating the smug and affluent.

In early December, in the spirit of the holiday, children dressed in red and green, and the march had an air of improvisational theater. Baxter happened to catch the attention of a young couple with a cute young boy. They sat at the table at the front window. The little boy waved at the bearded man. Baxter waved back. Since the boy and Baxter were center stage—one on each side of the window—all the protesters outside and the clientele inside watched them.

The mother and father refused to look at Baxter. They had a brief conversation, the father pointing his fork at the mother and then at the boy. The mother cut off a tiny piece of her omelet and ate it. The father tapped the boy's plate and told him to eat his pancakes.

The father, his hair parted in a perfectly straight line, wore black-framed glasses and a gray three-piece suit with a red tie. He shooed Baxter off with his hand. Baxter stayed put and offered a peace sign to the boy, who imitated him by putting up two fingers in a V. The protesters cheered.

The boy smiled back, enamored by the attention. The boy's father, his lips set in a straight line, eyed Baxter and jabbed his finger at him.

Baxter smiled. The dad gave Baxter the finger. The protesters booed.

All this time, the boy focused on the man with a white beard who kept smiling at him. His mother cupped her hand around the boy's back and pointed at his plate. The father stabbed one of the pancakes and shoved it at the boy, who winced and turned his head. The mother patted the boy's hand.

Baxter stepped back, put his hands on his hips, and gave a hearty laugh. The boy smiled. Baxter tapped the window, saying as loudly as he could, as he gave the boy a peace sign, "Let's exchange signs. You do this. Yes. There you have it. And I'll do this. Good." The boy made a V again with his fingers.

All the customers in the restaurant, as well as all the protesters, watched as Baxter gave the whole restaurant the peace sign.

The father glowered at Baxter and gobbled two quick bites of his pancakes. The tiny boy, not much older than four, looked once more at Baxter. His expression brightened. His father leaned forward to converse with his wife. The boy looked at Baxter and talked to him. Everyone could hear him. "You're Santa Claus!"

Baxter cocked his head back and laughed. He put his hands on his belly and cried, "Ho. Ho. Ho, I sure am!"

His father turned as red as the scarf around Baxter's neck. He shook his fist at Baxter and cursed, grabbed his son's head, and forced him to focus on his pancakes. The boy broke down in tears. The mother wrapped her arms around the boy. Baxter crouched by the window, looking sad, as if to show the boy he sympathized with him. The father called the waitress over to the table. The mother took her son in her arms, but he waved at Baxter as the family made their way to the back, while the protesters cheered and waved after them.

After the protest, several of us went with Baxter for coffee. He'd lived a remarkable life. When John Kennedy flew into Dallas, Baxter greeted him. Kennedy asked him if he should ride in a covered or an open vehicle. Baxter told him that the people of Dallas loved him. "Ride in the open vehicle."

"There is not a day I do not regret my advice," he said. "Think of what would be different now. No Nixon. Bobby would be alive." He brushed something off his jacket. "There's no way you can get out of this life without getting dirt on you."

Someone asked him about his work with Dr. King.

"I'll tell you something you've never heard before," Baxter said. "You remember the sanitation strike in Memphis?"

Some of us had, some hadn't. He gave us some background. The FBI organized disturbances to provoke public outrage against the protest. It was unsettling for King. He was supposed to speak to rally the workers, but he'd been ill, so he sent Ralph Abernathy instead.

The crowd clamored for Dr. King. Abernathy called to tell King he had to come.

The crowd roared their approval when King arrived. But he hadn't prepared remarks and, unlike himself, at first rambled about Abernathy, about history, about Egypt and the Promised Land, struggling to find his way, leaping from topic to topic—Aristotle, Martin Luther, Abe Lincoln, and even Franklin Delano Roosevelt.

That's when his tone changed. Became darker. He spoke of Jerusalem and of the road Jesus walked. But he paused, changed topic again, as the topic became more personal, about his being stabbed in New York, the tip of the blade near his heart. If he had sneezed, he would have died. He spoke about all the major civil rights events he'd have missed.

Someone whispered that King was being rather morbid. Baxter agreed. It wasn't like him. He didn't talk in public about threats to his life.

King paused again. His voice became more impassioned. Something had struck him, and his voice rose as he spoke about the threats to his life:

And then I got to Memphis. And some began to say the threats or talk about the threats that were out there. What would happen to me at the hands of our sick white brothers?

He shook his head as if trying to shake something out of it, spoke of mortality, wanting to live a long life, then abruptly ended with those famous lines:

I just want to do God's will. And He's allowed me to go up to the mountain…I've looked over. And I've seen the Promised Land. I may not get there with you…I'm not fearing any man. Mine eyes have seen the glory of the coming of the Lord.

"What happened next," Baxter said, "was eerie. When he spoke the last words, he turned hastily, almost as if he'd lost his balance. At first, we didn't rise to greet him. We thought he was at a fever pitch and was going to go on and speak more about the strike. He lunged at us, not waiting for applause. We knew something must be seriously wrong for him to cut off a speech. His eyes looked strange, filled with fear, as he made his way to his seat.

"Abernathy stood and hugged him. We took his arms and led him to his chair. He confided that he had seen his death. He looked ashen in color.

"We tried to lift his spirits and say, 'It's all right. We'd heard that before.' But he said, 'No, this was for real.'

"Later, he asked to be left alone. He needed time. By the next day, he had recovered from the shock. Lively and engaged, a burden seemed lifted from him; he was his ebullient self.

"That was the day he was shot."

Baxter sighed and said, "I often wonder if I…if we'd been more vigilant, if we'd kept him off that balcony, whether he might be with us today."

As Baxter spoke, I recalled reading that Lincoln also had a premonition of death, and I wondered whether Bobby Kennedy had had one. The hatred in the eyes of the father at the Pancake House came to mind. Such hatred fueled violence. But there was also the boy waving at us, as if he knew something was wrong and he wanted to make it right.

Cut Short

"I'M LATE," ANN SAID. "Two weeks."

She sat on my dorm room bed; her legs folded beneath her. I sat in the desk chair across from her, holding her hands. Early that day, she called and asked me to talk. With all the weeks we'd been apart, except for several nights after Tom in my room, and with her upcoming graduation, I thought she wanted to break off our relationship. But not this, not being pregnant.

"Have you seen a doctor?" I asked.

"No. I was hoping—"

"Sure."

"What'll we do?" she asked. She looked at me intently.

"Punt," I said.

"What?"

"It's a joke. You know, in football, if you don't know what play to call, you punt."

"Not funny. This is serious, Jason." She jerked her hands back. "We need to decide what to do."

"Sure."

"Well?"

"I don't know," I said. "I mean, can't we wait a little longer?"

When the door slammed, I wanted to get up, go out, embrace her, and tell her that I would stand by her no matter what. But my feet stuck to the floor. I sat in my chair and gazed out the window at the yellowish-green leaves.

I called her later, but she didn't answer. I went over to her apartment; her roommate told me she wasn't in. I remembered Travis, who sat in my lap and talked about everything costing a penny. Having a kid in my arms didn't seem too bad. I'd have to find a job, risk getting drafted, and settle down. I hated the idea. But it couldn't be helped. I wanted to tell her I'd changed my mind and knew it was serious. She didn't call. One week, two. No word from her. Maybe she was going it alone. It was most likely my child. As far as I knew, she'd been exclusively mine. I had to start acting and looking like an adult. I went to a local barbershop and asked the barber for a haircut. "Long or short," he asked.

"Short," I told him.

He cut it short. My ears stood out like a new army recruit. When I got back to the dorm, the kids asked, "What happened to you?"

I wondered the same. Ann would be surprised. But she wasn't at her apartment.

I attended a party that a mutual friend had invited us to weeks prior.

When I arrived, Ann was with another student, a young man I'd seen at antiwar protests. With long, wavy hair, he was strikingly handsome. I walked over to her.

She glanced at me and said, "Oh, hi," before continuing to talk with the man.

I grabbed her arm. "Can we talk?"

She pulled my hand off her. "Later. Can't you see we're involved here?"

After three bottles of beer and a shot of whiskey, I was more drunk than I'd been in months. I bumped into the table with the refreshments, lost my balance, and put my hand in a bowl of onion dip, licking it off my fingers.

Ann avoided me most of the night. She must have seen me staggering around. I was singing to myself, "We shall overcome…" and dancing in a circle, holding onto a bottle of beer as if it could keep me upright.

Someone stuck an arm under my arm and pulled me to the side of the room. "You're making an ass of yourself," Ann said.

"You bet I am."

"And the haircut, it looks awful. You look like a frat boy."

"You don't like it?"

"Are you kidding?" she said. "Lower your voice, please."

"It's my responsible father look," I said.

"I said, lower your voice!" She jerked me toward the front door. We went out and stood on the stoop. A cool breeze wafted across my face.

"Listen," she said. "You don't have to do the dutiful father routine with me."

"But—"

"You already made it clear where you stand."

"Sorry, I—"

She smiled. "Besides, I'm back on my cycle."

"You're what?"

"Not pregnant," she said. "Now, go back to your room and sober up." She kissed me on the cheek. I leaned over to hug her, but she stuck her arm out. "Whoa, horsey. Not so fast."

I lost my balance and fell into a hedge. She laughed so hard she bent over and put her hand on her stomach.

"Perfect," she said. "That's perfect."

I struggled out of it, straightened up, and walked away. The traffic on the streets quietened, and only a few cars passed by. I felt a strange exhilaration, yet I felt like a fool. She had made me see how petty and insensitive I could be. Why she had not called me earlier, or when she had known, seemed immaterial.

Free. I could do what I wanted when I wanted. No kid. No marriage. I rubbed the stubble on my head. In a few weeks, I'd be myself again. Maybe even date her again.

Nixon

DICK AND PAM ASKED me over to watch the Kentucky Derby.

Dick made a mean mint julep. He explained how to make them. The night before the race, he got out three chilled silver cups and placed them on the counter.

"Must make them the night before so the ingredients make love with each other in the cool quiet of the night," he said. Then he added two cups of sugar to a pitcher, stirred in two cups of water, and crushed ice.

"Now the important ingredient," he said, pouring what seemed to be an entire bottle of bourbon into the mix. He stirred it with a spoon. "Can't forget this," he said, adding sprigs of fresh mint. He put crushed ice in a glass and poured the mixture over it—the rest of the mix he set in the refrigerator.

"This is to die for," he said. He passed the glass to Pam, who took a sip.

"Wonderful, honey," she said. "Decadent southerners. That's why I married him."

We passed it around, each letting the sweet-bitter taste wash over our tongue. Dinner consisted of chicken with a Dijon mustard sauce, served with carrots in a honey-ginger sauce. With these two, I saw how a marriage could work, how he, even with his misgivings about his sexuality, seemed quite happy.

Even though he was against the war, Dick was excited because Richard Nixon was to be the first president to attend the Derby.

"It's nice that he's coming. Our Derby is a national institution. But I'm afraid if he thinks we southerners are going to welcome him with open arms, he's in for a surprise," Dick said. "Protesters will greet him. He'll not have an easy time of it."

The next day, Dick's predictions proved correct. Nixon had to be escorted in a decoy car to and from the race. Once he had gotten onto the track grounds, some patrons cheered him. He waved and made the best of their support. But the antiwar movement had reached a fever pitch. He couldn't go anywhere without someone shouting at him to end the war.

After the scare with Ann, I worked on an exegesis of the saying from Christ's Sermon on the Mount in Matthew:

You are the light of the world. A city set on a mountain cannot be hidden. Nor they light a lamp and then put it under a bushel basket; it is set on a lampstand, where it gives light to all in the house. Just so, your light must shine before others, that they may see your good deeds and glorify your heavenly Father.

I'd been thinking about it since that last night with Cheryl and had come to see it in a different light. The saying seemed ironic, almost a play on words. Of course, a city cannot be hidden on the hill.

Why would that be important to Him?

What could it possibly mean to his followers?

Perhaps if someone didn't want to hear what He had to say because it disturbed their worldview, their established way of thinking, they could deny it and hide it from themselves. He could go on believing what he'd always been told and, using a modern analogy, could go on acting as if the penthouse he lived in, the swank restaurants he frequented, and the wealthy friends he hobnobbed with were all there was of the city. If he wanted to see what was really happening around him, he had to let the lamp shine on the whole city, places he may not even want to look, places on the Southside where people were living in poverty, as many Black people were in Chicago.

My ruminations jived with what was happening on campuses. Ever since Nixon ramped up the war, campuses rebelled at a higher pitch. What he said to justify the escalation didn't help.

President Nixon appeared on all three U.S. television networks to announce that "It is not our power but our will and character that is being tested tonight," and "the time has come for action."

He launched American forces into Cambodia. Their objective was to capture "the headquarters of the entire communist military operation in South Vietnam." Behind Nixon's high-minded rhetoric was a ruse to escalate the war more than he already had. Students saw it for what it was. Protests broke out. Kent State students ignored Ohio Governor Rhodes' threats to bring in the National Guard. His statements only incited them. Pounding on a desk, he sounded like a petty tyrant, calling protesters un-American revolutionaries set on destroying higher education in Ohio. He said,

We've seen here at the city of Kent, especially, probably the most vicious form of campus-oriented violence yet perpetrated by dissident groups...who were worse than the brown shirts and the communist element and also the night riders and the vigilantes...the worst type of people that we harbor in America...They are not going to take over the campus. I think that we're up against the strongest, well-trained, militant, revolutionary group that has ever assembled in America.

To him, the students were worse than Nazis or revolutionaries and didn't warrant respect. He didn't care about their reasons for protest. He couldn't acknowledge that students were saying the opposite thing: The United States was acting as Nazi Germany did in Poland, with our incursion in a sovereign nation that was, according to international law, illegal.

Rhodes and Nixon wanted students to remain silent, as they didn't want their foreign policy shaped by protesters on the streets of Washington or on campus. Instead, they wanted students to unite behind them "for peace," while they waged war. When he claimed student activists were "Bums...blowing up our campuses," we felt insulted, unheard.

❧

At Vanderbilt, students threatened, as they had at Kent State, to burn down the ROTC building. Not a bad idea, I thought, although the building was adjacent to the Divinity School and right across from the Law School.

At the time, I was enrolled in a class on contemporary poetry. I sat next to Jackson, an undergraduate, poet, and antiwar activist who was interested in the Divinity School—what I studied, who I knew, if I'd met James Lawson, because he was thinking of going into the ministry.

His rusty brown hair fell over his shoulders. He wore Army fatigues and a bandana across his forehead. During class, he scooted his chair next to mine, nudged me, and whispered commentary about Yeats's "Leda and the Swan." "Have you ever had sex with a swan? It's great." He rubbed his fingertips like feathers across my thigh.

I chuckled and whispered back, "Not yet."

"It's fun!"

I remembered how Tom had lured me into having sex with him, but I felt relaxed with Jackson's playful touch.

After class, he asked me to have coffee so he could fill me in on the protests that had occurred that day. He was worried about the students in Ohio. The governor had declared martial law and brought out the National Guard. "He's a major nut case," Jackson said. "Not to worry. It's all talk and no action. We have big plans for today. You should come. Allen Ginsberg is going to speak at an anti-war rally. You want to come?"

ᘐᘏ

A phalanx of students surrounded Ginsberg as he, arm in arm with his lover Peter Orlovsky, walked across campus. Wearing loose, multi-colored pants, sandals, and a white shirt, Ginsberg, once on stage, chanted a long anti-war poem. He played his sitar and danced, his arms waving back and forth over his head.

The crowd let out a loud "OM." Jackson slung his arm over my shoulder, put his cheek next to mine, strutting and prancing to the sound, grabbing a Peace sign and pumping it up and down.

After the protest, Jackson told me to come over to his dorm room. He had a new poem that he wanted me to read. On the eighth floor of the new high-rise dorm, he asked me to sit on his bed while he rummaged through his papers. His room looked as if someone had detonated a bomb in it: papers, magazines, books, clothes on the chair, bed, and desk.

When he found the poem, he told me to lie down. He jumped on the bed beside me, lifted my legs, scooted underneath them, and then let them down over his legs. He leaned over to read his poem. He had lovely hazel eyes.

His poem was about a man lost in a dark wood. I listened intently as he rubbed his hand on my chest to keep rhythm to the poem's oracular beat.

"What do you think?" he asked

"I like it. Love the image of the creek. 'It shimmers under the dark ash.' Perfect image," I said.

"You have a nice body." He rubbed my belly.

I put my hand on top of his. I'd become aroused and didn't want to let on. "You do too." I rubbed his fingers.

He scooted close and ran his fingers through my hair. He placed one finger on my lips. "I've wanted to do this since you first came into the class. Did you know that?" he asked.

"No," I said. He reached behind my head and pulled me upright. His head was now resting on my crotch.

"You feel good." He rubbed his cheek on my erection.

"I don't think I should go there," I said.

He pressed himself up, his chest against mine, and put his lips on mine and kissed me. He swung his legs around, so he was sitting next to me, and said, "I get it. It's all right. Let's just cuddle, you know, hold onto each other, man to man."

He lit a joint and offered me a toke. I took it. He stretched out, his body against mine, his chest against mine, his leg nestled between mine, and brushed back my hair and kissed me lightly on the cheek, putting his head next to mine and looking into my eyes.

"We could be good friends, you know," he said.

"I think we already are," I said.

He leaned over and kissed me. "You may be right. You know if other men felt as we do about each other, there wouldn't be any wars. We'd be seeking how to connect and make love. And the only thing we'd worry about would be if the other guy was as attracted to us as we were to him."

I could feel that he, too, was aroused. He took my hand and let me rub his chest, face, and legs. He did the same to me. Eventually, he leaned up on an elbow, asked if he could kiss me harder, and I told him yes. He pressed his lips against mine, his teeth hard against mine, and slipped his tongue inside my mouth. I moaned. Then he stopped.

"Need to check on the protest for this afternoon," he said.

"We'll meet again?" I asked.

"Anytime," he said.

I told him I had to get to my Synoptic Gospel class, but I wanted to continue being with him.

❧

At two o'clock, after I left my second class, I heard shouting on the campus lawns. A large group of students carrying North Vietnamese flags marched toward the ROTC building.

Outside the ROTC building, an officer and twenty cadets stood in front of the entrance. They had set up a barrier. Arms crossed and legs spread wide, they looked imposing.

I asked one of the marchers what was going on.

Word had spread about Kent State. Students had marched toward the National Guard; shots were fired.

Dean Harrelson rushed down the hill from the Divinity School with James Lawson and several other students, including Penny, the student I'd met at orientation. He motioned for me to join them.

"Come on, Jason. There's going to be trouble," the dean cried.

As we raced down the hill, he explained that the Ohio National Guard had fired at antiwar protesters. From news reports, several students were killed.

The dean and Reverend Lawson arrived at the ROTC building before the protesters. They spoke to the officer in charge. He'd called Nashville and campus police. Sirens screamed, and four cruisers charged up the drive of the ROTC building—a one-story building with windows on each side. It looked more like a maintenance building than a military training facility. The police officers kept their sirens on. Eight of them strode up to the front entrance, armed with rifles. They spoke with the dean and the ROTC officer.

The protesters shouted, "Burn it down! Burn it down!"

I noticed Jackson standing in front of a group of protesters, a Peace Now sign in his hand. He led the chant to burn it down. He saw me standing with the dean and the police and narrowed his eyes.

The dean turned to us. "Do you know any of the activists?" he asked.

"Yes, one of them," I said.

He turned back to the officer and pointed toward the Divinity School. Sweat poured off his forehead. He took out a handkerchief and wiped his brow. The police officer approached me. "Do you know one of these…thugs?"

My fist was clenched.

The dean interrupted, "Officer, I told you he did."

"Okay. Here's the deal," the officer said. "We don't want trouble. Your dean here says he'll give up his office if you and some of the other ministers can calm this down. Think you can do it?"

Reverend Lawson put his arm on my shoulder. "Yes, officer, we'll do it. We have some other students who are on their way to help."

The officer stepped back. He conferred with the ROTC officer and then signaled the dean with a simple nod. The dean and Reverend Lawson asked me to introduce them to the protester. We walked up the embankment.

The crowd had expanded to several hundred students.

I called out to Jackson and motioned for him to come to one side by a large magnolia tree, where I introduced him to the dean and Reverend Lawson.

"THE Reverend Lawson?" he asked as he shook his head.

"The same," said the reverend.

Jackson looked at me. "You know him?"

"Yes."

The dean and Reverend Lawson explained to him that they'd like to see whether he and some of the organizers would be willing to meet with other students who are also against the war. The dean wanted to stem the violence and not escalate the encounter.

Jackson looked at me. "Will you be there?"

"Yes."

He asked if other authorities on campus, including the chancellor, could be involved.

"Yes," said the dean. "We can arrange for it. You will have access to my office, day or night. I assure you that you'll have access to the people you need."

"I'm not sure I can stop this," Jackson shouted. The chanting had increased, as had the number of protesters.

The police force had expanded to eight cars. Eighteen armed police officers stood in a line in front of the protesters.

"Look," Lawson said. "I've seen worse. Would you let me talk to them?"

Jackson nodded. Pressing my hand on his shoulder, I thanked him. He pulled back and shook his head, wary at best.

Reverend Lawson was perfectly composed. His whitened afro showed his age and his experience with violence. He went over to a police car and asked for a bullhorn. The lead officer went to his car and retrieved one.

Lawson strode up to the protesters with Jackson beside him. He draped his arm over Jackson's shoulder. Jackson gazed up at him, clearly stunned by the strange turn of events. Lawson told the crowd who he was and how he had stood with Dr. King against the war. He believed it was an unjust war. He despised the recent incursion into Cambodia. But he also believed in nonviolence. He told them that they should be mad. Students were shot, killed for doing what every American had a right to do: protest against a war that they believed was immoral. The students listened intently. He said that the dean (whom he introduced again) had graciously given up his office so that leaders of the antiwar efforts could meet and find a nonviolent way to resolve the issue. He encouraged them to protest peacefully.

He offered Jackson the bullhorn. Jackson put it to his mouth, but no sound came out. The officer showed him the switch to press. Jackson laughed and then told the crowd how angry he was, how other students, innocent students, had been shot down. He said that he wouldn't back down. There were cheers.

"Burn it down!" someone shouted again.

"No, no," he said. "I'm a longtime admirer of Reverend Lawson. I'm also grateful the dean has offered us his office. I, for one, would be willing to give it a try." He held up his sign: "Peace Now." "Will any of you join me?"

Several others raised their hands. With support for the negotiations, Lawson asked that the protest move away from the ROTC building—there was to be no vandalism—and he would gladly lead them to the Student Union building, where he'd let them speak.

Three students joined Jackson. The dean motioned for me to join them. He also asked three ROTC students to join us. Jackson glared at them. Ten of us headed to the Divinity School. While the protesters headed to the center of the campus, the officers, armed and in a line, stood their ground.

The four protesters, three ROTC students, and three divinity students headed to Dean Harrelson's office. He asked his secretary to have the cafeteria set out coffee and snacks. He pointed to a long boardroom table and suggested that we sit down.

But Jackson interrupted him. "Mind if we sit in these chairs?" He eyed the leather chairs surrounding his desk.

The dean chuckled. "You don't mind luxury, do you?"

"We have a heap of work to do. We might as well be comfortable," Jackson said.

"Go to it," the dean said.

A girl who wore a red bandana and had been leading the march took one of the chairs. Jackson sat in another. Other students sprawled on the rug; some sat in the large chairs around the table. Penny sat by me and winked.

Once we'd all settled, the dean spoke to us.

"It seems to me," he said, "that you need to have a plan. The others, both those who value their ROTC experience and those who oppose the war, need to feel you have a better alternative to burning down the building. I suggest appointing some members to serve as facilitators to ensure everyone's heard, some to keep track of your proposal (you can use the blackboard over there), and some to address the crowd once you've agreed. You don't have much time since that crowd isn't going to be put off for long."

We introduced ourselves and informed the others of our stance on the war. One ROTC student, a freshman, opposed the war. The other two believed that the president should never be questioned.

We decided that Penny should be the facilitator. Jackson became the scribe, writing down our proposals on a whiteboard. Coffee and doughnuts arrived. The dean excused himself to keep the chancellor and police briefed about our proceedings.

Nothing came easily. Inflammatory accusations flew around the room. An ROTC student with a crewcut refused to listen to the protesters. "You're anti-American," he blurted out.

"Cut the crap," Penny said. "You're no better than the president. And look at what he said got him!"

"But we have an oath," the crewcut said.

"Listen, if I remember right, you took an oath to defend the Constitution, not the president, right?"

"Yeah."

"Well, can you set aside your loyalty to him and focus on what might be right for your country?"

The crewcut nodded his head in agreement.

Penny said, "One of the rules: no name-calling. Let's cut the bullshit and work together."

Jackson proved to be a significant problem. He demanded that the university make a statement against the incursion into Cambodia. "That's why we're here," he insisted.

"Not me," the crewcut said.

"Well, you're a—"

Penny jumped in. "Jackson, not another word!"

The freshman ROTC member offered a compromise. He suggested that the university sponsor a forum to allow students to hear different perspectives.

"You miss the point," Jackson said. "You're acting as if Nixon's view is legitimate. It's not. You know it. For Christ's sake, how can you offer such a proposal?"

"We need to compromise here," I said. "There are others who don't share your point—"

"Share?" he burst out and stood up. "Share?! My God, he's invaded another country without the consent of Congress. Fuck compromise. Fuck this whole process. We need to make a stand."

Penny stood up. "Let's have a break, shall we?"

She asked Jackson if she could talk with him. He grabbed a coffee, and they walked into the hallway.

After meeting with Jackson, she asked the dean to obtain some soda for us. He also had pizza, chips, and coleslaw delivered. But he said, "Not a word about this."

As we helped ourselves, Jackson sat next to me and whispered, "Sorry."

"Hey, this is intense," I said. "Hold your ground. But let others hold their opinions too."

At the Dean's suggestion, we broke into subgroups with members from each faction. Penny divided the groups, with members from each faction mixed together. She put Jackson in my group. We met in different parts of the room.

Penny told me, "Work with him. I think he has the hots for you."

"No!" I was startled that she'd seen something going on between us.

"Oh, yes," she said. "And I believe you are quite aware of it." She smiled. "He's cute. I don't blame you."

I headed to a corner with large windows facing the central campus. Jackson, another protester, the crewcut, and I sat in a circle on the carpet. Graduate students were the group's facilitators.

Before the subgroups met, the dean asked us to have a moment of silence. Before that, he said he wanted each of us to dwell for a moment on what brought us to this room.

"When you came in here, you came as part of a group." He glanced around the room. "When you entered this office, you were just twelve 'I's, separate persons with your loyalties and faiths. Now it's time for you as an individual 'I' to find something in common, a 'we' that respects each of the 'I's, including yourself."

I thought of Jackson, who sat beside me, and of Will, and of my torment about being attracted to them. I thought about the war, how my dread of serving in it had brought me here. I knew that some, like my high school friend Duffy, who wanted to serve his country, had died. I needed to respect that call to serve.

The group's consensus was that students wanted the university to issue a statement denouncing what happened at Kent State.

The dean told us that a statement from the university would require a board meeting. It was unreasonable to think that it could be done quickly. Jackson offered the idea that the university sponsor a forum where both the pros and cons could be heard. He also advocated for the university to allow protesters to present their concerns about the war to the board. I was surprised how he'd taken on the role of conciliator.

The dean got the chancellor to hold a special board meeting where the protesters could be heard. The university would sponsor a forum that the dean agreed to spearhead. The Dean congratulated us.

We left to inform the protesters about what we'd done. There were cheers and celebrations that their protest had led to some action. Reverend Lawson, who had been with the group, told us the gruesome details of the Kent State shootings and the chaos on campuses across the nation.

After the crowd dispersed, Jackson took me by the hand. "You want to go back to my room?" he asked.

When I hesitated and said, "I need—" he added, "We could always compromise and go to yours." I laughed. He could be so charming. We went to his and I spent the night in his arms.

Start Up

THE SEMESTER DREW TO a close as my work with the Folk School intensified. My big worry was my relationship with Jackson. As much as I was attracted to him, I wasn't sure how I'd negotiate being with him and working with Erling.

As it turned out, Jackson took his exams and left early, going home to upstate New York, where he wanted to join in more antiwar activities. He promised to write, and, much to my surprise, he did write short letters about his hometown, the antiwar organization, the grocery store where he worked, the local fair, and his boyfriend. They'd been together for years, and well, he said they would continue to be.

Ann was still in my life. I held onto her because she made me feel all right. A man. A lover of women. We studied together. She told me about her job applications and an interview she had with a company in Connecticut.

Meanwhile, Erling and I made plans for the summer. We brought boxes of books for the library to our newly owned Folk School building, purchased from Peggy. Erling had four new students and more faculty to work with us, but we needed more students, so I was told to find them.

Earlier in May, Dr. Compton, my former philosophy professor, invited me back to Ashbury College to read my poems at his house and recruit students for the Folk School. Thirty students came to his house for my reading and my pitch about the Folk School.

Three students volunteered to come to the Folk School. One, a member of my fraternity, Stephen, was a pledge son, and I knew him well. Sensitive and thoughtful, he made a perfect fit. The other, Adam, a son of a friend of my parents, was a freshman but wanted, as he told me, "to do good," so I accepted him. The last one, Alicia, was new to me, but she seemed to be inquisitive and wanted to talk with me privately about the program.

Attractive and petite, I met her at the Double Decker café. She was taking a course in modern poetry and, contrary to inquiries about the program, wanted me to explain "Sunday Morning" by Wallace Stevens instead. She read it aloud, her soft, sensual voice enunciating every word.

I told her, "Listen to yourself; you are the poem." Line by line, we talked about what was meant by

She dreams a little, and she feels the dark
Encroachment of that old catastrophe,
As a calm darkens among water-lights.
The pungent oranges and bright, green wings
Seem things in some procession of the dead,
Winding across wide water, without sound.

I asked her what the "old catastrophe" could mean. She deciphered what the poem meant to her, how she'd often felt constrained as a sorority girl. She acted as if she were just some pretty object, but inside, she was full of loss. Despite the bright colors and elegance of her sorority house—one of the most beautiful on campus—it didn't seem very sensible to her. She became excited about how the poem spoke to her. She called her parents to convince them to let her go to the Folk School.

❧

After a brief visit home to drop off my books and records and to see my parents, I headed back to Nashville in my air-conditioned car. I pulled into the driveway of Dick's house and walked to the door. In seconds, my shirt was drenched with sweat.

Dick and Pam had gone to Louisville, but left the key under a ceramic frog.

I planned to spend the night resting before heading to Rose's Creek, where I would meet Erling before the students arrived.

We had seven students. Two young women, Grace and Betty, came from Maryland. Stephen, my college friend; Adam, a cross-country runner; and Alicia, the sorority girl. A foreign exchange student from Sweden, Ingrid, came from a college where Erling taught American Literature.

Maddy, a local girl who played guitar, attended Bethel College and later headed the music program. Erling enticed a divinity student, Dylan, to come. A first-year student, who wanted, as Erling told me, "to explore the primitive heritage of the mountain people," was the latest find.

We also had one faculty member, Erik Cline, a professor of history from Vanderbilt University specializing in American Studies, who used many three-syllable words but had a genuine interest in history as a lived experience. His wife, Ellen, a tall, thin woman who bore a resemblance to Audrey Hepburn—she exuded sensuality—was the activities director, a painter, and would coordinate craft programs.

That left Erling and me to run the school, assign tasks so that meals and festivities happened each day, and provide instruction in American literature.

Everyone would stay at the new Folk School. Erling had purchased bunk beds for co-ed dorms. A library was in one room that also served as Erling's bedroom, a meeting room, and a living room.

Since the house sat on the crest of a steep hill with a great view, some of our group sessions were to be held on the front porch. Despite the desolate quality of the immediate terrain—a few pines, some shrubs, weedy grass—there in the moonlight, you could see far beyond the soft slopes of the mountains to the grayish blue light on the horizon. On cool evenings on the porch, Erling and I would discuss how we would organize our daily schedule. I couldn't wait to get there to start a new adventure, this time more seasoned, better known, and more assured of my role.

I opened the door to the narrow flight of stairs to Dick's apartment. Stale, hot, dank air slammed into me. I turned the air conditioner knob on high and stood in front of it, my shirt lifted. It would be the last time for months that I'd have the luxury of cool air.

My mind wandered to my second year of graduate school. What had it gotten me? Sure, I'd gotten out of the suburbs, gotten out of the draft, gotten far from my parents' prying eyes, yet I was still mired in uncertainty. Will. Tom. Jackson. Ann. Julie. Cheryl. A dabbler. Never committed. No one true passion.

It would be good to return to the mountains, where I felt comfortable.

Erling called so we could make final arrangements. His voice seemed distant, almost as if we had a bad connection.

I told him I'd gotten more money from the church. "Another grand. They like what we're doing. Mr. Hook may come to visit us!"

"Hold your horses," Erling said.

"What is it?"

"Bad news," he informed me.

"What?"

"The Folk School burned down last night."

The air conditioner droned on. I stared at it.

"Arson," he said. "By the time the fire department came—and they didn't rush—it was engulfed in flames. I couldn't get in. Old as it was, it went up like tinder. Nothing left. Nothing."

"Shit," I said. I crumpled onto a kitchen chair.

"You got it," he said. "Shit is the right word. 'Damn' would work too, and 'fuck'."

"What will we do?" I asked.

"Already on it. Peggy told me about a house not far from the Folk School that's empty. We may be able to rent it. It's furnished—beds, furniture, kitchen, the whole works. I looked in a window to see if it had enough room. I believe that it would hold most of us, not all. Some would have to sleep up in the log cabin, which is nearly done," he explained. "The grand may make the difference."

"Do I need to get anything?"

"No. Drive up as fast as you can. We can outfit the house if I can rent it."

After the call, I drank some cold water and sat in the lounge chair.

Dick and Pam told me, "Don't wait up," since they'd be home late. But I did.

When I heard the door open downstairs, I helped them carry in their luggage.

Pam seemed tired and excused herself, citing the long drive. When she closed the door to the bedroom, Dick said that she hadn't been well.

"Is there a problem?" I asked.

"Not exactly," he said.

I waited for him to continue. Restless, he picked up something on one counter, set it on another, and then moved it back again as he unpacked.

"I might as well tell you," he said. "You're the first. She's pregnant!"

"Really?"

"Early on. But it's real."

Since he stared at me without expression, I didn't know how to read him. "And..."

'She's due next fall."

"Dick, how are you feeling?"

"Oh, that," he said, wincing. "That's more complicated. Still have school to complete. A parish to find. Being a dad, you know, that's hard for me to get my head around."

"Mixed reviews," I said.

"Very."

"Let's have a drink," I said. "You can unpack later." We spoke for several hours. His father had been absent, consumed by his job. Dick didn't want to be like that, but he was starting a new career, having to learn the ropes, not the best time to be a dad, but the longer we talked, he became convinced it was for the better, and that he wasn't, and would never be, like his dad. He'd be there for Pam and his child.

By the time Pam came back into the room looking surprisingly refreshed, he seemed more relaxed. He fixed us cheese dip and corn chips.

I told them the bad news. They were shocked and let me speak of my disappointment. They offered to write a check. I told them we had enough cash, at least I thought we did, and would let them know if we needed more.

Eventually, Dick excused himself to unpack his bags in the bedroom.

"He's a bit nonplussed," Pam whispered. "Men don't get pregnant the way we do. I mean, for us, it's there. What can we do? For them, it's like inviting a stranger into the house. He'll get used to it."

She had such a unique way of putting things. I suspected that she wasn't exhausted at all but just knew that Dick needed to talk. She was right about our bodies and as I listened to her, I was reminded of a brief encounter I'd had with a woman in Chicago months ago.

Last January, I went on a double date with my friend, a medical student, to a drive-in. He introduced me to a nurse who worked at his hospital, where he was an intern. Before the movie previews, she had her hand in my pants.

Her name was Darla, but she preferred to be called "Pussy." She slipped off her panties. If I hadn't been inhibited by my friend and his girl in the front seat, I would have had sex right there. Later, she invited me to a party at her house. Before the guests left, we'd hopped into bed. I was amazed by how willing she was, how much she enjoyed having me enter her body, how comfortable she was making love. I began to feel that maybe my confusion about sex grew more from my inexperience or not finding the right woman than my attraction to men.

After all, Dick had found Pam. He seemed happy. Maybe that could happen to me.

The next morning, after Pam fixed a big breakfast of hash browns, eggs, sausage, and toast, I wished them well and gave Dick the address at Clearfork Post Office. He hugged me, whispered, "Thanks." Pam hugged me, too. She escorted me to the car. "You worked your magic. He's fine now. He'll be a great dad."

V

Footfall each in the memory
Down the passage which I did not take
Toward the door we never opened

—"Four Quartets," T.S. Eliot

Fire

WHEN I ARRIVED AT the location where the Folk School was to be situated, the hillside was blanketed with white ash. The person who torched it had done a good job. Only a brick chimney rose from the middle of a slab on one side of the house.

Just a year ago, on my first visit to Peggy's house, my heart filled with optimism, and now I sat in the same place, my books burned and ash all around me. The surrounding trees were scorched and dead; the stovepipes twisted like melted plastic tubing. The hillside was denuded, red clay like a wound.

I picked at chunks of ash and realized that they were burnt books, each page like flakes of French pastry dough. One book seemed intact. Chardin's The Divine Milieu. As I broke the pages from the spine, they blew away like white wings of a moth. I remembered bringing boxes of books to the house, setting up a bookcase, and alphabetizing them: James Agee, Teilhard de Chardin, Henry David Thoreau, Thomas Wolfe, and countless others. I opened my journal to make notes about how beautiful yet delicate the book ashes were, almost more stunning than the books themselves.

The afternoon sun was at its apogee. I wiped perspiration from my forehead. Still had to find Erling. Find out what he wanted me to do for orientation.

A car came up the hollow and turned into the driveway next to mine. Out popped Bobby and his sisters, Valerie and Katie. They scampered up the driveway and called out, "Jason! Jason!" I almost burst into tears at the sound of their voices and their pleas for me to go swimming in the strip mine pool.

I raced down the hill to greet them. Bobby had gotten his driver's permit. He pointed at the keys in his hand; I patted him on the back. The girls tugged me, "Come on, come on," and told me to hurry. I got my suit.

Bobby and I chased after them and scooted behind a crop of saplings, stripped, put on our suits, and jumped into the cool water.

Bobby hopped on my shoulders, and Valerie hopped onto Katie's shoulders. We tried to topple each other. My being a foot taller than the girls, the girls shouted, "No fair!" I intentionally fell so the girls would win. Bobby glared at me, I winked, and he smiled. We played for an hour. Then they took me to the house that would be the Folk School's replacement home.

Erling greeted me at the front porch, which was less than five feet from the road. The house hung over a gentle ravine, its back supported by four posts. A set of stairs out the back door led to a backyard and a meandering brook.

Erling hugged me and, pointing up the road, said, "Sad sight." While the kids roamed around the new location, he told me what he thought we should do to organize the house. Bobby, the girls, and I helped Erling move some bunk beds into different rooms. He'd bought some more cooking sets—pots, pans, fry pans, and kettles—along with dishes, glasses, and silverware for fourteen. We dusted and washed the cupboards, installed new yellowed shelf liner, and arranged the plates, bowls, and pots on the shelves.

Toward evening, Erling met with Marie Cirillo and told me that I could do what I wanted. The Metzler family had moved to their other home deep in the hollow. Bobby invited me to visit. I drove up the road that, in some stretches, was hundreds of feet above the creek bed. The farther I went into the hollow, the steeper the drop-off became.

We took the right branch of a fork to their house. Constructed much like their other home, it had a front porch that led into Peggy's and the girls' bedrooms. Across from it was another room with a bunk bed where Bobby and Tommy slept. Just beyond Peggy's room was the kitchen with a wood-fired cookstove and a kitchen table. There were no gleaming white porcelain toilets. Couldn't just push the handle and flush. Couldn't step to a mirror, smile at my face, and wash and dry my hands. Couldn't open the door, step into a hallway, and go back to where everyone pretended nothing had happened.

In the outhouse, some twenty yards from the house, the olfactory senses told a different story from the hygienic bathrooms in the dorm or at my home. Bodily reality couldn't be denied.

But at the same time, I realized that my presence wasn't based on social status, political affiliation, the deodorant I had, the clothes I wore, the car I drove, the money I had in the bank, or the name I had. It was based on my being with other bodies. Martin Luther, the German radical and theologian, wrote graphically about this bodily communion with others. To him, it was a great equalizer.

As I scampered to the outhouse that night, stepping carefully down a path, the stars overhead, the quiet of the trees above me, I believed him. One's body was a primal connection. Being with Peggy brought back that awareness.

❧

We oriented the new students and set up the house, then determined that Stephen and I would sleep in the new cabin that had been constructed on the Folk School property. The program began with morning classes. Lunch. Outdoor activities in the afternoon by the burned-down school or in the new cabin. On Friday evening, a campfire was held. For the first two hot and humid weeks, we spent many afternoons in the pond.

The new students organized the arts and crafts program under Ellen's guidance. The two Maryland students, Grace and Betty, both athletic, joined the boys in the football games. Dylan liked to play checkers and chess in the shade of a maple tree.

In the morning group discussions, I soon learned that I had an adversary, someone who wanted to prove that he was smarter than I was and, to boot, would be better at what I was doing as Erling's assistant. Dylan liked to upstage me anytime he could by responding to Erling's questions during our morning sessions or by doubting what I suggested. Short, with the remnants of acne splattered across his face, he impressed Erling with his familiarity with the day's reading. If I made a statement about Thomas Wolfe, he interrupted me. "No, that's not what he said. Haven't you read him? In the chapter you're referring to, he said..." and, riffling through the book, recite the passage to prove he was right. I had an urge to punch him in the face, but decided, instead, to ignore him, a decision I'd come to regret.

The Swedish student, Ingrid, led writing workshops and taught students to paint watercolors. Everyone, including Erling, joined in. He said he was interested in short story writing. That Ingrid was stunningly beautiful may also have attracted him. I was sure that the three younger and two teenage boys who joined the group never complained when she leaned over their shoulders to see what they'd written.

With a larger crew of five men and four women attending the Folk School, we had managed in three short weeks to build even stronger community allegiance than we had the year before. The core of our community events was the Friday bonfire. People brought potato chips, potato salad, chicken, fresh-made loaves of bread, and cookies—plenty to eat.

Erik, the history professor, and Mandy, the musical wizard, played the guitar along with Bud Terry and Otrel, two local musicians, who played the fiddle and guitar with such bravado that, soon, everyone, including kids, were up and dancing.

We'd sing folk tunes and dance around the fire. Robbie Metzler, a cousin of Bobby, and a teenager, became a regular in the day program, brought his banjo, and soon enough, we had a jamboree.

Before the bonfire, we had baseball. To allow the younger kids to play, we used a Wiffle ball. Erling played with a vengeance, baseball being his passion. He'd pick the teams and pitch for his team. If his team were down, he'd slap their backs and embolden them to play harder, run faster, score more often. He'd stand at the pitcher's mound, slap his fist in his mitt, lean, eye the batter, and whip the ball to home plate. His motto was, "No one on, no one scores." When he batted, he crouched so low it was hard to get a strike across the plate. On offense, he batted balls over everyone's head and charged around the bases with his arms up, chiding the runners on base to hurry up so he could plant his foot on home plate.

Horseshoes brought serious betting for some adults. The locals would challenge members of the Folk School, betting five or ten dollars. The horseshoe pit would be lined with kids watching the horseshoe fly end over end toward the stake.

To draw more local men who could pass the word that we were not communists, and who could protect us from threats, we added a turkey shoot contest. We put bull's-eye targets on a maple tree. Everyone chipped in a buck to fill up a lineup. The one with the highest points won.

The first round went to the younger set. Tommy and Bobby had two bull's-eyes.

"You young Turks are whipping these old guys," I said.

Tommy shook his head, put his hand over his mouth, and whispered, "Don't be fooled. Shady John will clean house. He's the best shot in the county, probably the state."

Squatting on his heels beside his red Ford pickup, Shady John worked his plug tobacco in his jaw and spit on the ground. He wore a baseball cap low on his forehead. His piece of land was down the hill from the Folk School—it had a small pond next to his driveway and, beyond it, an extensive garden with a sizable corn crop, squash that twined among the corn, beans, carrots, chard, lettuce—you name it. Most of the day, he posted himself under a pin oak that loomed beside his house, held a rifle in his arm, and picked off any varmint that snooped around. His face, like the land he labored on, was worn like clay, streaked with crevasses that ran along his eyes, down to his massive jaw. He could have been any age—forty to seventy.

Rarely one to smile or even speak, he came to church every Sunday and sat in his front pew, dressed as he did most days in bib overalls and a white work shirt. Rumor had it that in his youth, when he was rowdy and mean-spirited, he'd shot and killed a man. But he met his wife, had a son, who was his pride and joy, and settled down. He had palsy, a slight tremor in his hands, and, as a result, kept his hands in his lap, or, as he did at the turkey shoot, on the butt of his rifle.

I laughed out loud when Tommy told me that Shady John would clean house. "Christ," I whispered, "He can't keep from shaking. How's he going to sight a gun?"

"Watch him."

I called Shady John up to shoot. Everyone stopped to witness a legend. He set his legs wide and lifted the rifle to his shoulder. The tip of it jittered up and down. He put his eye over the barrel and sighted on the target, must have stood for several minutes, then squeezed the trigger, and everyone looked at the target. Bull 's-eye. He rested his gun. There was applause. A smile creased one corner of his mouth. He squeezed off two more shots, bull's-eye each time. "Much appreciate the turkey," he said. "And what you are doing with my boy." He came back every week.

Squeaky

RUMORS SPREAD IN THE third week of the Folk School: Squeaky wanted to kill me. I couldn't believe it. Who was this guy?

Squeaky, a young man newly released from prison, didn't like our being in the hollow. Thought we were communists. Didn't like my looks. Resented that I had taken the boys skinny-dipping in the creek. Called me a "faggot." He had a knife, and I was going to get it.

Erling told me., "Don't go off by yourself. Keep someone else around. Let's check it out and play it safe until we identify if he made the threats."

With Shady John on our side, and more people coming each Friday, Squeaky's threats surprised us. The trouble was that, having been in prison, we had no idea what he looked like. He carried a switchblade and had a proven record: having gone to jail for knifing someone. Manslaughter.

Stephen, Erik, and Adam were to be my bodyguards. One was in front of me, one to the side, one in back. Wherever I went, they followed me like the Secret Service. They kept their distance, so they didn't look conspicuous, but I was aware of them as I passed the football, when I got up to tell a folk tale, or during the folk dance. They were there, joining in but also looking for Squeaky.

One evening, Grace told me that Squeaky had arrived. As we were doing a circle dance, she kept hold of my arm when I was supposed to swing her to her next partner and, instead, pulled me aside.

"That's him," she pointed to a young man standing at the outskirts of the campfire.

Short, with long black hair and a plain, almost childlike face, his head darted back and forth and up and down like a startled turtle peeking out of its shell. He wore a plaid shirt open in the front, jeans, and cowboy boots. Self-assured, even cocky with his hands shoved in the front of his jeans, he chatted with several guys his age. An unfamiliar girl hung on his arm.

Grace signaled my bodyguards. They moved closer. Stephen came over to me and put his hand on my shoulder.

"Erling suggests," he said, "that I take you back to the cabin, just to avoid trouble. Okay?"

I told him to wait. "He's not making trouble, let's see what he does."

I spoke with the fiddlers, then squatted on a log and fed the fire. The Metzler kids—Bobby, Tommy, Donna, Katie, and Valerie—gathered around me. They took turns tossing sticks into the bonfire, but I realized, without telling me, they were protecting me, too.

Squeaky and his friends came over to the campfire and stood on the opposite side, laughing, tossing sticks in the fire, and stomping their feet to the music. His friends clustered around him. Squeaky eyed me. I crouched and gazed into the embers; an orange light welled up from the gray ash. As the timbers and logs burned down, the fire hushed as if sleepy, no longer snarling and snapping.

Stephen came over again, knelt beside me, "You sure you don't want to go?"

My neck was tense. For a week, I had kept my guard up, careful not to go anywhere alone. I was easy prey, sleeping outside the cabin on the hillside on hot nights without someone with me, worried Squeaky might sneak up and stab me. I imagined what it must be to be the president, knowing that someone could take a shot at you. Dr. King and President Kennedy joked about it.

I picked up a stick, broke it on the ground with my foot, and aimed it at the fire.

"What is it?" Stephen asked.

"Wait here," I said.

I walked toward Squeaky's group. If Squeaky were going to knife me, he'd have to do it in public. He saw me coming and nudged one of his buddies.

Katie was at my right shoulder, Tommy at my left, Bobby next to him. Stephen, Erik, and Adam watched from twenty feet away.

I came up to him, extended my hand, and said as calmly as I could, "Hi, I don't think I know you. What's your name?"

He had a soft, cautious grip. "Squeaky."

"Mine's Jason. Nice to meet you," I said. I wasn't sure what to say next, but I followed the script that I had used at cocktail parties that my mother held for my dad's corporate friends: ask something personal about them.

I asked him where he lived. He told me that he was staying with his uncle for the time being. I thanked him for coming.

"We do this every week," I said. "We need help in getting the bonfire going.

You good with an ax?"

"Yeah. Pretty good, I'd say, but even better with a chainsaw." He smiled at his friend. He stared at me, his face fixed.

I felt an odd affection for him, for his boyishness, his soft, round features, and long curly hair, sticking out in several directions. No more than five-two, nearly half a head shorter than I was, he had a frail build—slight shoulders and skinny legs—seemed vulnerable, as if he had been picked on and had a chip on his shoulder. I could have picked him up with one hand. He must have been easy prey in the prison system. I took a risk and touched him gently on the shoulder.

"It would be great to have your help—and your friends too!"

I introduced myself to his friends: Taylor, Billy, Joe, and his girlfriend, Jean-May.

"Hey, we are going to roast some marshmallows. You want to get some sticks for the kids? We need a lot of them."

He frowned at first and shoved his hands in his pockets. His girlfriend nudged him. He agreed. "Sure, anything for the kids."

Becky approached him and began chatting. She asked him if he played guitar. He did, and she invited him to come to the cabin sometime to play. Tommy, Bobby, Squeaky, Taylor, Billy, Joe, and Jean-May joined her; they all headed to the saplings on the edge of the strip mine, pocketknives in hand.

Squeaky had a theory about not letting the marshmallows get too dark, and with his friends Taylor and Jean-May, he toasted two bags of marshmallows and passed them out to the kids.

They didn't come back the next week, but Squeaky went to the Folk School to play his guitar with Becky and became a regular and a friend, confiding in me that he wanted to get his GED.

Fires of Hell

FROM THE FOLK SCHOOL porch on Sundays, we could hear faint fragments of hymns from a Pentecostal Church. Being such a small congregation, they imported different preachers each week, mostly lay preachers wanting to get a shot at the pulpit. Peggy knew I was a divinity student and urged me to come. She couldn't understand how a man of God could avoid coming to church. I didn't have the heart to tell her that, at best, I was a man searching for God.

After weeks of pestering, I finally relented, donned my best slacks and white dress shirt, and walked up the crooked road to the church.

Peggy greeted me at the door. The church consisted of one large room, twenty feet long and fifteen feet wide, with a platform in front with a makeshift pulpit, painted white, and a vase of Queen Ann's lace and wild daisies on a little table by the pulpit.

Nine people filled the first row of folding chairs, and others took their seats here and there, like checkers on a board game. Shady John leaned against the back wall.

Peggy ushered me to the front.

A local boy who worked in a collision shop was the preacher of the day.

"You'll enjoy him," she said. "He's lively."

When he arrived, she introduced me and told him I was attending Vanderbilt Divinity School.

In a gray suit too large for him—the sleeves hid his hands—he had to extend his arm full length for me to locate it. For a moment, I thought he might be missing a hand, but catching my mistake, I shook his hand. He had a rotund face. A slab of black hair looked glued in place across his forehead. He bounced from one foot to the other as we talked, his eyes focused more on my Adam's apple than my face.

Peggy sang the first line of the hymn "He has the whole world in his hands." Everyone followed, repeating the line. Her firm, deep voice reminded me of Mahalia Jackson's.

As the service continued, three toddlers wandered in and out of the building, scampered into their mother's laps for a while, and, when tired of the service, toddled out, their playful screams outside the open windows.

The boy preacher read several New Testament verses from a worn, leather-bound Bible, thanked the congregation for the chance to preach "The Word." He emphasized those two words, his voice pitched high in a falsetto. He recounted how, living in the hollow, he had fond memories of the church, though he admitted he had been a wayward boy.

Peggy called out, "You certainly was," and several women echoed her sentiment, saying, "Uh-huh."

With the Bible held high, he slapped it with his hand. "I've come to Jesus." His voice stronger, he crouched down, knees bent, and leaped up high in the air, still saying, "I've come to Jesus. I've been saved by Jesus." His face flushed, the slab of hair on his head broke loose and flapped up and down as he jumped up and down. He managed to break the phrases. "I've come," called out at a lower pitch as it steadily rose, "to Jesus" as he leapt in the air on one word and landed on another.

Peggy and the other women shouted, "Praise the Lord!"

He stared at me and asked, "You ever seen an acetylene torch?"

I shook my head. "No."

"Well, I'll tell you I work with one every day, put a match to the flame, and it's mighty hot, so hot it melts iron into liquid, a flame as hot as the flames of hell. Yes, it is! Hot as the devil's temptation, a flame that'll burn the flesh. I see it burn metal black as tar, black as the soul without salvation. I know you're tempted—" He was still staring at me. Besides Shady John, I was the only male, the only one who might have been tempted, as he had been tempted. But I wondered if he suspected something else about me.

He kept on dwelling on the fiery damnation, "Yes, charred souls. The skin peeling off black as the sinners go against the word of God," and, each time, he said "sinners," he jumped straight up so the floorboards shook. When his shoes slammed down, his legs wide open, he popped right up again, up and down, calling out, "Yes! Yes, ah, yes! Ah!" as if he was out of breath. But he wasn't because he kept right on preaching. "Hot as an acetylene torch. God roasts sinners! Burns them black as coal! Sinners!

Mark my word. Yes, ah he will, ah, yes." Another jump. "Sinners, yes he will."

My head bobbed up and down.

Sweat poured from his forehead. He stared at me.

I was sure he knew I was one of those sinners that he had in mind, or because he was a young man, couldn't imagine a woman having sin as he had. Whatever it was, he liked looking at me, and I kept nodding my head.

As he continued leaping—his stamina mighty impressive—he looked like a man whose feet were being scorched on a skillet and had to jump to prevent getting fried as black as his shoes.

He must have thought I was agreeing with him, or perhaps he only felt comfortable talking to a man, as he described the torch, its blue flame, and how God could intensify the flame. He held the Bible out in front of him as if it were a torch, aimed it right at me, then scanned the congregation. Heads turned away, afraid to be scorched.

He sweated so much that he had to loosen his tie and shed his jacket.

Peggy enjoyed the performance, saying "Amen" and "Speak the word."

Children gathered on the seat beside me and seemed pleased with his calisthenics. His last pronouncements were about the wages of sin. He went back to the pulpit, put his hands on it, stared up at the ceiling, and offered a prayer. He asked us to accept the love of Jesus.

I was surprised. Up to that point, I was convinced that our fates were sealed, doomed to hellfire, burnt by an acetylene torch.

But the boy preacher came back to love, said Jesus's love washes away sin and quenches fire. He thanked us again for the chance to preach "The Word."

Peggy called another hymn. A basket was passed around. I put in ten dollars. The preacher shook my hand. I told him that it was inspiring.

He said, "I've been changed by the Lord."

I'm sure he had, but from what, I couldn't tell. I suspected that it was rough for him. Short as he was, most likely bigger boys picked on him as they probably did Squeaky. Now he had his torch, a decent job, a new jacket, and Jesus, too.

How someone "found Jesus," as if Jesus had been lost, never made sense to me. Jesus was a historical figure with a distinct message: to heal the poor, to see the kingdom of God in the world before one's eyes, and to see everyone recognize that they are children of God.

For that reason, I considered him, at best, a role model, and at worst, a tragic figure who had become lionized by a small group of followers and, as the centuries passed, was made into a savior. Jesus was never an intimate friend nor a personal savior for me. I had several people who saved my life. Two were professors at DePauw University. Both very much alive. Not dead for over a thousand years. The mystery of how Jesus, as a real-life personage, became vital in some people's lives eluded me, but I knew it was true for them, and that was enough.

Peggy asked if I'd come again, and I did. She introduced me to several other women who were regulars at church. Bonnie Hatfield lived a half mile from the Folk School. Her boys —Jay, Tyler, and Jesse —were regulars at the Folk School. I visited her house several times, picking up and dropping off her boys. She ran a household of six—her daughters worked, while all the boys were in school, from elementary to middle school.

"Church," she said, "gives me some peace and quiet."

Peace and quiet. That was never what I experienced at church. Most preachers had stentorian voices and ranted about our failures as mortals. They may not have been as entertaining as the one with the torch, but they spoke of sin and damnation, calling for us to repent. No one came forward to repent while I was there. But the congregation enjoyed themselves and sang gospel tunes that lifted our spirits.

Being there gave me credibility within the community. Only lasted an hour or so, depending on how revved up the preacher was, but it was refreshing.

Bonnie and Peggy knew I didn't care much for the message most of the time, and neither did they. They had enormous faith in people's goodness and enjoyed getting out of the house to visit their neighbors. That's what you did on Sunday mornings. Probably the only time Peggy and Bonnie got away from chores was when they were at church, not taking care of children. A day of rest. Something blessed about being free from the household, just as it was good for me to be away from the Folk School.

I skipped a few services as the summer days shortened. My wages of sin were getting the best of me. Much as I tried to deny it, my attraction to Stephen, who slept in the log cabin with me, became an obsession. I'd been attracted to him in college. Loved watching him undress before we crawled into our sleeping bags. A momentary pleasure. Relief from the daily excursions to the stores, the preparation for meetings, the drives to the laundromat, and the games with the kids.

❧

One evening, after supper, I went alone and followed the stream up the ravine to where I could see the water at its source flow down into the valley. I was haunted by something that happened the night before. I examined what I had done like a puzzle from different angles, but the more I thought about the incident, the more confused I became.

Late at night, after I thought Stephan had fallen asleep, I slipped my hand into his sleeping bag. The wages of sin. But not sin. I was out of sync.

I climbed farther up the mountain to a graveyard and examined the gravestones, which dated back to 1840. The sun was steep in the sky at midsummer. The heat on my body was like the lust I had felt last night. I felt a compulsion to be naked, to strip off my clothes, and to sit naked, free of all veneer, to unbutton my shirt, doff my sandals, and slip my jeans off. Low to the ground in case anyone might see me, I let the sun bake me. My shyness—almost instinctive. The wind fingered across my legs and my jockey shorts as if it was wanting to tell me something I failed to understand—how I could be naked with guys in the swimming hole as if it meant nothing at all, and yet, in the dark by myself on a hillside, I felt drawn to touch Stephen. When I was with other guys who enjoyed being naked, I felt no shame, but now I felt shame for what my hand had done.

I lay back, let my mind wander to the previous night when I snuggled next to Stephen and placed my hand lightly on the cotton of his underwear. I waited. Stephen was quite still. The moon showed through cracks in the logs. A milky yellow light spread over our sleeping bags.

There was a stirring. My hand snapped back.

Stephen rolled over to face me. "What are you doing?" he asked.

I pretended to be asleep.

"You awake?" Stephen said, nudging me. He leaned over me, propped on his elbow. Getting no response to his question, he turned over and slept.

The wind stirred. I put my hand back on his sleeping bag, feeling the rise and fall of his breathing. I was aroused and groped for the warmth of his body under the palm of my hand.

He sat up, turning to me, "What are you doing?'

"Nothing," I stammered.

"How long have you been awake?"

"Awake?" I looked at my hand as if it were a foreign object. I cringed. "My hand must've fallen on your sleeping bag."

"I don't think so."

"Sorry."

"What is going on?"

"Must've reached out in my sleep."

"But you were awake. Weren't you?"

"Yes." There was no avoiding it; I had to admit it. "I was. I'm sorry."

Stephen looked at me and shook his head back and forth. "Keep them to yourself, okay?"

"Okay."

I rolled over into a ball, closed my eyes, and wondered what Stephen would say the next day. I wanted to creep off into the night and disappear.

In the morning, Stephen's sleeping bag was empty, with its corner folded back. I sat on my elbows, while he sat on the front stoop of the log cabin, watching the sunrise. When I unzipped my sleeping bag, he turned around. With a beautiful smile, he said, "Good morning." I wished him the same.

The Runner

ADAM AND I WERE OUT on a run one afternoon. Although I could not keep up with him if he kept a regular pace—as a cross-country athlete, he could run for hours—he slowed down so I could point out where different people lived. When we crested the hill, I could hear Bud Terry's guitar playing, and we slowed down to listen to it. He waved for us to come in. We pushed open the gate, went to the front porch, and chatted about the heat.

He showed us a pistol on a table next to his chair. "Feel it. That's the best gun in the hollow. Rests in your hand like a glove," he boasted. He picked it up and asked Adam to place several bottles on the fence. Once they were perched there, he aimed and hit one, missed another. His hand trembling, he shattered one more and missed again.

"Twern't the gun," he said, apologetically. "My hands ain't no good. My breathing's so bad I wonder if I'll ever catch another breath."

When he started to complain about his health, Adam turned away and walked to the other end of the porch.

Bud handed me the gun. "You much of a shot?" he asked.

"Don't know," I confessed. "Never shot one, except toy pistols when I was a kid."

He told Adam to line up a set of six bottles in a row. "Let's see what you can do."

I asked him how to aim the gun. He told me to use my dominant eye to focus on the target and to squeeze the trigger gently. I held it out in front of me, closed one eye, and aimed. Shady John at our shooting contests said that a light touch keeps the gun working properly and prevents jerking it off the target. The gun fired, and the bottle shattered. Proud of myself, I shot one after another: six bottles, six shots.

Bud laughed. "Well, I'll be. For a city slicker, you've got a steady hand."

He coughed several times and complained again about his lungs. Adam moved off the porch and was pacing back and forth. I apologized for Adam. Bud said, "Oh, I remember that age when it was hard to sit still. Be off with you."

I handed him the gun, and Adam and I returned to the run. After two hundred yards, I told Adam that it was rude of him to ignore Bud when he was complaining about his illness.

Adam said, "He's not ill."

"Yes, he is. He's got emphysema, compounded with black lung," I told him.

"He's fine. He's just fine." He picked up his pace, jogging yards ahead of me.

I looked at him, his lean body and the scars on his legs like marbled rock. When he was twelve, a chemistry experiment at his house exploded, splashing his legs with a flammable liquid. He ran down the street and collapsed in a neighbor's front yard. The neighbor covered him with a blanket to put out the flames. The doctors said he'd never walk again because of his third-degree burns. However, he walked, ran, won the state cross-country meet, and also became a Christian Scientist, claiming that the religion had saved his life.

Earlier in the spring, when he visited Nashville for the weekend, he stayed in my dorm several nights. One night, we had a heated argument about how, in my opinion, decisions were neither good nor bad. He stood up—his arms crossed, face flushed—and started to leave the room.

I told him not to walk out in the middle of a discussion.

He changed direction and leaned against the window, his feet tapping the floor. I told him, as an example of how good can be bad, that producing more energy to help the economy grow damages the environment.

He shook his head, claimed that there was only good, the right way.

He was standing by my window when I noticed a large magnolia with a shadow beneath it. I pointed to it and said, "Look at that tree. See the shadow under it? Notice how dappled light mixes with the dark? That's how it is for most things: it's not just dark and light, good and bad. There is always a gray area where most decisions are made."

He looked at the tree and shook his head, "All I see is shadow and light."

I put my hand on his shoulder and pointed at the light changing under the tree from the branches blowing and shifting the light. He refused to see it. That's where we left it.

As I followed him up the road, his legs pumped in long strides, I knew that his running gave him a way to block out anything that interfered with his reality. I also knew he'd keep running for miles and miles, keep going higher up the hollow, onto steeper, more rutted sections.

I called out to him to let him know I was turning around. Sweat streamed down my back, and my shirt was soaked. I thought about how difficult it must be to see the world in a strict black-and-white, right-and-wrong way, but how convenient it was too.

As long as you were on the right side, there was only shadow and light. The dappled subtleties of life couldn't exist; they were ignored.

❧

At night, I often went off to read, sometimes spending time with Alicia. When I was with her, I could ignore my grey zone, my feelings of attraction to Stephen, and the conflict of being at odds with those feelings. I could simply be with a woman I liked and who, from what I'd seen, liked me back. We walked along a creek behind the Folk School, dipped our feet in the water, and talked about the other members: how Ed, the history professor, made up words to sound more impressive, like the "thwartedness of the American Dream." We wished he'd speak more from his heart than his head. We also discussed what we would do after graduation. She had one more year at college. I had one year at the Divinity School.

For us, the future seemed bleak. I'd probably be eligible for the draft. She majored in history and had no idea what career path she would choose. She slipped her hand into mine and said, "We have now. That is what we can count on." She remained the one person I felt I could truly talk to and who reminded me of Ann—thoughtful and genuine.

Vibrant, with long brown hair and an impish expression on her face, she wanted more out of life than what she had been told was her destiny: marriage, housework, and children. She wasn't about to let that happen. Sometimes, I felt I could fall in love with her. But I knew that couldn't happen—at least while we were at the Folk School, with me as an administrator and her as a student. Still, I kept going off with her, partly out of affection and partly to ease my doubts about myself.

Security

MIDWAY THROUGH THE summer, we heard that a local group claimed we were a bunch of "communists" and "outsiders" who had come to Rose's Creek to introduce "socialist" programs. They threatened to root us out and planned to crash our Friday night bonfire. They had guns and meant business. Being targeted once again made Erling and me fearful that we had set up a program that endangered the students and faculty. We discussed ending the program, calling it quits. But Peggy told us that everyone supported us and no one would let them harm our program.

Erling took her advice and spoke with several members of the Folk School's board about it. They told him who it was and to confront them.

But they also said that this new threat came from a gang that had guns and clubs and committed serious assaults up and down the valley with anyone who crossed them. They'd even assaulted members of another baseball team that had beaten their squad.

Erling and I considered calling the police, but Peggy, Bonnie, and other board members told us that local police often secretly collaborated with federal agents, and many people in the hollow made a living or earned extra income by brewing moonshine.

Peggy downplayed our fears and assured us that everything would be all right. "We'll provide security," she said.

Friday night, as I was walking up the hill to set up the bonfire, I noticed Cecil Marlow, the biggest and most successful moonshiner in the hollow, on the side of the road.

I was in his debt. Last summer, he sold me a quart of moonshine, which I brought home to my father. He told me he loved the taste of it. He poured it into a shot glass, took a sip, and claimed it was the best shine he'd ever had. After we each took a couple of shots, I learned that during Prohibition, my dad drank a lot of moonshine in Ohio and even set up a small still himself. He patted me on the back and said, "Next summer, be sure to get some more," showing his implicit support for what I was doing.

Cecil's black 1967 Lincoln Continental, parked at the base of the hill, partially blocked the road. He was an enormous man, broad-shouldered and well over six feet tall, with white hair that was in stark contrast to his young, sturdy face. He wasn't someone you'd fool with.

I asked why he had parked his car on the side of the road.

He smiled and said, "Don't worry about tonight. Everything is going to be fine."

"What do you mean?" I asked.

He motioned for me to look in the back seat. A long baseball bat leaned against the seat.

"That should take care of them," he explained.

"I heard they have weapons," I interjected.

"Well, I wouldn't worry about that," he said, lifting his shirt to reveal a revolver. He took me by the arm and led me to the back of his car, flipping open the trunk. Inside, he had a range of rifles, some with clips attached. He told me that if our country were invaded, I should come straight here to Rose's Creek. There are more arms per capita than anywhere else in the United States.

"We could hold an army off for months," he claimed.

I didn't doubt it since, on most weekends, when they had dances at local bars, inevitably someone was wounded. Cecil was never involved in those altercations since he was well-respected and well-armed.

When I got to the top, Stephen, Adam, and Alicia, along with Jay, Bobby, and several other boys, had piled up wood in tepee-like fashion for the bonfire.

Erling was pacing back and forth.

"Worried about tonight?" I asked.

"Yes, who wouldn't be. It's one thing if they take a potshot at you like they did last year. But there'll be thirty or more of us tonight. Cars drive by all the—"

"Don't worry, we'll be—"

"Hey, don't tell me not to worry, I'm—"

I put my hand on his shoulder. "Let me finish, Erling." I told him about Cecil, who was parked down the road, being the only entry into the hollow.

Erling laughed. "Best moonshine in the hollow, they say."

"Best armory, too!"

Erling drove down the hill to thank Cecil. They drank moonshine while stopping each car to check its occupants. Erling was gone for almost an hour, and by the time he returned, he was in a good mood.

If anyone came into the hollow to threaten us that night, I never heard about it.

The following week, Erling and I found out the names of the boys who had made the threats, checked with the postmistress, found out where they lived, and drove fifteen miles to meet with them.

Erling acted like a career diplomat. He "calmed their fears" and, to my surprise, challenged them to play softball.

I told him they didn't take too kindly to losing a game.

Erling brushed me off. "It will be just a friendly game." He winked at me.

The wink bothered me. When it came to baseball, Erling was like a rabid beast, unstoppable. He'd do anything to win. And, if we won, I suspected that we'd have a real gunfight.

~

A group of young men from the hollow—Tommy, Bobby, and some of their friends, along with some of our staff—formed our team, which included eight guys and four women. I wasn't concerned about the women because Betty and Grace had played softball in college. Mandy could hit the ball hard. The professor was quick but uncoordinated. Dylan hated team sports. Adam could run, but that was about all.

Our opponents, all burly young men between eighteen and twenty-six years old, made us look tiny. When I shook hands with several players, I got my hand crushed.

Erling positioned us deep in the left and right fields, expecting our opponents to hit the ball a long way. And they did. He had a relay team ready to bring the long balls back to the infield. If the bombs went out of reach, he had players stationed every twenty feet to relay the ball and stop them from reaching third base. Erling pitched and knew how to spin and jig the ball so the batters couldn't get a smooth swing at it.

They hit enough home runs to keep them comfortably in the lead most of the game. I was relieved.

By the seventh inning, I suggested that we concede the game.

Erling wasn't willing to give up. He'd wagered a keg of beer on the game.

By the eighth inning, we were down three runs—13 to 10 because Betty, Adam, and Grace were quick and stole bases any time they got a hit. Erling had the shorter girl, Betty, come to bat and told her, "Don't go for a home run. Get on base."

When I came up to bat, the other team had their players deep in the outfield because I had hit a home run in the third inning. My line drive got me on first base. Stephen followed me and did the same. We batted one single after another, scoring three runs and taking the lead 14 to 13.

The next inning, their big hitters knocked balls over the tracks, putting them up by three.

Erling, unfazed, in the bottom of the ninth, had another plan. He wanted us to load the bases, leaving him the fourth batter up. A good hitter, Erling had swung from his heels and hit a home run, a double, and a triple in his last three at-bats. Their pitcher, a tall, lanky kid with a powerful arm and graceful athleticism, enjoyed winning just as much as Erling did. He planned to shut down our lineup quickly.

Grace, another short player, stepped up to the plate. Erling told her, "Crouch down as low as you can." She walked. Manny, not one to miss a good pitch, knocked one over the fence. Adam struck out. I hit a line drive for a single. Betty popped out. Stephen's long fly ball allowed me to reach second base.

With a flair for the dramatic, Erling took fierce practice swings like Babe Ruth. The outfielders backed up. On the first pitch, Erling made a mighty swing, catching himself with his hand before he fell over. On the second pitch, he swung again and missed. The infield moved back slightly in case he grabbed hold of a line drive. On the third swing, just as Erling planned, I took off as soon as the pitcher threw his pitch. Erling bunted the ball, dribbling it down the first baseline. The pitcher sprinted after it, hoping to make a quick throw for the final out. Erling ran past the ball, causing the pitcher to slow down to avoid him. When the pitcher grabbed the ball, Erling screamed "Ahhhhhhh." The pitcher, startled, looked up to see what was wrong and missed the ball. Erling dashed toward first base, his arms out at his sides. The pitcher threw past Erling's outstretched arms over the head of the first baseman. Meanwhile, Stephen and I crossed the plate with my hands raised in a victory salute.

The pitcher slammed his mitt on the ground and charged at Erling, shouting, "You fuckin' asshole, you can't—"

Erling held up his hands and said, "The victors must buy the keg."

What might have been a disaster turned into a celebration. He had already bought a keg, and once we opened it, Erling offered it to the other team. They became drinking buddies, and we played with them again at Clearfork Park, and despite Erling's scheming, we never won again.

The Invitation

ON HOT AFTERNOONS, the boys skinny-dipped in the basin below the falls. Local men often sat, watched, chatted, and joked about the nudity:

How we looked like we'd been chased out of a whorehouse. Some joined us. They'd strip off their shirts but keep their pants on. When they climbed out and sunned on the hillside, their wet pants clung to them like a snake's skin.

Jonathan, Bonnie's oldest son, who met me several times at Bonnie's house on nights I stayed for dinner or slept over, became a regular visitor.

Bonnie worried about him. "He takes too kindly to the drink," she said. "And not enough to work. His wife's the one who makes things work. Afraid he takes after his dad. Most of the time, he's up to no good."

One afternoon at the stream, he invited me to come with him to a good whorehouse. "They have really pretty girls there," he said. "None of your old biddies."

"Nope. Although I appreciate the offer," I replied. I learned that anything you did in these parts became common knowledge and visiting a whorehouse would be too risky.

"Hell, I wouldn't say a word. My wife don't even know. It'd be between you and me. I promise," he whispered.

His secrets were known to pretty much everyone. His wife, from what I heard, didn't care about his trysts: She hadn't much use for him.

I told him that I would love to do it and let off a little steam, but not tonight. The younger boys went off with Erik—he offered to drive them home. Jonathan told me, "Just you wait here. I'll be back in a spell."

"I need to head—"

"Just a spell, you hear?"

"All right."

I pulled on my jeans and sat by the stream, listening to it lapping over the rocks. The afternoon light glinted off the water. Adam paddled around in the water, off in his own world, imagining the positive ions radiating into his body.

Jonathan returned with a brown paper bag, a bottle—probably moonshine—and his cousin, Barry. He was a familiar face, a regular at the bonfires. A slim man with soft brown hair parted down the middle, he'd been married to Jonathan's wife. The marriage didn't last long. No hard feelings; it simply didn't work out. Rumors said he couldn't consummate the marriage.

"Since you don't want to take me up on the chance to meet some real sweet girls," Jonathan said, "at least join me for home brew. I'll show you the best way to drink it."

He took a big tomato out of the paper bag, sliced it in half with his pocketknife, and salted it—holding it up to me like an offering. With his other hand, he brought the bottle to his mouth and took a swig. Immediately, he bit into his tomato—one smooth, quick motion.

"That's the way to do it," he gasped, twitching his head back and forth. Barry followed suit, then passed me the sliced tomato and the moonshine, clear as the stream.

At first, I backed out because I was too nervous about embarrassing myself. However, Erling told me to take the night off and do whatever I wanted. Nothing was planned. Most Folk School members were hanging out at the house, playing guitars.

A little drink wouldn't hurt. I took the sliced tomato, sprinkled salt on it, and, as deftly as possible, took a bite, then took a swig. My ears popped. Eyes watered. Gasped and coughed.

Jonathan and Barry laughed.

"We make it strong," Jonathan said.

Barry patted me on the back. "There you go," he said. "You got it."

I had to admit that the tomato's acidity took the sting out of the alcohol. I had more tomatoes and took more swigs. Night balanced on the edge of the mountain. An hour, maybe longer, passed.

We went back to the Folk School and saw if anyone wanted to drive to the top of the mountain, where you could see the faint lights of Kentucky. Three girls—Maddy, Ingrid, and Alicia—joined us. Adam tagged along, too. They packed up hot dogs, potato chips, and soda.

Jonathan took me aside. "Sure you're not interested?"

"I'm sure."

"Well, much as I like picnics, I need to take care of business, if you know what I mean." He grabbed his crotch, stepped into his truck, and hit the accelerator. Dust roiled across the porch.

Adam, Alicia, and I jumped into Barry's jeep. The others followed us in Maddy's Chevy, an old, dented 1965 Impala.

At the top, we piled out, got the Coleman stove lit, and put on a pan to fry the hot dogs. Maddy pulled out her guitar, played Bob Dylan songs, "Blowin' in the Wind," "Mr. Tambourine Man," "Like a Rolling Stone," and "It Ain't Me, Babe," while our off-key voices occasionally blended in harmony.

Barry, Adam, the girls, and I foraged sticks and a dried-up log to start a campfire. Its embers emitted a gentle light.

Maddy's large, sweet face lit up as she stirred the coals and looked up at the stars, content in the moment, just as she went about her day—helping in the kitchen, sitting with the youngest children, teaching them crafts—without drawing attention to herself. I wish I knew her better.

Alicia, bending over the fire, stuffing in little sticks; it glowed on her face. She asked if I wanted to talk.

We strolled to a rock overlooking the ravine that ran along the road.

"What brought you up here?" she asked.

I was frank. "I hated my life: playing golf, going out to get drunk—"

"Like you are now," she jested, sliding her arm inside mine and pulling me close.

"Yeah, like now."

"Sorry, I couldn't resist," she said, leaning over on my shoulder. I put my hand on her shoulder and pulled her close.

I asked her, "What brought you here?"

"When you explained what we would be doing—working with mountain people, learning about folk traditions, and studying the American tradition—it seemed like an adventure, something I'd never have a chance to do again, so I jumped at it."

"I'm glad you came. You're the one girl I can talk to," I told her.

"Why is that?"

"Oh, I don't know. I feel awkward with girls," I admitted.

"I thought you did. You spend most of your time with the boys and Stephen, and, when you're all business, Erling."

"Is that weird?"

"No, most guys aren't really comfortable with girls." She looked up at my face and brushed back my hair.

I leaned over and kissed her lightly.

"Hey, what are you two lovebirds doing over there?" Barry called out. "You having an affair?"

He came over with a bag of potato chips. "Here, have some before Maddy and Adam eat them all." He dropped the bag in my lap.

I looked over at the campfire where Maddy and Adam were poking at it. Little sparks rose, wavered in the air, swirled around like fireflies, and went out. Ingrid was standing, her arms folded across her chest, gazing at the fire. With her blond hair flowing over her shoulders and down her back, she seemed to be made of moonglow.

"Beautiful, isn't she?" Alicia said.

"Amazing," I said. "Yet she wears it so naturally. It almost comes as much from inside as outside."

"When you get to know her, and I have these past weeks, you appreciate how unpretentious Swedes are, not caught up in appearances. Or so it seems from being with her. She's quite thoughtful."

"I wish I had more time to get to know her. By the time dinner is over and everyone has settled down, I'm heading up the hill to sleep. I don't get as much time as others to be with you at night in the house."

"Why not make more time?"

"I may."

"Always on guard, huh?"

"You got it."

"A loner, right?"

"Something like that."

"We should be getting back to the fire," Alicia said. Holding hands, we returned.

In that moment, as we walked back, I felt close to her. I should, as she suggested, spend more time at the cabin, just hanging out, rather than working, doing errands, going to the store, and preparing for classes. I hardly knew Ingrid, Alicia, Erik, Ellen, or Grace at all. I felt like an outsider whenever I arrived, as if I'd walked into the middle of a conversation and didn't know what to say.

Because our new quarters were so crowded, I had volunteered to sleep in the cabin. Stephen agreed to join me in case someone threatened me again, and as he admitted to me, because he was an introvert—he liked being by himself. We both missed the late-night socializing, sitting on the porch when locals came down, parked their cars, and played their guitars.

For the next week, after the spell on the mountain top, I spent time on the porch, singing along with everyone else, and grew fond of the regulars at the cabin. One was a local guitarist named Otrel who lived several miles away in another hollow, loved country music, played a mean guitar, and arrived before we ate supper. He always stayed most of the evening, and told stories about bears and raccoons, about the feds chasing moonshiners, and about endless feuds.

He was a gaunt man with a light spring in his step, and rarely sat still. He invited me to dinner several times. He had five kids—four of them living at home, one off in Vietnam.

On the hillside behind his house, we gathered buckets of blackberries that his wife turned into a thick preserve we spooned onto ice cream. On his porch, he talked about starting a band and how he would help me with the Folk School next year. He warned me about J.B. Terry, Squeaky's uncle, who came to the Folk School jam sessions but never said much, just chewed on a toothpick and spat on the ground—looking sullen.

"Trouble," was all Otrel said.

❧

That night, although I didn't know it, as I was sitting on a log by the fireside, looking over the valley below, and the faint lights of cabins off in the distance, I was about to have my own trouble.

Everyone—Adam, Peggy, Ingrid, and Alicia—seemed mesmerized by the way the sky, drawn closer to us on the mountaintop, pressed down on them, but they also wanted to head back to the Folk School since it was almost ten. Yet no one tried to get up. Too beautiful. Far off, the black outlines of mountain ranges stretched across the orange-tinted sky—the moon over the mountain and the stars close enough to touch.

Maddy, tired of strumming, poked at the fire. Silence settled in. The fire crackled and spat up sparks.

Barry turned on the radio. We could hear a Chicago radio station broadcast a Cubs game that traveled from Lake Michigan, far from the northwest of us, across Indiana and Kentucky to us—my hometown team.

Barry offered me another drink. I took a sip. Although I hadn't drunk for an hour, the amount I'd drunk before had begun to hit me. It made me feel woozy. I stood up to pee but lost my balance and stumbled against the front hood of the Jeep.

Alicia hurried to me. "You all right?"

"Perhaps too much so."

I held onto the jeep as if it were a tilting ship. She took me by the arm and steered me toward the woods.

Barry called out, "Might be better for me to do that. Let me help you." He swung quickly around the Jeep to where I was standing and put his arm around me. I slung my arm around his shoulder. We walked to a ledge. I tried to unzip my fly, but couldn't find the zipper.

He said, "Mind if I help?"

"No, go right ahead," I replied.

He unhitched the tab and pulled the zipper down.

I fumbled, trying to find my penis.

He asked again, "Need more help?"

"Help yourself," was as much as I could say.

He deftly opened the slit in my jockeys and fished out my penis.

"Steady as you go," he said as I leaned back and let out a long stream, the arch of it disappearing in the dark.

After I finished, he joined me. He found his zipper like a pro, even while holding me up, and peed like a racehorse.

At the campfire, Alicia put her arm around me and kissed me. "We need to go. Too late. Early morning," she said. "Be good." She hopped in the back seat of Maddy's car. Ingrid slid into the front seat beside Maddy, who waved at us. The red rear lights snaked down the mountain, dimmer and dimmer, and vanished around a curve.

Barry plied me with several more sips as we listened to the ball game. The Cubs were losing 6-5 in the ninth inning. I pressed my head onto my knees. My head felt as if someone had yanked part of it off.

I awoke to find myself in the jeep.

Adam had wandered off and was perched on a rock up the side of an incline. His silhouette looked like a scarecrow. He called out, "Hey, the girls have gone, time we get back."

Barry called back, "Hold your horses. We've got some serious drinking to do. Moonshine always tastes better when the moon shines overhead. You can touch it."

I must have passed out again because I woke up with Barry slapping me gently on the face. "Come on, don't be a spoilsport," he said. He offered me a tomato. I chomped into it. The juice dribbled down my chin.

The stars pressed down from the sky. I started counting the stars in one corner of the sky and got to 358 when Adam interrupted me.

"Jason, you're drunk and need to get off this mountain now." He used the same condescending tone as my father.

"Why don't you loosen up, Adam? Cool your heels. We've got some serious…" I raised the bottle in the air. "Have a drink."

"I don't drink," he glowered at me.

I took another swig and offered the bottle to him again.

"I said I don't drink."

"Oh, I forgot."

Adam whipped around and grabbed Barry by his shirt. "Listen to me. You got the assistant director drunk. You'd better get him back to school. I don't want to hear any excuses. We need to get off this mountain now."

"Yes, sir. We're getting ready to go," Barry said, saluting Adam. "Just get your big mouth in the Jeep."

Adam guided me to the front seat. He got into the back and said, "Hurry. It's late."

The road, mostly one lane, gripped the side of the mountain like a rope stitched around a tree trunk. On one side, the rock wall rose straight up and clear into the clouds; on the other, a ravine, hundreds of feet down, pines and saplings clinging to it.

The cool night air caressed my face.

Barry's jeep was humming along when it jagged, jerked, made a wheezing sound, coughed several more times, and sputtered to a stop. Barry pressed on the accelerator.

Nothing.

"What the hell is going on?" Adam called out.

Barry tapped the gas gauge and raised his shoulders. "Plum out of gas."

"Well, coast down," Adam implored.

"Not a good idea. No lights either."

Adam jumped out of the jeep. "I'll get some help. We can't stay here; some logging truck might hit us."

"Do many come this hour of the night?" I asked.

"Not likely. Some do, ones that want to get ahead of traffic," Barry said. "Don't worry. We'll see 'em coming. Might as well enjoy the pretty night. We can camp out here and get some help at sunrise."

"Are you nuts? I'm not risking my life," Adam cried out. With that said, he charged down the road, his head bobbing as he jogged. I had little doubt he could negotiate the four or five miles down the mountain. It would take some time. Who knows who he could scrape up at this hour of the night?

Barry brought out his bottle and toasted Adam. "Here's to Mr. Do-No-Wrong!"

❧

An hour passed. Rescuers never showed. We drank the last of the moonshine.

Barry asked, "It's chilly. Mind if I lie down?"

"By all means," I said. "Go ahead."

A long, angular man with no fat on his body, he leaned over, snuggled on the seat, near my thigh, his hands under his head. I patted him on the back and let my hand rest on his hip.

"Make yourself comfortable," I told him. "We are going to be here for a while, I suspect."

I stretched back in the seat and extended my legs. I lifted his head onto my lap and fell asleep.

The sky was punctured with lighted holes.

He shifted several times, turned on one side, then another, trying to get comfortable, and finally nestled into a somewhat comfortable position. But not long. His head rubbed one way and another.

I felt aroused, shifted my hips to the side.

He tilted his head. His cheek was against my erection. It felt good—his face against my crotch. Here I was with another guy, aroused when hours before I had felt close to Alicia, behaving like a guy should.

If I hadn't been so drunk, I would have gotten up and strode down the mountain.

I must have passed out again. When I awoke, I felt Barry's head on my lap, asleep. But he tilted his head up and then put his mouth right where my erection was sticking up. Ever so slightly, he moved his head back and forth. I put my hand on his head. His hand loosened my belt and unzipped my pants. He wasted no time and got right to it. He got my pants partially down and hooked his lips on my erection.

"You okay?" he asked, pausing.

A thin flicker of light darted back and forth in the trees. A vehicle is charging toward us.

"Shit. Lights!" I pushed him off me, pulled up my pants, buckled, and shifted upright in my seat to try to see what appeared to be a logging truck moving fast, with the headlights bobbing up and down.

Barry moaned, "Shucks, just when it gets interesting."

I shouted, "Let's get out of here!"

I hopped out of the jeep, stumbled, and fell to my knees. Although dizzy, I managed to stagger up the road to clear the jeep at the turnout and pressed against the side wall, hoping Barry would follow.

A logging truck would obliterate the jeep.

Barry scampered behind me on his hands and legs like a dog.

"Hurry up, it's coming fast!"

The lights barreling toward our jeep swung around the bend. I put my hands over my ears.

Nothing happened.

A large Ford truck with someone standing on the sideboard came around the curve and then stopped. Adam leapt out, followed by two figures—Bobby and Tommy Metzler. Tommy was holding a gas can.

"Mission impossible!" Tommy yelled at us. He poured gas into the jeep's tank. Bobby told Barry to get in the back of the Jeep. He hopped in the driver's seat. I sat in front.

He glanced at me. "You alright?" he asked.

"Fine."

"You don't look fine."

I admitted, "You're right. I'm out of it."

He said, "I can see that."

Bobby drove down the road. Tommy backed the truck up and reached a turnout where we could pass. Then, he moved the car back and forth and followed us. Four lights crisscrossed the trees. I closed my eyes. The jeep swayed and its engine moaned as we approached the bridge over the creek and headed up the hill to the log cabin.

Bobby held me up, brought me to the cabin, and stretched me out next to Stephen, who had opened my sleeping bag. Stephen took off my shoes and pants and stuffed me into the bag. He patted me on the head and said, "Go to sleep."

Bobby, kneeling beside me, held up my head and put the pillow under it. "Careful," Stephen said, "put his head down real easy."

Bobby asked, "Is he going to be all right?"

Stephen whispered, "He's not going to feel so good tomorrow. But he'll be fine. Thanks for taking care of him."

Bobby walked away. Barry asked where I was. He wanted to say goodnight. Tommy told him to get back in the jeep. A raised voice. A smack. Then the gears grinding. An engine loud, then fading, and soon as it slipped over the hillside, silence.

My hands were between my legs, where Barry had been. I turned on my back, felt my cheek where Alicia had kissed me, smiled, said "She loves me," and thought, but what kind of love is that when I can't even control the love inside myself?

The Conversation

SOMETIMES, ERLING WOULD join Stephen and me to sleep in the log cabin or outside on the ledge beside the cabin under the stars. With mostly women in the house and guitar music playing until eleven at night, he needed quiet time. We read by a kerosene lamp in the log cabin until the mosquitoes, beetles, and moths became so numerous that it was impossible to read.

When morning crested the hill, its rays muted by firs, and with Stephen asleep in a corner, his pillow pulled over his head, Erling sat up on his elbow next to me and said, "It's like old times."

I mused, "Yes. This is how it was every morning."

"That was a great year, not as crowded as this year. It had a more leisurely pace. I miss that."

I remembered how, after sunrise, we took turns washing, shaving, and brushing our teeth on the side stoop, looking out at the pasture down to the road and listening to the lull of the cars, each with its unique sound along the route. We'd spend several hours writing in our journals, chatting, and drinking coffee brewed on our kerosene burner. Unlike this year—with an infant mewling, guitars playing, and people chattering from dusk to dawn, Erling and I barely had time to talk to each other.

After folding up the sleeping bags, sitting on the porch and gazing at the scraggly trees and vines that wove through the hillside, I asked where he was going at the end of the summer since, as far as I knew, he had no place to call home.

He said, "Oh, I'll do a pilgrimage to Sandburg's house in Flat Rock, North Carolina. I'll also visit his birthplace in Galesburg, Illinois. I can visit you if you'd like."

"That would be fabulous," I said.

"That'll work out. From there, I suppose, I'll go back to Iowa and visit my mother. Nothing fixed. Just traveling." He asked what I was going to do when I got back. I told him that I would play some golf and visit with college friends.

A scowl creased his face.

"What?" I asked.

He stood, shifted his weight on the porch, and bit lightly on his cheek.

"I don't see how you can keep on going back there and calling it 'home.' Down here, do you hear them?" Erling said. "The people tell you to come back, to stay here with them because this is your home."

"It's lovely that they feel that way about me," I said. "But I've no job. No place to live."

"Bonnie or Peggy would put you up if you stayed. You know that."

"I suppose I do."

"So?" Erling asked.

"Not ready for that. Not yet."

Erling tapped my chest. "Not ready, huh? There's something I'd like you to explain to me: How can a guy raised in upper-middle-class America, within the capitalist economy, keep going home to a place tarnished by all its false values? I ask you, how are you going to live in that society and still manage to separate from its claims on you?"

"I don't know," I said.

"I can explain: You've never truly challenged their false ideals and tastes, and by avoiding that, you sidestep having to reject that world. I would think the very idea of playing golf would disgust you now. It's a game for the wealthy elite, a game for fat cats. They play it on the backs of the poor."

I knew that he didn't understand how complex golf was, because he'd never played it.

"I don't have to explain why I like golf. But if I did, and it sounds like I do, my reason is simple: I'm good at it. I enjoy the challenge. It's a demanding game. I work hard to play it well."

"If you were good at killing people at war, does that mean you should keep killing them when you leave the Army?"

I stood up. "That's not fair. We're not talking about murder here. You don't get it. When I play golf, I can do this solitary thing—hitting shots, seeing how many balls I can land close to the pin. For a while, I'm in my own world. I can let go of expectations of me—acting and looking nice.

I'm just a kid with a club, perfecting a move."

He laughed. "The quest for perfection is one of the last remnants of religion. Since we've abandoned the idea that we are flawed sinners and replaced it with a sentimental notion that all we need to do to be saved is strive for perfection, we can pretend religion doesn't matter. Look at yourself. Look at how you dress. Look at the luxury car you drive, a Volvo no less. You copied your elders, falling in line, conforming to some belief that doing something well excuses you from responsibility to those who suffer while you play," he told me. He tilted his head, peered over the edge of his glasses, and raised his eyebrows. "Right?"

What was I supposed to say? He had a point. I'd seen how the club's ground crew lived in near poverty. Many of them were alcoholics, perhaps their only consolation.

"I'm not giving up a game I love. Not now. Playing it doesn't make me into some monster. I'm getting pleasure, just as you do, going on your pilgrimages. And, besides, when you play baseball, you love it. Admit it. And you're good at it. What's the difference?"

He tried to interrupt me, but I went on. "For me, golf has kept me sane. I go into an altered state, a place of my own, where I can put aside the world. And that is not a bad thing."

He stood up, shook his head, picked up a stick, and broke it, tossing half of it aside. "To my ears, it sounds as if you use this private spot for yourself, separate from family, work, and friends as a way to escape," he said. "We all need that, I agree. That's why I come up here some nights. And, you're right, baseball does that for me. It's fine to indulge in occasional self-affirming activities in the pursuit of perfection. But where does it lead you?"

He turned back to me, drew a circle in the clay, and tapped it.

"Here's Jason Follett, the lawyer, a member of Glen Oak Country Club, part of the establishment with a charming wife and obedient children. His son is a star halfback on this fall's Oak Lawn High School team. Oh, he'll have a life outside of that where he writes poetry. He takes pride in a game he plays well. While he hits shots, he distances himself from the world. That works if you want to be an aesthetic writer, making pretty verses, but not if you want to write about larger moral issues."

He walked back to his sleeping bag, picked it up, and shrugged his shoulders. "We need to get back to the school. I need to prepare for our discussion of Eugene Debs. You might find it interesting."

I put my sleeping bag back in the log cabin. "I'll be there," I said, and added, "I hear you. It's just that you're asking me to change some things that are dear to me."

He turned and nodded. "I know. That's my job," he offered, smiling out of one side of his mouth. "I'm a gadfly in the ointment of complacency."

As he strode off, I woke Stephen, who was still asleep, his hair tousled from tossing and turning.

Materialist

DURING THE DISCUSSION about Debs and the labor movement, Dylan, who often sat across the room, moved next to me and asked if I enjoyed sleeping up on the hill. I told him it was fine unless it rained. When we took a coffee break, he asked if he could borrow my car, since Erling had asked him to run into Jellico to pick up some supplies.

"I do that," I said. "That's my job."

"Well, I also need to meet a friend who's coming into town," Dylan said.

"Sorry, it's not a rent-a-car."

"So the rich boy won't let anyone play with his toys," Dylan snarled.

"Right," I said. "You got it."

"Listen, I'm sorry. I didn't mean that. I would really like to see her. We're close, if you know what I mean, and she—"

"I'll think about it," I said.

Later, Erling asked if he could talk with me on the porch. "I heard you're not letting Dylan use your car."

"First of all, Erling, it's none of your business. And secondly, not really. I told him that I have to think about it. It's new. I don't know what kind of driver he is. And—"

Erling grabbed my arm forcefully. "Look," he said. "Remember what we were talking about this morning? It's time you let go. He needs your car. It's no big deal. Besides, all you've done this summer is ignore him. Why don't you give him a break?"

I pried his fingers off my arm. "I'll think about it. And as to why I avoid him, that's my business."

At lunch, I asked Dylan if he'd ever driven a stick shift. He said, "No problem."

"That's not what I asked," I said, staring at him.

His eyes shifted to the right. "Yeah, several times."

❧

When he came back later that day, he parked the car and tossed the keys to me. "Thanks," he said and strutted into the front door.

From the porch, I noticed a mark on the car's back panel. I inspected it. Dylan—or someone—had dented the car. A foot-long crease ran along the panel an inch deep.

"What the hell did you do to my car?" I yelled at Dylan, who was helping himself to a cup of coffee.

He laughed. "Took a curve a little too fast. That car has a lot of pep."

"Is that all you have to say?"

"Yeah, what's the big deal? It's only a scrape. I didn't wreck the car."

Before I knew it, I had him by the collar. "You little bastard," I shouted. "You will pay for it. Every cent."

He shoved my hand away from him. "Hey, cool it, man. I'm not paying a dime. You let me use it. I did—"

I pointed my finger at him. "You think you don't have any obligation to pay?"

He laughed again. "I'm a fuckin' student, man. I can barely afford to pay for my tuition. I'm not some rich dude like you—"

"Rich dude?"

"Right, Erling says you come from money."

"He does? That's interesting."

Erling heard the fracas and came into the room. "What's going on?"

Dylan stepped toward Erling and said, "He's all fuckin' uptight because his pretty car has a dent."

"A dent you caused," I said.

Erling looked at me and then at Dylan. "So what's the problem?"

In a whiny voice, Dylan said, "He wants me to pay for it!"

"You're damn right," I said.

Erling put his hands on his hips. "Let me see it."

We walked outside, and I pointed to the dent.

Erling groaned. "Jason, that's nothing. Hey, look at Mabel! She's got so many dents and bruises she looks as if she'd been in a roller derby."

"What are you saying?" I asked.

"I'm saying you need to let go of your materialism. It's no big deal."

"It's not a big deal that he—" I pointed to Dylan, who stood on the porch smirking. "That he isn't responsible?"

"He doesn't have the money—"

"Money, is it?" I said, barely able to control my temper. "It's okay to damage someone's car if he has the money. Isn't that, Erling, a bit of a contradiction? What if I didn't have the money and he did? Would he have to pay?"

Erling winced and said in a low voice, "But you do. And probably insurance, too."

"You're right, I do, and it's okay for you to use me to raise money for the program. Is that right?" My fists were clenched.

"Yes. But that's—"

"Yeah. That's the point, when it's convenient to you and Dylan. You..." I started to say something else, but stopped. I opened the car door and hopped in. There were two cigarette butts in the ashtray. Dylan didn't even ask if he could smoke.

I headed out of Rose's Creek on the main road, going nowhere in particular. The word "materialism" throbbed in my head.

Was I materialistic?

Sure, I was. But what was so bad about that? I respected people's property. It seemed to me that Dylan was no better than a coal company: he took my property, damaged it, and blamed me for being upset.

When I arrived in Jellico, I parked at a motel, paid for one night, and pulled out my journal. I wrote for hours, feeling a sea of doubts inside me. On one hand, I wanted to break away from my family and become someone different. But I had no idea who that person was. Perhaps I was too much like them, too materialistic. On the other hand, I valued my belongings: the record player, my books, golf clubs, clothes, and shoes. Maybe I was too focused on my appearance and how I presented myself. Still, I cared about others and respected what they had, even if it wasn't of the same quality as mine. I felt like driving away, getting as far from the hollow as possible, but I wondered where I would go and what I would do.

I had to go back to the Folk School. It was the closest thing to home that I had. But I had to let go of my rage. I wanted to punch that snotty, smug face of Dylan's, to tell Erling off, to let him know that he was dead wrong. Yet I wasn't so sure he wasn't right.

I walked to a local diner. A stocky waitress with a large, round face and a soft Southern drawl asked me, "What'll it be, hon?"

"Not sure," I said.

"You look like you need some good loving," she said.

"You're right about that," I said.

"Well, I can't offer you that. But I can get you some good food."

"That'll have to do," I said.

"We have a great burger here with everything on it—tomatoes, onion, cheese. And our fries—I swear they are the best in the state," she said. "How about it, hon?"

"You're persuasive," I said.

"What's that?"

"The burger it is, and fries, and whatever's on tap."

In the cool yellow light of the diner, I listened to customers chatting and watched the cook work behind a window, sweating and flipping burgers. My rage was doing nobody any good. I sipped the beer, and another, and put my fingers around the giant burger and lolled away an hour.

The waitress kept coming back. "How's it, hon?"

I told her, "Great," and it was.

"You look a mite better," she said. "That's what our burgers and fries do to ya!"

By the time I got back to the motel, my rage had cooled into a simmering frustration. I turned on the TV. All the buzz was about astronauts walking on the moon. No one mentioned Kent State. I had even managed to forget about it. I changed the channel. A Cary Grant movie was playing. He dodged an airplane. Most of the film, he was on the run, fleeing from some guys trying to kill him, much like I was running from mixed feelings.

The next day, I drove back to Rose's Creek.

Kids ran up to me, crying out, "Where were you?"

I said, "I don't know."

I didn't want to tell them about a strange place called rage. I passed the football and got involved in what mattered to me.

❧

Midweek, after dinner, when we all sat on the Folk School porch to play folk songs, Erling sat by me and said, "Glad you're back."

I nodded.

"I talked to several other people. They told me what Dylan said. I spoke to Dylan, too. He owes you something, and not just an apology," he said.

"We'll see," I said.

"I need you here. I count on you more than I can say," he said.

"Even though I'm a materialist?"

"I was wrong. I overstated my case," he said, pressing his lips together. "You had a point, and I respect it."

I didn't look at him. Several people had pulled up outside the house. They hopped out of their trucks, guitars and banjos in hand.

❧

Dylan spoke with me at the bonfire. He had talked to his parents. They may be able to cover some of the repairs. "They don't have much money," he said, not looking me in the eyes.

I kept my mouth shut.

"You expect me to pay, don't you?" he said and kicked something on the ground.

I didn't say a word.

"Fuck it," he said. "Just tell me what it is."

"Give me your phone and address," I said. "I'll let you know."

We shook hands, but I had no use for him. I'd become bitter, and my resentment toward him never quite left me.

More Bad News

AT OUR CAMPFIRES, Otrel and his band member, Bud Terry, called the folk dances. Bud would stand on a log and call the steps. His deep, gravelly voice carried well into the mountains around us. Then he'd join Otrel, and they'd do a medley. Not much of a looker, Otrel—often unshaven and swarthy—had uncommon charisma. He managed to keep his house on the mountain top together by doing odd jobs, by driving trucks across the country, and back home, by performing whenever he could. Give him his banjo or guitar, and he was a happy man. Talented and able to pick, strum, and play practically any song, his high-pitched nasal voice made every song a celebration. His thumbs, callused and dry, were split from fingering and strumming the strings, but people whooped and joined in whatever he played.

Every evening, Otrel joined Maddy's songfest on the porch of the Folk School. With new cowboy boots and a western shirt featuring gold buttons, he was pleased that his band had performed five shows and generated some good money. He spoke to me about coming to Nashville and securing a record deal.

After Dylan dented my car, I withdrew from the staff and spent many afternoons alone, spending fewer evenings on the porch listening to the music. Otrel sensed something was up with me and joked, "Come on, sourpuss. Sing a few bars."

He asked me to come over to his house—he had something else to discuss besides Nashville. Betsy, his wife, poured her blackberry preserves over bowls of ice cream. Otrel and I stood in the middle of the front room with the TV off by itself in the corner. The alabaster sky blended with the dusty earth: the grass, stiff and dried out, needed rain.

Before we finished the ice cream, from out of nowhere, a heavy rainstorm trampled the roof. When the rain stopped, his boys scrambled up an apple tree and picked ripe apples.

Otrel said, "Erling is worried about you."

"I imagine he is," I said, not letting on about my resentments.

"He needs you. We need you. You're too important to drop out now."

"Oh, Otrel, it's no big deal. Doesn't someone have a right to be upset?"

"About your car?"

"How'd you know?"

"Everybody's talking."

"I just—"

Otrel interrupted me. "You know what I'd have done, had it been me? I'd have punched the squirt in the nose."

I laughed. "I thought about it."

"You're too nice, that's your problem. You take things to heart."

"I suppose I do."

"Well, piss on 'em."

We sat on the front steps. He mentioned Bud Terry, the fiddler who consistently played at the campfires, and reminisced about the fun times they'd had playing at the Friday night bonfires and gigs around the state.

"You talk about him as if he were dead," I said.

"He is."

"What?"

"He died Wednesday," Otrel said.

"But he just played last Friday!"

"You know he was pretty sick."

"I knew he had the shakes."

"I told Betsy he'd not make it this time. His eyes were set back in their sockets. You notice?" Otrel asked.

"Can't say I did."

"They were, believe me. He shook sometimes like a headless chicken," Otrel continued. "He lost weight. Couldn't eat. He went to the hospital on Monday. What killed him was his stomach. It burst, folks say, from moonshine. Drank pretty near two quarts a day."

"I liked him. He let me shoot his pistol once. He made our bonfires something special." I tossed a pebble into a puddle. "Shit."

"He liked doing it. But folks called him a drunk. No one paid him much mind. He wasn't like his relations. That J.B. Terry is always out to get something. Bud never hurt no one. An alcoholic, I suppose. But he was a good man, too. Never an angry word from him. And he played a mean fiddle. I'll miss him. Won't you?"

I nodded. "Yes." I'd never seen him drunk. But I'd probably never seen him sober. He could talk, look you in the eye, and walk as steadily as a marine. His death wasn't unusual. Many men had lost their jobs, had little to do but make moonshine, and had filled their lives with drink and died quietly and young.

Before I left, Otrel shook my hand and said, "Now you and Erling need to mend your fences, hear me?"

I tried to pull my hand away. He held on. "Hear me?"

I smiled. "Okay. Okay."

"I weren't supposed to tell you," he said and pursed his lips.

"Tell me what?"

"Erling wants to move on."

"What!?"

"That's what he told me," he said. "So now you know why it's important that—"

"Christ! Why didn't he tell me?"

"You haven't been yourself lately, now have you?"

"Not exactly."

He smiled at me but then turned his head to the side and squinted, signaling that what he had told me was serious. "There, my job's done." He patted me on the back and handed me the quart of blackberry preserves. "Get back there. See that you talk with Mr. Duus!"

I intended to do just that. I was irate.

Why didn't he tell me about his plan?

Had he decided to have someone else run the school? It better not be Dylan. Why was he quitting? We've just gotten started.

I drove down the mountain, careful to slow at the switchbacks so I wouldn't spill the preserves on my car seat. I knew I needed to get over my anger and wondered what I'd do if Erling left. It would be a big change. If he wanted me to take over, I'd have to handle all the recruiting. But by next summer, I'd be finished with Divinity School and would need a salary, no longer relying on the church to pay my way.

The slow back and forth—taking a curve to the right, then to the left—made me pay attention to each turn and released tension in me. I kept thinking that nothing is as straightforward as it seems.

❧

Erling and I took the next day off and drove up to Cumberland Falls State Park, a place he loved and I had never been, to watch the water cascade over the rock ledge and fall to the pool below.

I told him what Otrel had told me.

"Sorry you got it indirectly," he said. "But let me say that if the Folk School is to continue, you're the man to keep it going."

"You want out?"

"I need to move on. Don't get me wrong. I think we've had a great two years. But I need to see if I can make it work somewhere else. I believe you'd be better off going it alone."

"I don't think I'm ready."

"Don't underestimate yourself. You've got what it takes. You've learned a lot in the last two years. Besides, I think you can find the funds better than I can."

"Materialistic, huh?"

"It has its merits."

"Glad to hear you say it."

"You were right. Dylan can be a stuck-up little bastard. But let's be done with that. We have more pressing issues at the moment. I need your help in making some hard decisions."

"Shoot away."

"It's this year's program. We're almost out of cash," he said, looking at the falls. He went on to explain that, due to the financial shortfall caused by the fire and the high cost of renting the house, we needed to close the Folk School in mid-August. He wanted to stay longer, as did others, but we couldn't afford to feed everyone. After a lengthy discussion, weighing the options, we decided to end it with a big campfire and cookout the following Friday. The next day, the students and staff would pack up and go home.

Erling and I would stay behind to plan for the following year.

&

The Folk School staff cooked all day: pies, macaroni, beans, corn, and squash from our garden, hamburgers, and hot dogs on the grill.

As cars filled with kids and their parents arrived, Erling gathered us for one last softball game. The kids, as usual, helped start the fire under Squeaky's watch: pour gasoline on it and watch it explode. After dark, beside the bonfire that lit up the sky, Otrel played his guitar. We sang, danced, and roasted marshmallows.

Throughout, a sadness hung over us because we knew that, come morning, we'd all pack up and go our separate ways. During the campfire, I sat beside Alicia, letting her know I would write and wanted to stay in touch, though when I thought about Ann, I wondered whether I should start a new relationship. She told me that, whatever happened, she had enjoyed herself, and her life, as she now saw it, would be different.

&

The last morning, early before everyone headed off, when Stephen woke up, he slipped out of his sleeping bag that was several feet from mine, pulled it over to mine, and lay on it.

"You awake?" he asked.

"Getting there."

Stretched out only a foot from me, with only his white briefs on, his body was tempting to look at, but, conscious of how I had violated his privacy, I averted my eyes. He propped himself on his elbow, stared at me, nothing hidden. I glanced at him again.

"You like to look at me," he said.

"Yeah."

"I figured. It's okay. I only wish I felt the same way. But I don't, and I'm sorry. It might have been nice."

He was looking right at me, not flinching. I didn't say anything.

"Hey," he said, amused. "You're a complex and different guy. I get it. I just wanted to thank you for inviting me here. I love the people. If you rerun this next year, I'm willing to come back. Might slip into your role. Not sure I'll ever think about where we were brought up—the suburbs—in the same way again." He reached over and pulled me close to him, holding me as I nestled into his neck, smelling his early morning musk. Then, he stood, dressed, and washed his face in a basin of water while I got up, dressed, and shaved.

"Thanks," I said. "That meant a lot. I mean your understanding. And I'm sorry."

"No sorry. I told you this has changed my life. All there is is 'thank you'."

He put his gear in his car, turned, gave me another hug, and headed to the Folk School to say his goodbyes to the others.

Cars pulled out onto the dirt road as the staff left, leaving the house empty, Erling and me the last ones to figure out how to make the program work without him.

Erling was right. People liked me, and I had a home in the mountains. Marie Cirillo, who was on the Folk School board, suggested an idea for funding next year that, if successful, could give me a salary and keep me there long-term. The Folk School board could apply to the federal government for a daycare grant. It would provide year-round childcare and fund a position that, if the board chose, I could apply for and, it seemed logical, secure. I could direct the Rose's Creek Daycare Program and, in the summer, run my own Folk School, gathering students and staff, including Stephen if he was interested, and Alicia, who I had no doubt would return. I needed to convince the other Folk School board members that it was a good idea and earn their approval.

On the last day, I drove around the hollow to say goodbye to everyone. I also helped clean up the house for the new tenants who would arrive a week after we left. We stored supplies in a shed at Peggy's house.

The Visitor

I SPENT THE REMAINDER of the summer at my parents' house. I worked in the yard, dividing my mom's iris beds, and, when I could get a tee-off time, played golf.

Erling promised to come by and spend a few days before I went back to Vanderbilt.

Returning home was a welcome relief. I could shower every day, swim in the pool, play golf, and read. Dad worked most days. My mother was busy with projects or her bridge club. I often had the house to myself. I even got an estimate to repair the car and sent a bill to Dylan. A check arrived a week later.

❧

I'd nearly forgotten that Erling planned to visit until I came home one day, and Mabel was parked beside the garage. Erling was stretched out under a maple, reading. My mother and I were on our way back from the grocery store.

"Who's that?" my mother asked.

"That's my friend Erling," I told her. "The one who started the Folk School." He was wearing an old, wrinkled white shirt, open at the neck, rolled up at the sleeves and old wrinkled white slacks.

After I pulled into our garage, I raced over to him. He roused himself from his spot under the tree, closed his book, and greeted me with an extended hand.

"Good to see you," he said and added, motioning to the yard with the long blacktop driveway. "It's what I expected."

"What do you mean?" I asked.

"Bourgeoisie," he said dryly. He curled up his mouth in a grimace.

I ignored. "Let me introduce you to Mom."

My mother, ever gracious, asked him to come in. She hoped he could stay for dinner. We were going to the club and she was sure that I would like to show it to him. He stood by, chatting and gazing at the cathedral ceiling in the living room and out to the back deck. I helped Mom put away the groceries.

She told us to get a drink and go downstairs to relax with Erling in the game room, where we had a billiard table. Erling loved to play pool. We played several games.

When my father came home, dressed in his blue suit, he came down to meet Erling. They eyed each other, noting the relative size and strength of their opponent. They chatted for a few minutes.

My father glowered at Erling's attire and said, "We're going to the club, Mr. Duus, and, well, we need to dress up. I would hope—"

I interrupted him, "I know, Dad, we need to dress up."

"Good. Coat and tie."

"Right," I said.

My dad went upstairs to have a martini. When he was a young executive, he went to the Mayo Clinic for a check-up and was advised by the doctors to have a martini every day upon returning home from work. He never failed to follow this advice.

I explained the martini ritual to Erling, who smiled, nodded, and said, "As expected." We played another game of pool, then, before we went to the club, I had Erling bring his suitcase —a wicker contraption tied together with rope —to my room. I told him that we really had to wear a coat and tie.

Dumbfounded, he looked at me. "Coat and tie?"

"Yes."

"To dinner?"

"Yes."

"What is this club?"

I explained that it was the Glen Oak Country Club. It had a full dining room, swimming pool, tennis courts, and an eighteen-hole golf course.

"Oh," he said. "'How the other half lives.'"

Erling pulled out a wrinkled white jacket, like the one Bogart wore

from Casablanca, but yellowed and frayed. I asked if he had better pants, and he did. Though cleaner, they were still wrinkled. He wore tennis shoes and no socks. I gave him a pair of socks and a tie with tiny yellow elephants, but he said that he never wore them. They caused him to choke. I showed him how to keep the top button open and still wear the tie.

He shrugged apologetically, "It's the best I can do." I nodded, realizing this was his only option, and helped him smooth out the jacket as best we could. With both of us now properly—if not perfectly—dressed, we headed downstairs to meet my parents.

When we came downstairs to greet my parents, who had finished two martinis, they stared aghast at Erling as if contemplating where to leave him off on the side of the road. I stood beside him in my blue blazer, red tie, brown slacks, and dress shoes.

❧

When we arrived at the front entrance of the club, just before my dad got out of the car, a senior valet opened his door, and two valets my age opened the doors for my mother and me. My dad left the keys in the ignition, and we went inside.

Erling whispered to me, "Aren't you allowed to open your own doors?"

I explained, "It's a service."

In the clubhouse, my parents went right past the Green Room, where on everyday occasions we stopped to chat with other members and even had another drink, then headed straight for the dining room. My father approached the maître d', who smiled and greeted us, "Good evening, Mr. Follett. May I help you?"

My father pulled him closer and whispered, pointing to a corner table.

The maître d' said, "Certainly, Mr. Follett. Come this way." We headed to the far corner where we'd never eaten before; my father generally enjoyed eating by the bay windows where he could watch any late golfers coming up to the eighteenth hole.

Over dinner, we batted polite conversation back and forth, talking about golf, how I'd finished second in the club championship, how lovely the summer had been, and how happy they were that I'd done some good work with the people in Appalachia.

To engage Erling, my parents asked him what his plans were for the rest of the summer.

It was a mistake.

He explained how he'd wander, planning to see Eugene Debs' home. He asked if they knew who he was. My father said that he'd certainly heard of him. Over salad and drinks, Erling explained how Debs was a labor organizer and socialist.

My father said, "Mr. Duus, if I recollect, I voted in those elections when he was a candidate. I can't say I thought much of his views."

"You didn't? May I ask—"

My dad shot me a dagger-like glance that I knew meant "change the topic." I did.

We discussed the Folk School, how well it had gone, and how we managed despite the fire. By the end of supper, I could tell that my parents had had enough of Erling, who could tell that discussing the poor, social class, and the inequities in society was off-limits—not something you mentioned at dinner, or, for that matter, anywhere.

After dessert, my parents suggested that I show Erling the clubhouse and golf course while they excused themselves to talk with some friends. I showed Erling the Oak Room, the exclusive men's room, with its wood-paneled walls, ceiling-high mirrors, and a wall-length mahogany bar stocked with every liquor imaginable on glass shelves behind it. There was a painting of the eighteenth green over the bar.

We ordered two more beers while Erling surveyed the scene—the men at the tables drinking and playing cards, the large bay windows showing the putting green and practice range beyond. I led him into the men's locker room through two swinging doors. For forty yards, on either side of the room, there were lockers, many with polished golf shoes in front of them and plaques bearing members' names.

Samuel, one of the attendants, greeted me. "Good evening, Mr. Follett, how are you?"

I greeted him and turned to Erling, "Sam, this is my friend Erling," and they shook hands.

"Can I do anything for you, sir?" he asked.

"No, I'm fine, just showing my friend around," I reassured him.

Erling sipped his beer and gestured to the long row of lockers and the white-tiled bathroom, "So this is where Mr. Jason Follett calls home."

"Well, yes, you're right. I do feel at home here. I've spent more time here than at home," I admitted.

"I suspect you would. Why people treat you as if you were important! That must be gratifying," he said, giving a sideward glance at me.

"Never thought much about it."

"No, I suspect you wouldn't," he said. He noted the wood paneling, the gold-plated faucets in the bathroom, cloth hand towels, hand lotion, a glass jar containing combs, and a bottle of aftershave. Every need was anticipated, every amenity there for the asking. He looked at a pair of shoes in front of the lockers. "Do these attendants shine your shoes?" he asked.

"Of course. Why do you ask?"

He stared at me. "Why don't you ask?"

"I don't get what you mean," I admitted. I looked around the room I'd been in hundreds of times since I was a little boy. I changed clothes here, took a shower after playing a round, and got dressed up to eat in the dining room. Sure, I knew that it was a privilege, but I also had long-standing attachments here.

"This whole place stinks of money, of privilege, and pampering," he said. "It's the conspicuous consumption, the inflated materialism, that leaves people who you and I know, those people in Rose's Creek, with nothing and people like your father and like you with everything you want just for the asking."

"That's not fair," I retorted. "My father didn't cause their poverty. You know as well as I do it was those mining companies, some of them British firms."

"But he's a part of the system, the larger system of greed that makes it possible for those companies, and ones like the one your father works for, to use the workers, to wring sweat and blood from them at the lowest wage. Then they reap the profits and build these palaces to their enormous egos," he said, swirling around, looking at the stained-glass windows, filtering in red and blue light.

I didn't know what to say. On one level, I agreed with him and resented how many club members acted as if they were better than everyone else. But that wasn't how my family behaved.

He spoke in a hushed tone. "Oh, I'm not blaming you, Jason. Not for this. This is amazing. I've never been in a place like this before. Yes, it would be nice to come in here and have an attendant say, 'Is there anything I could do for you, Mr. Duus?' calling me by my last name, while I call him, a man older than I am, by his first. But if I did accept it, and didn't question it, and went on living in this illusory world, I'd be fooling myself and betraying my own beliefs."

"Well, you don't have to because you're not a member here," I said. "We need to go."

I felt disappointed that he didn't like the club and angry that he was making me feel defensive about the club. Despite my misgivings about my background, I felt proud that I belonged, that people, yes, even attendants, recognized me, knew I was a good golfer, and that I was my father's son.

We walked out of the locker room, and the bartender called out to me. "Oh, Mr. Follett. Your father was looking for you. He wants to go."

I hurried into the lobby where my parents were chatting with the Johnsons. There was Hilda in her purple dress who eyed Erling and me, then turned back to finish her conversation with my parents.

Without bothering to acknowledge Erling, Mrs. Johnson said, "Nice to see you, Jason." She smiled weakly, took her husband's arm, and walked out to their car.

My dad went outside to hand his ticket to the valet, who ran off and retrieved the car. My father, a martini glass in his hand, had added another drink to an evening that, I suspected, he wanted to forget ever happened.

On the ride home, my father asked whether Erling enjoyed the meal and what he thought of the club. Erling said that the meal was fine, and the club was quite impressive. My dad nodded his head, pleased. Although I did not like to admit it, I felt as if I'd brought a rube to my high school prom and felt embarrassed.

I left Erling in the basement to play billiards with my father while I changed clothes. As I walked down the stairs, I could hear Erling in his calm, measured voice criticizing the business mentality, how corporations care little for individuals, and how profit drives them solely. My father was hunched over the table, cued up behind the white ball, not responding to Erling, who leaned against the paneled wall, arms folded, face scrunched up, gazing intensely at my father, waiting for a response and simultaneously sizing up the shot my father was about to make. My father executed one of his classic spin shots, which pocketed two balls, leaving him only one more to win the game. He stood and studied the table, then spoke to Erling without looking at him.

"You know, Mr. Duus," he said. "Who was it you called a capitalist? Did you say, 'the privileged class' when you were talking about me? Let me tell you, I had to work my way up. I understand what it's like to be poor. My father's restaurant went bankrupt during the depression. I worked as a clerk to pay for college. Oh, I had fun—spent more hours than I care to admit in a pool hall to pass the time. But I worked for next to nothing for years. Twenty dollars a week. Couldn't even afford a car."

Erling said, "I'm sure you did, Howard. That wasn't my point. What I was saying is that the economic system, as it is set up, creates a sub-class who do all the heavy lifting so that an elite class can enjoy it."

"Elite class, you say," my father said, mulling over the term.

I knew that my father didn't like anyone calling him "Howard" if they were younger. Earlier this summer, another friend of mine, a junior member, had played golf with my dad and me, and called out, "Hey, Howard, nice shot."

My father glared at him and said, "My name is 'Mr. Follett' to you."

My friend, startled by his steely tone, said, "Yes, sir," and never called him Howard again.

My father glanced at me, settled into his next shot, and smacked it into the pocket. He took his stick and handed it to me, "Your turn."

Without looking back at Erling, he said, "Nice to have met you, Mr. Duus." He headed up the stairs.

Erling had a puzzled smile on his face. "Well, your father plays a tough game of pool," he said.

"Did you win any?" I asked.

"I skunked him in the first game," he said, pleased with himself. "But then he got down to business. Based on our conversation, I think he'd just as soon cut my throat. I must hand it to him; he showed me a thing or two."

I wanted to find out what Erling had said because I knew my father would certainly tell me his side of the story.

Erling said, "We discussed inequities of the economic system. He made some points, good ones, but ones that confirmed his views and the narrow-mindedness of corporate leaders who only see the bottom line—profit." He shook his head and hung his pool stick on a hook on the wall.

"What's wrong?" I asked.

"To be frank," he said, "I'm shocked to see how much you feel at home here. I don't think that you are being honest with yourself. The question isn't whether you'll love and seek to understand your parents, but whether or not you will declare your independence."

"I have," I protested. "I have committed to working in Rose's Creek. I haven't taken a job here, as I could, in the business world like my brother."

Agitated and not wanting my parents to hear me argue with Erling, I said, "Let's go out for a beer."

⁂

We said goodbye to my parents and drove to a local bar, a quiet spot with booths and a few people. I told him that I had broken away from my parents, refusing to cut my hair as they wanted, not dressing exactly as they preferred, and not doing what they wanted by attending the Folk School for two summers.

"Yes, yes, you have taken some measured steps, but they are only half measures. What shocked me was how easy it is for you to blend into their world, how thoughtlessly you expect others to wait for you, even call you Mr. Follett. In my mind, you haven't even come close to making a real separation. You would rather go through hell than deny them. Yet, isn't it clear that all men who want to be their true selves must do so, must separate? With each year that passes, you are quickly approaching an age where it can no longer be done, and you will find yourself trapped."

"What do you want me to do, tell them off?" I shot back. I looked at my clenched fist. It surprised me. He glanced at it, too.

"Have another beer. Calm down. Let me explain. Just hear me out, okay? What I experienced in you was a near-paralysis of will around your parents, and you might see that as just an obedient and respectful son. But it seems much more than that. Of course, I know that you maintain an important measure of individualism." He took a sip of his beer. "Do you want to order some potato skins? Do they serve them here?"

"Sure."

He called the waitress over and ordered one item.

"I dip them in ketchup. Left over from my childhood. Now, where was I?"

"Individualism."

"Right. I think that's good: you're your own individual. I can see that, especially compared to your older brother, who has resigned himself completely to the expectations and values of your parents. But here is the thing: I found in the things your parents said to me a striking lack of respect for you. I could see little resemblance between the Jason I know and their own view of Jason. It's not just that they don't understand you, but that they are unable or unwilling—I'm not sure which—to see you as a person separate from their perspective. Do you hear what I'm saying?

"Yes," I said. "Sort of."

"Here's how I see it: they judge you by your ability or inability to accept and be at ease with their world. And so—this is hard to say—your mother sighs tolerantly and says, 'Oh, Jason has so many things to learn,' while your father self-righteously upbraids you for the language you use at the dinner table. That they can do this so confidently shows that you have not made a break with them. They are unaware of any rebellion."

"What am I supposed to do? Tell them to get fucked? I'm not going to do that."

I glanced over at the counter behind the bar. Our potato skins were sitting there. I tried to catch the waitress's eye. My fist clenched again.

"They've paid for my schooling," I said. "I do have some obligations to them. And that they don't understand who I am, yes, it frustrates me. But I don't know that there's anything I can do about it. They see the world through their lenses and only their lenses. I do too. So, quite frankly, I don't know what more I need to do to break with them."

The waitress brought the potato skins with dipping sauce, but Erling asked for ketchup.

Erling followed up my question, "I broke from my father, and, yes, it was difficult and painful on both our sides, as I imagine yours will be, but now I'm treated with respect, and instead of his world imposing on my world, my world imposes itself on my father. He has come to know who I am. I was about your age when this finally happened."

I drank some beer, cooling my mouth after eating several spicier potato skins.

"I don't know how I would start. I just don't—"

He interrupted me. "Jason, it's not just what you say. It's about what you want them to say about you. You do know, don't you, what you want? Tell them."

"I'm not sure I know."

"That's important to understand because the character of this independence is that it cannot happen just internally. It requires outward expressions. The authority of the father over his son, especially a father like yours who is so successful and aware of his success, must be openly and outwardly challenged, or it will stay in place. There's no way you can avoid confronting him or yourself."

I leaned on the table and looked at him. "You make it sound inevitable. I'm not sure it is. At least not for me. My parents have their reality. I have mine. How is it that I'm going to change their life? It's so all-encompassing. You don't know. Its demands literally possess them: going to this party, that party, this meeting, that meeting, traveling to Portugal and Hong Kong, and being caught up in all the demands of their lives. Even if I tried to make an outward break, they probably wouldn't notice. And, well, I'm still beholden to them right now financially. I never told you, but they made a sizable contribution to the church's funding of the Folk School, and, on the side, provided me with a living allowance. I won't have a real job until we get that grant for the daycare."

Erling dipped a potato skin in the ketchup. "You should try this," he said. "Nothing better."

I poured ketchup on my plate and tried one. I preferred mayonnaise and went back to dipping them in it.

"If that's how you see it, you seem resigned to living as you do. But remember, having a job is a choice you make. Not making a clean break outwardly, you are pushed inward into a psychological struggle and inner rebellion that play out in your soul. As a result, you suffer, while others only see the public mask you wear and assume you are okay, which is what you're doing now. You can keep an inner life that belongs solely to you. However, there's also an outer life, which can influence your inner world. Sure, you can be like Wallace Stevens, whom you admire, and focus on outward appearances of success—being a well-paid corporate lawyer for an insurance company. To most of his colleagues, he was just a lawyer, not a poet. This wasn't unusual since they didn't care about art. He led a compartmentalized life. While he was a poet pursuing an aesthetic life, he also lived in a different reality—the corporate world—which was unrelated and meaningless to his artistic pursuits. He separated his outer life from his inner one.He dabbled in poetry on the way to work and at home. Due to his immense genius as a poet, he managed to balance this split life rather well and successfully. You could follow his example, but I'm not sure you have his genius. Or you can move toward a compelling view of reality that calls forth your whole life and effort."

"I like his work," I said. "It's amazing that he could live in those two worlds. But I agree. I'm not sure I could do it."

The discussion revealed something I didn't want to tell him—my own duality about my sexual life, feeling one way at one moment and completely different at another. Instead, I said, "It's nice to know that it's possible to be possessed by one reality and still live in another."

Erling held up a potato skin and pointed it at me.

"I cannot believe that you really mean it when you speak of reality as something to possess. When you speak of it in terms of this man's reality and that man's reality, that would, of course, be convenient; but is it truly what's going on?"

"For me it is," I said, thinking about how I felt about Alicia and how I responded to Barry.

Erling's voice rose and tugged me back from my reverie.

"I don't buy your premise about reality. For me, reality possesses us to the extent that we live close to it, and that must be the case for you, me, Mr. Stevens, or an Alabama sharecropper, or Mr. Howard Follett, Vice President of some corporation."

I drank my beer, not looking at him, my brain stuffed with too many thoughts I didn't want to have, least of all talk about with Erling. We ordered another beer and finished the potato skins.

"Listen, Jason." He reached across the table and tapped my hand. "The problem is serious and demanding. Very demanding. It's maybe your misfortune that your parents have been so loving and lovable, and that your dad is so confident in his authority and his right to decide what's best for you. They've given you enough freedom to grow intellectually, but you have to do the hard part: rebel. Your existential freedom seems to be seriously limited to me."

He shrugged his shoulders. I must have looked distressed because he then said, "It's not the end of the world. You don't have to do anything. There are plenty of people who would give their eyeteeth to have what you have."

I told him I wanted to change, but now wasn't the right time.

"And one other thing," he said. "It's not good news."

"What?"

"It's never the right time."

We paid, and he asked me where the nearest river was—where I used to go ice skating—and where, in the summer, when I was in elementary school, a friend and I used to take his boat to an island on the river and pretend we were Native Americans, living as though we had no obligations and could be free, running around half-naked.

We walked down to the river and sat on a wooden bench.

"When I'm not sure what to do with my life," he said, "I go to a river and watch it. Look at it. It moves gently through these trees, finding its way. Oh, the Army Corps of Engineers may try to force some rivers to bend to their will, but, in the end, rivers make their own way. They don't take any prescribed path. They meander. My life is like that. I go where I can find my way, which is, by analogy, to say you don't have to live as your parents think you should live."

The water's surface shimmered with flecks of light that danced on the current as it swirled around some rocks. The moon skated over the water, seemingly suspended and still.

What Erling had said about my parents was true. Their love had demands built into it. Maybe his bringing me here was his way of saying that I would, as he had, find my way as the river does. We sat quietly for an hour, then walked upstream where I pointed out several islands where I had spent one summer, and to the inlets where two kids had fallen through the ice and drowned.

When we got back to the car, I said, "Thanks."

He looked at me and winked. He stayed the night, left early the next morning, well before my parents awoke, and headed to Terre Haute, Indiana, to the grave of Eugene Debs.

❧

Before he left, Erling shook my hand. "Glad I had a chance to meet your parents. Let's stay in touch as you make plans for next year's Folk School. I'll be in North Carolina at the Joseph Campbell Folk School. You're invited to come any time. And if you ever want to go there," he said. "Debs is buried in the Highland Lawn Cemetery in Terre Haute."

"I may just do that."

Mabel left the driveway, turned right, and disappeared.

❧

When my parents woke up, they didn't mention him, but asked what I planned to do. I told them I was going to the club to hit some balls and maybe find a game. My dad, dressed in his suit, seemed remote and ate his cereal quietly, paging through the financial section of the Chicago Tribune. I could almost hear him thinking, "What in the world drew Jason to such a man?" I took the sports section and went out on the porch. As I read, a cardinal flitted from a lilac bush, and my old friend the squirrel, leaping from limb to limb, stopped on one limb and peered down at me.

"I know, I know," I said. "You want me to try it. I imagine Erling has been talking to you. Just be patient. I'm not ready yet."

❧

The following evening, my dad talked about Erling, told me he was worried that I hung around a person like that and had become his disciple.

"He's an angry man, not at all at home in this world," he said. "I don't understand, son, what you see in him."

I tried to explain, but ended up being tongue-tied, spouting platitudes that didn't reflect my indebtedness to Erling.

"I can tell you," Dad said. "I'm not willing to support your working with him for another summer. He's not a stable person."

"I'm not," I told him. "I'm writing a grant and plan to start a daycare program."

"That's a relief," he said. "I found him..." he searched for the right words, "...very misguided." He paused again. "And a very arrogant young man."

I went to my room and wrote.

Dear Dad,

After speaking with you tonight, I thought it was appropriate to lay down a credo and, at least theoretically, explain my relationship to Erling Duus, which is essential to me. But I need to start by making it clear that I am by no means a 'disciple', as you called it, of his.

First, Erling is an excellent teacher. Until I met him, I was very unfamiliar with the American intellectual tradition, especially that of Ralph Waldo Emerson, Willa Cather, Black Elk, Thomas Wolfe, Carl Sandburg, and Walt Whitman. Erling was the catalyst that made me read them. He has dedicated his life to studying these visionaries, particularly Whitman, whom he considers an American prophet.

Unfortunately, he cannot tolerate the economic and social disparities between the wealthy and the poor. He distrusts wealthy people because they represent the inequality in our society. For him, you, as an executive in the corporate world, are a threat to his ego. If he could argue with you and win with his arguments, he'd feel that he had defeated at least one corporate power. I didn't expect him to try to do that with you. I was disappointed when I walked into the basement and saw him completely twisting some of his thoughts to upset you. I later asked him why he did it.

He said that he had to express his contempt for our way of life. It was a moral issue. He told me I shouldn't live the way I do, but that I should give it up. I asked him what I should do and where I should go, if not here with you. He never could figure out where I should go or what I should be. I told him that his judgment was indeed correct—there are inequalities—but that I had to affirm, not deny, my own life. If I were ever to address those wrongs and work to change some small part of them, I'd have to choose to do that in my own way. Since that conversation, I have split with Erling.

I wrote this to appease my dad. If I were done with Erling, it would make the rest of the summer better for both my dad and me.

I learned a lot from his knowledge of literature, but I also realized that I have my own life. I saw that some wrongs are not just the fault of individual men but are the result of failed generations and distorted values that caused injustices no one meant to create. I know that you are a good, smart man and…

I broke off writing. It wasn't any use. My dad would grow more incensed that I had anything to do with someone who opposed capitalism. Even worse, he'd be enraged that someone was pitting a son against his father. I folded it up and stuck it in my journal.

I never discussed Erling again with my parents. It was as if he had never visited our house. Our life went on as usual. I played golf with my dad in a father-and-son tournament. We finished second, our best result since I was a teenager. I worked at the club helping the pro, went to dinner at the club, sat at our usual table in the middle of the room by the window overlooking the eighteenth green, talked about golf, the world I was used to, the world I couldn't seem to leave behind.

What Erling said felt like a dark splinter under my skin. He was right. Yet, for the time being, I had no idea how to break away or what, if I didn't belong here in their world, I could ever call home.

VI

What might have been and what has been
Point to one end, which is always present.

—"Four Quartets," T.S. Eliot

He understood that men were forever strangers to one another, that no one ever comes really to know anyone, that imprisoned in the dark womb of our mother, we come to life without having seen her face, that we are given to her arms a stranger, and that, caught in the insoluble prison of being, we escape never, no matter what arms may clasp us, what mouth may kiss us, what heart may warm us.

—Thomas Wolfe, *Look Homeward Angel*

Big Plans

I RETURNED TO SCHOOL and started classes, and saw Ann once before she left on her way to a lucrative advertising position with Gillette in New Haven. I promised to write and to visit, but when I kissed her at the airport, it was as if she'd permanently left, and, no matter how hard I tried, I might never get her back.

On Marie's advice, I began applying for a grant to establish a daycare program in Rose's Creek and to explain the grant's purpose to the Folk School board so that they could write letters of support.

My idea was that our Folk Center—the log cabin we built the previous summer—would be renovated to meet state daycare center guidelines. Several men agreed to insulate the cabin and install running water. We would also tear down the old Metzler house, which had level ground, to create space for a fenced-in playground. With a daycare center, mothers could work and help supplement their husbands' income. During the summer, if I could manage it, Folk School students could supervise daycare, as we had done in previous summers, while also studying American literature.

Helen Goya, who worked for the Department of Human Services, assisted me in writing a grant application. We also did fundraising in the hollow, with a Thanksgiving turkey shoot.

I'd brought enough prizes to make it worthwhile. We advertised at the local stores. We had eleven turkeys, ten hams, and six chickens as prizes. We raised $208.85.

The board—which included Peggy, Bonnie, Cecil, Marie, Greta (a mother with five young children), James, J.B. Terry, who expressed interest in the project, and Otrel—met to discuss next year's program. I reviewed how the grant could provide us with up to $60,000.00 to start the program, as long as we follow the federal guidelines.

J.B. had questions about the board's obligations—did they have to do anything? I told him that the board merely had to approve what I'd written.

"That's all you need us to do?" he asked.

"Well, yes. You need to approve the grant application. You will also have a representative hiring staff and monitoring the program."

J.B. nodded his head and offered a smile that didn't quite look like a smile, but more like the kind of expression someone gives right before they pull out a revolver to shoot you. I hoped Otrel would keep J.B. in check as we discussed building a rifle range on the property, a continuation of the crafts programs, and the Folk School in the summer. Everyone was excited about the possibilitiesand the three staff members that we'd hired from Rose's Creek if the proposal were accepted. I headed back to Nashville to write.

❧

Ninety-degree heat with eighty percent humidity had walloped Nashville. Based on Helen's suggestion, I met Linda Stone, who had a degree in early childhood education and might be interested in working on the grant.

"Sure. Sounds interesting. Why don't you come over?" she said.

Her third-floor apartment, hot and perfumed with the sweet smell of marijuana, had three guys lounging on her sofa, stoned. Chicago's third album played over and over.

I want to be free
I want to be free
I want to be free of all hurt
Free of all pain

"Want a hit?" she asked and passed me a joint as I joined the other three on the couch. She squeezed in next to me. With her hair parted down the middle and tiny wire-rimmed glasses, she looked like a female John Lennon. She didn't introduce me to the others, but I managed to pick up their names on my own.

Heat permeated her apartment. If anyone moved, sweat poured off their body. Linda filled our glasses with cold lemonade. Bill, a philosophy major with the body of a wrestler, suggested that we fill the bathtub with ice and take turns sitting in it.

I went to the grocery store and bought eight bags of ice to fill the tub. Linda slipped out of her clothes and hopped into the tub. Her eyes widened as she sank in inch by inch. Bill took off his shorts and shirt. Once Linda was out of the tub, he quickly got in after her. I followed Bill, and Jack, a short, stocky guy who played guitar, followed me.

For a few hours, we alternately cooled off and sat in the living room, smoking and listening to the traffic outside the window, and hoping for a breeze. No use. We got back in the tub.

Once the numbness from the cold water wore off, my skin tingled as if someone had tickled it. Soon, I started to sweat and spent several days alternating between the icy bathtub and lounging around, still going to class and returning. I was beginning to feel lazy and almost forgot how much needed to be done to finish the paperwork for the grant, as I enjoyed the relaxed atmosphere of her place and was nearly caught in a web of lassitude, and didn't bother, except to get my clothes and books, to go back to the dorm. It was as if I had finally gotten off my busy train and encamped in an apartment of indifference.

Linda used early childhood education language to write learning objectives. I wrote up the history of the Folk School and the property we had bought, along with the cabin that would serve as the daycare center.

Moonlight

ONE LONG WEEKEND late in October, I drove to Rose's Creek to stay with Bonnie and her kids. Her sons loved to play wiffle ball and football, and swim in the creek with me, and Bonnie felt close to me because I had saved the life of one of her children. The youngest, Jesse, nearly drowned one day the previous summer. He was paddling from one side of the swimming hole to another when his head dropped like a stone underwater. For several seconds, everyone waited for him to emerge.

"Where'd he go?" Bobby asked.

"Ah, he's playing around," Dylan said. "He'll come up."

I sensed something was wrong. He didn't dive under like someone who knew how to swim. I jumped in, grabbed his limp body from the bottom, dragged him to shore, and gave him mouth-to-mouth resuscitation. He coughed up water and regained consciousness quickly. Word spread, and Bonnie felt grateful to me.

❧

About a quarter of a mile into the hollow, a narrow lane followed a small creek to her house. I dimmed the lights and parked the car. The hum of tires on pavement still echoed in my ears. Snow fell lightly. One lightbulb hanging from a tree cast a damp reflection on their truck. I walked toward it. The stillness surprised me after leaving Nashville. A dog growled. The house, perched on a ledge up a steep incline and surrounded by pines, had the soft glow of moonlight on its porch.

I ascended the stairs, careful not to slip on the snow. The dog scampered off the porch into a stack of wood under the beech tree. Bonnie opened the door, welcomed me, and pointed at the couch. After I took off my jacket, she offered me a cup of coffee. She had brewed a pot just in case.

She eased herself into a large chair. We sat in front of a black-and-white image of a television program—some sitcom—which we ignored.

On some nights, when I came to visit, her family sat around the woodstove. Her family—all boys, Jesse, her youngest, Jay, a pre-teen, and Tyler, her eldest—sat in a semicircle, ignoring the TV, and told stories. Some about Shady John and his feuds with the Witcombs up the road. Some were about city boys at school who knew nothing about hunting and fishing. But this evening the boys were asleep.

Our conversation fluctuated between storytelling and concerns about the daycare program grant. I read her the preliminary applications. She liked what I'd written but wasn't sure everyone would. I planned to meet with the board the next day to go over the application.

She smoked four or five cigarettes while we talked, lighting each new one from the remains of the last. She recounted the time she had a rattlesnake in the kitchen that struck and bit her while she was reaching into the cupboard.

I asked her, "What did you do?"

She laughed and said, "Why, I killed it, of course! Wrung its neck." Instead of going to a doctor, she cut the bite, sucked it, and spat out the venom. For a few days, she didn't feel so good, a bit nauseated, but she'd been bitten before, so her body was used to it. She fried that snake up. Made a pretty good supper.

An hour later, we'd grown tired, and she told me to sleep in the bed on the left. "That's where Jay sleeps. He sleeps so sound, nothing can wake him," she said. While she prepared something in the kitchen, I slipped off my pants and shirt and slipped into bed.

Bedtime has always surprised me. Just like at Peggy's house, everyone respected each other's privacy there. Earlier in the summer, she told me I'd be sleeping with the boys. The three of them showed me the beds, two against the wall. I wasn't sure what to do. There were no changing rooms to undress in. I watched them. They slipped off their pants and shirts, folded them over a chair, and hurried under the covers. Tyler and Jesse went to the bed on the right, and Jay went to the bed on the left. I slipped off my pants and shirt, leaving on my T-shirt and jockey shorts, and flopped down next to Jay. He rustled and settled in, his small body with gangly arms and legs pulled in close to keep warm.

On this night, I whispered, "It's me, Jay. I'm staying over." He craned his head without moving his shoulders, offered a wan smile, and snuggled, as he did with his brothers, near me. I smelled his tobacco breath, pungent and sweet. His hair had a musty odor, the smell of clay and bark. He'd probably been helping his brothers cut wood for winter. The charcoal smell of the potbellied stove wafted through the cool night air. Tyler and Jesse groaned.

The cool lemon light from the kerosene lamp cast a faint glow from the other room where Bonnie changed into her nightgown, crawled into bed, and put the lamp out. The soft breathing of the boys pervaded the room, a lazy rhythm that grew quieter as a deeper sleep overtook them. Before I could fall asleep, Jay shoved his hand into my face, his little fingers brushing against my cheek.

My brother and I used to squirm in bed, fighting for the middle spot. I chuckled to myself. It was as if Jay, used to staking claim on his nighttime territory, unconsciously set his boundaries with a quick right to my head. Soon, he fell back asleep. I tossed and turned several times. My nose and toes were freezing. I pulled my head under the blanket. Jay scooted next to me, spooning his body into mine to get warm.

I looked across to Tyler and Jesse. They had crawled together, gathering heat from one another as the stove cooled, making the best of this small home, the beds.

Their futures wouldn't come easily. They'd have to prove themselves in a school system that considered them hillbillies, excelling academically or athletically, to find a niche outside the hollow.

Erling was right about me. I had become used to living a life where I believed people would take care of me and treat me as if I were important. I never questioned this. When I wanted to play a round of golf, I would pick up my shoes in the dressing room, retrieve my cleaned clubs from the pro shop, and walk to the tee. I expected the pro to make small talk with me and send me off to play as if I owned the course. I'd play as long as I wanted, hitting two or three shots a hole—being a member, one of the elite.

But here in Bonnie's house, I was also accepted as one of the family. I felt as comfortable here as in the Oak Room. They liked me, not because of who my father was, but for who I was with them.

Two worlds. Two homes. Two choices: the privileged life or this new life. I felt like a man holding onto a limb for fear of falling, unaware that he was standing firmly on the ground but unable to let go of the free golf at his father's expense, even as he longed to build a life separate from his work in Appalachia. Voices of Erling, Ann, my parents, and Will crowded my mind, replaying what I'd told them and wondering if I was acting, never quite sure of who I was.

I slipped out of bed, tiptoed to the kitchen, sat at a table by the woodstove, and looked out the window. After everyone had gone to sleep, the snow-covered ground, its shadows, and stillness became otherworldly in its timelessness—a feeling that, even as I looked at the scene, I was also not there. As I gazed out at the peaceful landscape, it was as if I could also look inward and quiet my thoughts. The snow was easing up; it had come early. Hours like these were perfect for introverts, while extroverts were asleep. Alone at the table, moonlight illuminating my journal, I felt more like myself than I did during the day—more present and whole.

For a moment, I was off the ambition train. I let my thoughts rest. Soon enough, my thoughts would be consumed with what must be done in the days and weeks ahead.

If the daycare project didn't work out or if we didn't get the grant, I could move on and find another job. My dad was right about work. I needed to have a job. He wanted me to be successful so I could keep living the good life I'd been used to, just like his other son. But these children sleeping beside me would struggle to find jobs that could support them. Their closeness eased their struggle—they snuggled close on cold nights—but such intimacy couldn't stop the accusations and obstacles they faced.

When I went back to bed, Jay held onto me. His embrace soothed me; sleep came easily.

The morning light filtered through the cracks in the walls. The frying pan sizzled with the smell of bacon. I lifted Jay's arm, and for a second, he opened his eyes and smiled at me before turning over and pulling the covers over his shoulder. I went to the kitchen and pulled out a chair by the stove. Tyler and Jesse sat nearby. Most of the snow had already melted.

They looked at me.

"Welcome home," they said like one of my kin. We sipped coffee and talked about school and the latest row at the dance. That's when I heard that Randy Hatfield—a blond boy who wanted to be the first in his family to go to college, whom I'd encouraged to keep working hard (because I saw a spark of keen intelligence in him) to keep his grades up—had been shot at the dance. It was bad: he lost his leg. But that wasn't all. When I saw him later in the day, he'd lost his ambition to go to college and seemed morose, dejected, acting as if his now being a cripple meant all his dreams were crippled too.

His story weighed on me as I met with the board. I told the board that I wanted a program that would give kids like Randy a better chance. They approved the preliminary application and agreed to meet again once I had completed it.

Mixed

WITH THE END OF the semester quickly approaching, Ann called me to ask if I would visit her in Connecticut during spring break. I wrote her a letter to share my ambivalence about any long-term commitment. I still felt close to her and, more than any other woman, felt safe with her sexually. I feared that if I kept seeing her, I'd fall so deeply in love that I'd want to marry her. I wasn't ready for that, not yet.

My parents, who had met her twice, liked her. Sweet and polite, she made it easy, knew how to carry on a conversation, defer to elders, and smile when she needed to do so. I spelled out my mixed emotions. I liked it that she got on so well, but I worried that if she did, that would only further incline me to avoid breaking with them, and fall in line, following her lead.

Dear Ann,

I'm not sure I can tell you this face-to-face, so I'll let you know in writing.

I have mentioned before that I need freedom. I must be able to go wherever I need to, whenever I need to. I feel like a sailor leaving the land he loves for the sea. But unlike that sailor, I have no distant port I'm headed for. I only have the promise of what might be.

What does this all mean?

I must be free of any long-term commitments. That is blunt. But it is true.

I do want to see you. I'm still in love with you. It's just that I'm confused. I need to sort out who I am before I commit to you. I don't want to disappoint you.

I'm planning to make a trip to Greenwich Village to see Father Flye, a priest. He's invited me to meet with him to discuss James Agee. My graduate thesis is on Agee's vision of tenant farmers as complex, authentic human beings. I'm excited to meet him.

We've talked on the phone. After seeing him, I'll drive up to New Haven. I really look forward to being with you.

Let me say I did and still do love you. I say this because, like it or not, I love you more than any woman I've known. But, because I cannot settle down, we can no longer go on as we did. We need to figure out, if you are willing, what our future will be.

It's much easier to say this on paper than to say it to your lovely face. My ability to set boundaries comes in waves. A large part of me resists letting go. I can feel your skin against mine. It's as if we're one.

For now, I speak of our lasting relationship, not as it was before, but as what we make of it.

I'm afraid the fault is in me. My heart is split. I must find the cause. I don't want to leave you with only half of my heart. I want you to have my whole heart.

Your friends Jay and Carol, who had us over to their house several nights last year, were right. You should have listened when they told you how I wasn't good for you.

Those who have never loved, or who have loved but never experienced heartbreak, cannot understand the pain I feel. There are no rings to return, no pins to unclip, just a word: "unsure." It's as if dark clouds hover over me.

You understood how I need freedom. Before, I said, "I must be free in a certain way. But the present is good. We have each other, and that is enough." Now I say, "I must be free. The present demands it. So, we must separate more than you would like." This is not "breaking up." I never liked that term. There is part of you that will never be separate from me. It will remain a part of me no matter where I go.

I'm afraid I've not been good to you. I have, however, been honest. You needn't read anything between my sighs. Let me know if I can visit. I say this with

Love, Jason

Ann agreed to meet with me. She wasn't happy with my letter and told me so, but she was willing to hear me out, to understand why I needed distance.

❧

I drove the same roads my mother traveled every summer when I was a kid, heading to Long Island to visit her parents and her brother. I found the correct tunnel, turned onto the right street, and parked two streets from

19 Perry Street, Father Flye's address. He had corresponded with Agee throughout his life more than anyone else and, including Agee's wives, knew him longest and best.

I was standing in the same Greenwich Village where the Stonewall riots took place. A tall man with long hair and the same stride as Will hustled across the street. If it were Will, what would he say? Probably keep on walking. I wouldn't blame him.

19 Perry Street was a four-story brownstone with six steps leading to a large black door. I pressed the apartment's three buttons. Footsteps hurried down the stairs.

A little man greeted me, his white hair sticking out as if an electrical current had just surged through him. He made a quick gesture with his hand.

"Come in, come in," he said. He wasted no time with introductions but took me by the arm. "You must be Jason. Yes? Good. Good. Now come on." He pointed up the stairs. "Two more flights. Be there in no time. I must tell you," he said, shaking his head, "I believe there are two types of people, don't you know. There are those who are concerned with material things."

We had reached the first floor. The staircase, narrow and dark, had a single bulb hanging from the ceiling.

"And there are those who are more concerned with spiritual things, the life of the mind," he said as we came to the second landing. "Now, I'm one of those who is more concerned with spiritual things," he said as he opened the door of his apartment.

Scattered on the chairs, the shelves, and the floor were piles of books and newspapers. Some piles looked as if they might topple over at any minute.

"Come in, come in," he said. His words came out in quick, scattered bursts, as if, had he not spoken them, they would spill out and escape on their own. He picked up a bunch of newspapers from a large brown wingback chair and, leaning over, carefully stacked them on top of another pile of newspapers on the floor. The kitchen, to the right, had books stacked in the sink, on top of the refrigerator, and on a small table. His reading tastes were eclectic: theology, literature, current events, poetry, and science.

"There you are." He motioned at the chair. "Sit down, my boy. It's so nice to meet you. I enjoyed your letter very much. Yes. Very much."

Being in his presence, knowing that he had known James Agee and, after teaching him in high school, how he had followed Agee's career throughout his life, overwhelmed me. Tongue-tied and nervous I'd say something stupid, not living up to the brilliant and expansive mind of Agee, I managed to say, "It's nice to be here. Thank you for taking the time."

"Oh, no. Thank you for coming all this way. Would you like some tea?"

"Sure."

He went into the kitchen, pushed the books aside, pulled out two cups, put a kettle on the stove, and came back. "Now, where were we?"

His hands clasped together in his lap, he leaned forward. Clad in his Episcopal priest's attire, with white collar, black jacket, and matching trousers that were too long, the cuffs covering his shoes, he was almost too much to absorb. His intense gaze made me flinch. I began to perspire and wiped the sweat from my forehead.

"Are you all right, my boy?" he asked. The kettle screeched. He pattered to the kitchen, talking over his shoulder at me. "Don't mind me. I'm always in a rush, it seems. Never enough time, you know."

Once he passed me the tea, he settled back on a couch, piled newspapers in one corner so he could sit on the other side. "Now, tell me, what do you find most interesting about Jim?"

I was not sure how to reply. I offered him ill-formed thoughts about my thesis on the imagination, explaining how, if he were an anthropologist, he could delve into the lives of the tenant farmers by immersing himself in their lives and conducting a clinical analysis of their plight. But he engaged with them as an artist and, most of all, a human being, becoming part of their family and absorbing their daily rituals, as well as their nighttime goodnights. As I started to speak, he held up his hand. "Now, would you mind if I recorded this?"

He pulled out a reel-to-reel recorder, tested it, and pressed the record button. The tape recorder made me even more self-conscious. I told him I thought Agee had seen more humanity in the tenant farmers than anyone else. He entered their lives so deeply that their daily struggles became, in a sense, his struggles, but even more so, how their struggles made them larger than life—far grander than people who live in mansions.

I asked him what he thought caused Agee's untimely death at forty-three. My question distressed him. He bent his head, rubbed his forehead, and repeated in an anguished tone of someone who had just lost a loved one, "I don't know. I don't know."

I changed the topic and asked if he had any recordings of Agee speaking.

"Why, yes, I do," he said. "He had a beautiful voice, rich and deep with a slight southern lilt. Here, let me play you a recording I have. Jim was as fascinated with the tape recorder, new back then, as he was with film, how it captured an image, made it, as it were, eternal."

He played Agee reading the Lord's Prayer and several poems. His voice, calm and measured, brought Agee into the room. Father Flye's face changed as he listened. His eyes crinkled up, and his thin lips curved up in a wistful smile.

"Lovely. Lovely. Isn't it? That was Jim. He made words come alive, almost sing. You know he played the piano. Had a wonderful singing voice. Much talent…" he sighed.

There was a knock on the door. A young Asian teenager came in. Father Flye stood up and motioned for him to enter. The boy carried several books under his arm. "This is Vinh. He's a student of mine. Wonderful writer," he said.

I stood and introduced myself.

He bowed.

"Be right with you," Father Flye said to Vinh, then turned to me. "He comes every day. We read together. Then he writes. Quite extraordinary."

From his enthusiasm for Vinh, I saw what the shy, fatherless, teenage Agee saw in him. Father Flye championed Agee, encouraged him, and, even when Agee's life went off track—failed marriages, dead-end movie projects, drunken nights, and a heart attack—stood by him, believing he had a calling. After Agee's death, Flye was his tireless advocate, published a book of letters, and, as he told me, had his voice recordings compiled into an album.

The student glanced our way, then perched on a chair and opened his book. Worried that I was taking up his time, I suggested that maybe I should leave.

Father Flye walked down the stairs with me. "Is there anything else you need?" he said as he opened the door. I thought how I'd love to sit for an afternoon with him to hear him recount more stories of Agee. But he'd given me enough.

"No, I'm fine. I really appreciate your taking the time."

"Time is the one thing we're all given," he said. He patted me on the arm. "We just have to take care how we use it."

I stepped into the street and saw a sign for Christopher Street, the one Will mentioned, and here I was, wondering if he was down one street in some apartment, and where, if I had said something that night, I might have been here too. Heavy traffic sped up one street; horns blared; pedestrians scurried across an intersection, darting past cars. Along the side streets, old, stunted maples shaded the sidewalk. It was a village—a mix of big city and small town—where other artists, later in their lives, like William Carlos Williams and Willa Cather, also lived. It was a place I might want to live. But for now, it frightened me. Too many avant-garde people, part of the fringe, and dangerous to someone like me.

Men walked arm in arm down the street. I must have stared, because a man passing by me asked, "You have a problem?"

∾

New Haven, only a couple of hours away, according to my map, is where I was headed. Northeast.

Ann's apartment complex, ensconced in a stand of majestic oaks on a ridge, was a new development. Three-storied brick homes with long driveways lined the street up to her apartment.

She shared a room with another woman who had a man's name, Sam, and exuded a masculine aura when she greeted me at the door, scanning me from head to foot and grunting as if convinced that what she'd heard about me from Ann was confirmed by the impression I made in the doorway.

Ann, quick to break the tension, offered me coffee and suggested we sit down. Ann and I sat on the couch in the living room. Sam squirreled herself in an armchair, her cup clasped between her hands.

"So what brings you east?" Sam asked.

"To see Ann," I responded.

"I thought that was secondary," Sam shot back.

I smirked at her. "I did visit Father Flye, a friend of a writer I know," I said. "Why aren't you honest?" Sam snapped.

I sipped my coffee and turned to Ann. "What do you say we go for a

walk?" Sam caught Ann's attention, shaking her head, which, in turn, immobilized Ann.

Sam pursued her inquisition. "Why don't you answer my question?"

I blew the steam off the coffee and stood up. "It seems like there are lovely views up here, perched, as you are, on a hill. Can you show me around?"

Ann stirred, leaning forward as I reached out to take her hand. Her fingers touched mine, but didn't close.

Ann turned to Sam. "Do you mind?"

Sam laughed. "Ann, you can do what you want."

"We'll be back in a bit."

"Yeah," Sam intoned, her thin lips turned down, scowling at me.

Once outside, Ann took me by the arm. "Let's go over there," she said, pointing to a pathway through the trees. The path went upward through broken light from the sway of leaves dancing in the sky.

"She read your letter," Ann said.

"What?"

"It was accidental. I left it on the kitchen table."

"That's great," I said, pulling away from her. "She had no—"

"She's a good friend."

"She's a creep."

Ann stopped. "You didn't have to come."

"I wanted to. I still love you."

"Really?"

"Really."

"You shouldn't send letters like that," she said and walked off, following the path to an open field atop a hill. I watched her go. Her body, strong yet soft, moved with the grace of a fine racehorse. Her brown hair, draped over her shoulder, caught the sun and shone with a glistening light. Quite beautiful.

I hurried after her.

"Ann," I said as I caught up with her. "I've been the creep. She's right. I'm sorry. It's just—"

She put her finger to my mouth, tapping it. "Shush. Let's just walk. It's lovely up here. You'll like it."

ɷ

After dinner at the Golden Wok and plenty of wine, the rapport we had at Vanderbilt came flooding back. She talked about how tough it can be to promote products that pressure consumers to buy the latest and greatest razor, even though their current one probably does the job just fine. "We always have to find the right sales pitch," she said, "to convince them that what they're using is outdated. What's new is always better—that's corporate philosophy. What is infuriating is that they know 33% of their products are mechanically no good, yet they still sell them. It seems everything about the consumer and what they want is so meticulously researched that it's nearly impossible for anyone to resist buying them. It makes me sick."

"That makes no sense," I said. "I use the same razor I've had for years."

"Profit," she said. "That's what drives it. New product, more sales. Higher price. Cheaper labor. It's tough. We focus on selling more and finding new markets. There's a strong desire for consumption, and a need to figure out how to encourage Americans to want more of it. That's what's frustrating to me. But I kinda like the work itself. It's fast-paced. The staff is smart. It pays very well. I'm going to buy a horse. Get back to riding."

"I'd love to see you ride!"

"I'm in another world. It's like profit and greed and 'hurry-up and do this and that' all recede. Would you like to go for a ride with me?"

"Wish I could. However, I do need to return to Nashville—grants to write. Classes. Papers to do. You know the routine."

"I remember. I miss academic life —the challenge of thinking deeply about ideas. People here don't seem to think. Yet they seem so happy and content. Sometimes I think that maybe ignorance is bliss, and I'll try that for a while—of course, to no avail."

"Can you quit?"

"No, not now. I keep thinking that somewhere there will be a thread of honesty and beauty, and I keep searching for that," she said, rubbing my hand between hers.

"Don't you feel as if you're compromising yourself?"

"I hope not. I must admit I'm still confused about what I'm doing. A few weeks ago, I thought I was having a mental breakdown because all I did was work late, come home, and read. I still don't know whether I want to go to graduate school, keep this job, or what to do," she said. She let go of my hand and scooted back. "But one funny thing." She laughed, putting her hand to her lips. "I met a man from Survey and Research in our company who knew your dad."

"Really?!"

"Yeah. And listen to this. You wouldn't have believed it. He started talking about the Vietnam War and came up with the brilliant idea that we shouldn't end it because all those boys would be brought home and there'd be a great rise in unemployment."

"Asshole."

"A big one. I told him I'd rather work to reorganize or redistribute the economy and industry, than have friends and family killed," she said. "But not him. That's the type of people I have to work with."

"Why don't you come down this summer, if just for a week or so, and meet the people in Rose's Creek. They're not like that. They're decent people."

"I'd like to. However, I'm still unsure what I'm looking for. It's like that quote you sent me about going nowhere rapidly, half-frightened that you'll reach some place and know it's wrong but not know enough to stop. Remember? Who said that?"

I was puzzled for a moment. "It might have been Rilke. Or maybe Camus."

"Anyway, I thought a lot about it and think it calls us to seek that which challenges us. For now, I want to cultivate the seeker, not the sought. I don't need another destination. I need to explore what I have here and see if I can do it well before jumping into something else. See what I mean?"

"Sure, I get it. I wish I had the same tenacity. But I don't."

"Jason, you'll figure it out. Be patient."

She curled up next to me, letting me hold her in my arms, her head pressed against my neck. I admired how she embraced living with uncertainty while staying focused on her work and remaining open to other possibilities.

After we came back to the apartment, Sam, who had stepped out to do some shopping, came in, paused briefly, and asked, "You're still here?"

"It's okay," Ann said. She kissed me on the cheek.

With a shrug, Sam said, "Catch you in the morning."

In the morning, after we made love, the light from the window covered us like a sheet. I felt complete. Her naked body coiled, leg over leg, around me. My cock nestled against her belly. She traced her fingers across my chest, circled my nipples, and down the narrow furry line to my belly. I cupped my hands on her breast, feeling its soft yet firm swelling. Her lips touched mine. The thick smell of love emanated from our bodies.

I wondered why I questioned my love for her. She caressed my chest and belly. I became aroused again. She slid back and I entered her again, slow and deliberate, feeling the light shining through the window embraced us.

We showered and dressed late that morning.

Sam sat at the kitchen table. "Well, here are the early birds," she said. "And he's still here!"

"Sam," Ann said. "It's fine, really."

"Well, lovebirds, I've fixed you French toast and bacon, just to show there are no hard feelings," she said.

Ann reached over and hugged her. "My special friend," she said.

I offered, "Thanks."

She smiled at me, the first time since I'd walked in the door. "Dig in," she said.

Warmed in a pan, the maple syrup perfumed the room.

Sam asked me about my plans. I told her about the daycare application and the Folk School. She wished me well and went off on an errand. Ann and I had the rest of the day together. I stayed one more night, making love again.

As I packed to leave, Ann sat on the bed, her legs folded under her. "I hate to ask," she said. "But where do we stand?"

"I love you," I said.

"I love you, too," she said, smiling softly. "But—"

"I know. You want me to say something and…" I couldn't bear to let her down.

She came across the bed, stared at me, took me in her arms, and kissed me. "When you can," she said. "When you can."

I kissed her goodbye again and again, tears streaming down my face, feeling as if the tug of my heart would tear me apart. She stood by the car, stepped back, and waved. I knew that what I felt for her was unlike anything I had ever experienced. It was real. Wise, compassionate, and honest, she felt like a soul mate. Yet I was heading back to Nashville, leaving her behind, and I wondered what, if anything, would bring me back to her.

"When you can," she'd said as if she knew nothing was set in stone.

I turned onto Interstate 95 and headed southwest. Well into the night, I pulled up at Linda's apartment. She let me curl up on the couch to sleep the few hours before dawn.

Grants and Strings

LINDA AND I MET WITH Helen, the regional director of the Department of Human Services, who helped us write the proposal. She had grown up in eastern Tennessee and wanted a good program up there. She knew from her own life the urgent need for better services. She suggested ways to improve the grant's chances of approval, including using statistics and a narrative that describes the region's poverty. Linda and Helen found unemployment stats for the Clearfork area. I wrote some descriptions of the local people and surroundings. Helen reviewed the grant application. It had good statistics and clear goals, but it lacked a better picture of the people and community, as well as a compelling narrative and descriptions to make it more relatable. Could we add some quotations? More vivid descriptions of poverty? The struggles of the people?

I added descriptions of Bonnie's house and included quotes from some people I'd heard during the summer. One man said, "Now don't just go off and forget about us." I described how Bobby, his shirt unbuttoned, greeted me with a handshake, and Peggy invited me in for breakfast. Linda added facts about the average annual incomes, the lack of health care, the incidence of mental retardation—all elements of the general poverty in the region. We filled out multiple forms and contacted local schools to find out how many students qualified for free lunch, which helped boost the grant's credibility. I made some notes and extrapolated from them, based on kids I knew who were struggling in school, like Squeaky, who'd gotten into trouble with the law, and other kids who had been suspended for various reasons, along with Randy, the boy who had been shot, and how he'd lost interest in college.

Helen read the next draft, shook her head. "Give me more numbers."

By the last draft, the picture we painted didn't look pretty, but it was what the grant required, and it would, if approved, funnel a substantial pool of money for the community. With Helen's thumbs-up, we planned to submit the grant application in May. I had had the board review the general concept of the daycare program and figured more approval for the application was unnecessary.

I put my energy back into completing my Agee thesis and several other papers. I also contacted students at Depauw and Vanderbilt who had expressed interest in attending the summer Folk School. I spent my free time with Linda, who visited Rose's Creek several times. We planned how to advertise and hire staff. She agreed to work as co-director of the program.

We invited a gospel choir to perform at the Folk School in early May and raised $60.00, which was added to the two thousand I had been promised by Mr. Hook to pay my salary for the summer, and which we could use as in-kind monies for the grant.

I showed the completed grant application to Bonnie, asking her to review it before I presented it to the entire board, and, if possible, share it with Peggy. I felt certain that we could build on what Marie Cirillo had started years ago: providing hope for a community that had lost its sense of hope and offering mothers the opportunity to work while we cared for their children. Bonnie looked at the grant and squinted, "Mighty big."

"Sorry. Federal applications require you to document everything. I mean everything."

"I'll give it a look."

~

A few weeks later, during final exams, Cecil Marlow, who had joined the board because he had several preschool grandchildren and liked the idea of the grant, called me. There was trouble. He claimed rumors were being spread. Several mothers—he wouldn't name them—said they saw a list with names of those who were "mentally retarded." It frightened them. I told him the application had no names attached. I'd included statistics and mentioned the difficulties some students faced in regional schools. Still, those details were part of the narrative, not connected to the statistics we gathered from local and state agencies. He told me I should get back to the hollow. They called a board meeting and elected J.B. Terry as chairman.

"J.B.? How the hell did he get the grant application?" I asked.

"Bonnie gave it to him. Seems he heard she had it."

"Shit."

The previous summer, J.B. had been released from prison, spent hours on the Folk School's front porch listening to impromptu jam sessions, but always seemed suspicious of what was happening. I had never spent time with him. I'd worried that he was more interested in Ingrid than in the program. Otrel had warned me about him.

Cecil told me that J.B. read to other board members a page that talked about "mental health." He claimed that I was saying mountain people were "mentally retarded." I knew the exact page he was referring to, the one where Helen suggested that we include more numbers.

At the meeting with J.B. as chair, the board voted to oppose any proposal that mentioned mental retardation. They also voted that any proposal had to be read by all the board members. In addition, they voted that Erling, not me, be asked to run the Folk School. What was it Otrel said?

Trouble.

"They're after your hide, Jason," Cecil said. "J.B. has them on the warpath."

That evening, I drove up to J.B.'s house. I wanted to go over his concerns, page by page, before the Board Meeting. I felt I could explain what the terms meant. Having driven from western Tennessee all the way across the state, I didn't arrive until 9:30, but I decided to see if he was up.

The air was heavy, and a thick fog rolled up from the valley onto the road. When I pulled into his driveway, my headlights illuminated J.B.'s front porch. I turned them off to avoid disturbing anyone and walked up to the porch. The gray glow from the TV lit up the interior, allowing me to see Karen, J.B.'s teenage daughter, and Squeaky cuddling on the couch. His legs were stretched out. They were startled by the dark figure on the front porch and sat upright quickly. Karen stood, adjusted her skirt, and stepped out of the front room, her arm resting on the door jamb.

"What you want?" she asked in a petulant tone.

"Wondered if your dad is up," I said.

"Nope. Went to bed a long time ago."

"Shit," I muttered and added, "sorry to bother you."

She leaned forward, straightening her blouse, softened her expression, and murmured, "Come in."

Behind her, Squeaky was adjusting his pants, tucking in his shirt, and buckling his belt.

I said, "Hi, Squeaky." He nodded in my direction. When my back was to him, he sat in a chair, closer to the TV, slumping low and motionless.

I gave her a copy of the latest revised grant application. I clarified the meaning of the term "mental health" in it and removed any references to people in the grant. I kept the narrative unchanged, but with those deletions, I worried I might not be able to convince the granting agency of the urgent need of the mothers in the region.

"This is the final copy," I told Karen. "Please show it to your dad so he can look it over before the board meeting."

She flipped through it. "You write this?" she asked.

"Mostly."

"A lot of words," she said.

"Yeah. There are."

Before I left, Squeaky got up and whispered something in her ear. She bit her lip, turned back to me, and asked, "You mind giving Squeaky a ride?"

"No problem," I said.

Squeaky kissed her. He held her by the waist, pulled her toward him, then hopped off the porch and caught up with me.

"Hey, I appreciate it, man," he said.

I told him not to worry. Glad to help. Once off the porch, he peed by the side of the driveway as I started the engine and turned the heater up. After he opened the door and sat down, the heat blasted across him, and I sensed a musty smell, like mushrooms.

His rump low in the seat, he said nothing. I put the Volvo in gear, then, sniffing again, recognized the smell: semen.

He looked over the instrument panel of the car. The red backup lights illuminated the narrow strip of gravel that curved down to the road.

"Cool car, man," he observed.

"I like it. It's safe and has a good repair record."

He nodded his head. We drove down the hollow, down along the dark curves in the road. Dust boiled up and mixed with a rolling fog.

I asked how he was doing. He sighed. "Hey, a good night, man, really good, if you know what I mean."

I did know. I could smell it.

We drove in silence. His silence came, I imagined, from the afterglow of his pleasure; mine from worry about the next day and what, if anything, J.B. would say. I pulled into his driveway.

He hopped out. "You take care," I said, leaning over the door.

"Hey, J.B., he's some riled up. Thought you should know."

"I do," I said. "Thanks."

Marie had invited me to stay overnight at her place. She'd left the door open, so I could use the guest bedroom. I settled into bed, but didn't sleep much, spending hours going over the grant and mentally highlighting sections I knew might cause controversy.

❧

The next morning, Marie and I drove up to the Folk School cabin. She told me Otrel couldn't make it; he was on the road. She warned me that she hadn't seen people as aggravated as this since the Folk School burned down. She agreed to do what she could at the meeting but advised me to hear them out before defending the grant.

A new wooden floor and three new windows had been installed in the log cabin. Folding chairs were arranged in a circle. I greeted Peggy and Bonnie when they arrived. They simply said, "Hi," and sat down. The only person who greeted me with some enthusiasm was Cecil. He wrapped his arms around me and whispered in my ear, "Don't worry." I tried to make small talk, asking about Jay and Bobby, and the girls. But Peggy and Bonnie only offered a polite, "They're fine."

With a new shirt buttoned at the neck, new pants, and shoes shined, J.B. strutted into the room. He greeted everyone except me. He didn't look well; his eyes had deep circles underneath them. His back was hunched, as if he had spent hours under a car hood. He sat in a chair opposite mine.

After everyone had taken their seats, he asked Freda, the secretary, to read the minutes of the last meeting. She said that the board had received a yellow and blue paper with a list of children labeled "mental health" or "mental retardation." She held it up and shook it. I wanted to contradict her, but I followed Marie's advice and listened. Freda was furious. Her son's name was on the list. Others had seen it too; no one was happy. The board denied the application and asked that whoever wrote the grant should explain why there was such a list.

Others shook their heads and looked in my direction.

I let her finish reading the minutes, then raised my hand.

J.B. nodded.

I assured them that I had indeed written the proposal. However, none of it involved mental retardation. It was a childcare proposal that required us to fill out all the forms and compile statistics the state had about the region. I listed families whose children would benefit from the childcare program, but those names had nothing to do with mental retardation. They just happened to match the state statistics.

JB turned to me, "So you admit that you filled in the form?"

"I had to. It was required," I retorted. "But that was one page. Did you read the rest of the proposal?"

"As a matter of fact, I did," he said. He sat upright and turned to a page. "You talk about us as if we're some no-good, ignorant people. Listen here." He flipped to another page. "You say we don't button our shirts." He lifted his hand to his neck to show me that, indeed, he did button his. "And you say we live in poverty." He flipped to another page. "And here you have statistics that prove we live in poverty." He looked up. "I don't like what you're saying about us. You make us sound like we're no good." He slapped the grant. "I think you're a two-faced liar. That's what I think. And, to boot, you have this director of the program and his assistant making a pretty penny. You're making a big salary so you can drive your fancy foreign car. And we get nothing. Nothing."

Marie said in a low voice, "J.B., I think you need to—"

"Much respect to you, ma'am, but this ain't none of your business," J.B. said.

He flapped the grant application in the palm of his hand like a preacher with a Bible. "This here's between Jason and the board."

"I'm a member of the board," Marie said.

"But you ain't in this grant like we are."

I asked if anyone else had read the new grant. No one had seen it except

Bonnie. I passed out copies to each member and asked that they read it, mark pages that were problematic to them, and reconvene the next day to revise the wording and make a final decision.

"I must tell you," I said, "that I had to write some things in the grant application to sell it to the feds. Most of you know me. You know how I respect you. I've already made some changes because Mr. Terry has brought up legitimate concerns. Language can be changed. No problem. Let's not make hasty decisions that could threaten our chances of getting the grant. It will provide, if approved, resources for you, other working moms, and your kids. That is what it is for, not to fill my pockets as J.B. seems to think. I would never do that."

Cecil, who'd been quiet through most of the meeting, spoke up. "I think that's a good idea. I respect Jason. I don't believe he'd do us any harm. And, J.B., you haven't been around much these last few years, so I'd suggest you listen to this here man." He pointed at me. "He's done a lot for our kids and this community."

After the meeting, I stopped by J.B.'s house to talk about the changes I'd made. I told him that if he wasn't satisfied with the wording, it wasn't set in stone—words could be changed. He expressed suspicion of government funds. I knew he had one of the better moonshining businesses in the hollow. The feds had arrested him after finding moonshine in his truck. He served time for it. He had assaulted an officer, bragging that he knocked him good, and he told me that any government program meant more inspectors. He made it clear he wasn't going to tolerate that, especially when it came to inspecting any daycare.

"In these parts, we don't want anyone snooping around about things that are none of their business," were his final words to me.

It was clear that he would be a hard one to convince, but his was only one vote, if I could convince the others.

I talked extensively with Marie about the language used in the grant application. She believed, as J.B. said, that it painted a picture of them as poor and helpless, especially when I described their clothing, which gave the impression of people who didn't care about their appearance. I remember how she rebuked the correspondent who wanted to produce a special on the region, emphasizing its poverty, and how she refused to do so. Somehow, without even realizing it, I had fallen into the trap of appeasing the federal government, criticizing things that were offensive to people I respected.

I mulled over Marie's comments and realized how powerful words could be. Thirty out of hundreds of words gave them the impression that I had no respect for them. I could do nothing about the words in the grant proposal that they had seen; they had already done their harm. Their poison was in the air and printed. I only hoped the board could look past them to what I wanted to do and how committed I was.

The Vote

THE NEXT MORNING, we met. Bonnie and Peggy were even less hospitable. They shook the grant application at me and said, "And we thought you were our friend!"

I sat down next to Marie, who whispered, "Keep cool; let them talk."

The meeting started with the reading of the minutes from the last meeting. Then J.B. criticized additional parts of the grant application. He read the sections that mentioned "mental health workers," "many serious health problems," and statements such as "anxiety among women, fed by fears of children's health, school success, and misbehavior."

"This here is slander. It's saying we don't know how to raise our kids!" he shouted. He slammed the papers on the floor. "I don't know what the rest of you think, but I'm sick of outsiders coming here and thinking they know best. We know how to raise our kin. We don't need no mental health workers to tell us how to raise our kids. We done it for years. We will continue to do it, feds or no feds."

I explained that, yes, it did sound bad, but it didn't reflect my true feelings. I wrote it to promote the program and to make funds available for the area, with allocation decisions made by the board members. It's just words, and words can be changed; sentences can be edited, and I can include what they would prefer me to say. We can review it now and make the necessary cuts and adjustments to the language.

"If you don't believe what you wrote, mister, then why'd you write it?" J.B. said, slapping the grant in the air.

Peggy spoke up. "We are terribly disappointed in you, Jason." She shook her head. Bonnie never looked up.

Freda said that maybe it was time for the board to vote. Cecil remained silent, paging through the grant proposal and shaking his head.

It was moved and seconded that they vote on the grant proposal.

I interrupted them. I had to make one more plea.

"Listen, everyone, you have the power to say yea or nay to the grant proposal. But you also have the power to rewrite it, to change the offensive language. I agree with you that the way it is written doesn't do you justice. So, let me work with you to make the change. If you vote no, the door is closed. You cannot get the money. Look at what'll come into this community—$60,000.00. That's a lot of money and it goes to you and—"

J.B. cut me off, "Bullshit. That money, much of it, goes to you, from what it says, and some director with a college degree. I don't see no one in the room with no college degree except you."

"Yes, that's part of the funding—I would like to work here, and I do need a salary. But much of—"

"That's a big part of it," he said. "It'll pay your way and that lady who was up here last fall, the pretty one who was hanging all over you. Is that it?"

I clenched my fist and stood up. But as I looked around the room at one face after another, I realized that it was over. Even Cecil wasn't paying attention to me; he was focused on the grant proposal. Sure, I wanted Linda to work with me. I knew she knew how to build a program. But those faces showed they had lost their trust in me. I was just another outsider trying to make them into something they weren't. And even worse, I would profit from a grant based on their poverty.

I sat back down, folded my hands in front of me, and said quietly, "That's not true. I would work with you, and you, as a board, would hire the candidate who applies. The federal government requires that you hire someone with a college education and experience running a program. If that is someone else, someone local, that is fine with me."

J.B. grunted, "Huh," and laughed. "That's a good one."

Marie put her hand on my shoulder. "Let it go."

Greta moved for the vote. Those who were in favor of the grant proposal were Marie, Cecil, and I.

Those opposed raised their hands, while everyone else remained silent.

Once the grant proposal was rejected, Greta raised concerns about what would happen to the Folk School summer program. I told them that much of the grant money would cover the costs for the Folk School, its staff, and myself. I also knew that the church's promise to donate thousands of dollars depended on my securing the daycare grant. I wasn't sure I could continue without the grant. I would check with Mr. Hook to see if there was enough money to run a summer program.

After the meeting disbanded, I went up to Bonnie, Peggy, and Cecil. I shook their hand and told them that I had the utmost respect for them. I was sorry that it ended this way. They seemed confused. They said they were sorry, too. They hoped I'd stay.

"Can't you do the summer program?" Peggy asked.

"I hate to say it, Peggy, but I need a job. I can't live on nothing."

"Well, we'll feed you. Why don't you come up for supper? The kids would love to see you," she said.

I said I couldn't. I had finals.

"Do stay in touch," she said. "The kids will miss you."

"I'll miss them, too."

As Cecil left, he pulled me aside and said, "Reckon I'll not be seeing you in these parts."

He knew the score. He'd lived in Illinois, Ohio, and Michigan over the years and knew, as my dad said, how important it was to have a salary. I heaved a long sigh, looked back at the Folk Center, the plowed hillside, the hills beyond, and nodded my head. "This may end it for me. I'll see if I can make something happen, but it doesn't look promising."

He patted me on the back. "Come by. I'll give you something to take your mind off all this. I think you may need it."

He drove off in his black Lincoln.

I chatted with Marie and admitted that I had no backup plan. She shook my hand and told me she was here and that I could come by anytime.

When I drove up Cecil's driveway, he was on the porch and invited me up, and we drank from a pint of moonshine. He showed me his pistol and revolver collection and rifles—twenty of them—and told me, as he had before, that, should there ever be an invasion, I should hightail it right to the hollow.

He told me that he trusted me. "As for J.B., well, don't put a mind to him," he said. "He'd block anything good from happening here. He is always up to no good." As I left, he walked to the dump beside his yard, out past his eight-hundred-pound pigs. We stood there talking and gazing out over a ridge to the valley, where the main road cut through the trees. I wondered what we were doing there when he said, "Wanted to give you a gift." He bent over, lifting an old tire, and reached into a little chamber under it, to fetch a fifth of moonshine.

"You take this and forget about today. You need to move on. I suspect that's what you'll do," he said and reached out his hand to shake mine. We stood there, hands clasped, for a moment. He stepped back and patted me on the shoulder again.

As I walked to the car, I said, "See you."

"Yep," he said as he headed up to the porch.

My chances of working in Rose's Creek were over. I had alienated nearly everyone with what I had written in the grant.

Days after I got back to Nashville, I informed Helen that the board had rejected the grant. Linda suggested that we try to secure a grant for the Clearfork region and not keep it under the Folk School's aegis. I didn't want to write another proposal if it meant writing disparagingly about people I respect. I called Mr. Hook and told him about the grant. He extended his regrets and said he'd talk with the church council. Later in the week, he called back. By his voice, I knew that it wasn't good news. They rejected the funding plan.

My father called and asked if I'd made any decisions about work. I lied to him that I was still exploring the possibility of starting a daycare program. He offered to set up some interviews with some of his friends. His voice had a kind, sympathetic tone. "It's what I did for your brother. It may help. You might be surprised and find something you like to do," he said. "You want me to see what I can do?"

"Go ahead," I said. He may have sensed my futility. "I'll let you know when I will be home."

"Outstanding," he said. "I think there are some real opportunities for you!"

When I hung up the phone, I stared out the window. The traffic moved steadily down the street. People going to work. People doing what they had to do to make a living. People like me. But somehow it didn't feel right. Not for me. Yet I didn't know what to do.

Exam preparation and writing my final thesis took up my time. I expected that I'd never hear from anyone in Rose's Creek again, since the grant and what I wrote had alienated them. But I was surprised to get a flood of letters from my friends in the hollow, particularly the kids.

I wrote to Otrel, told him what had happened, and wished he'd been at the board meeting. He might have turned it around. I told him I was devastated by how everyone seemed to turn on me and asked if he still supported me. I explained that, although we had planned for him to teach guitar at the summer Folk School and I had told him I had money, I didn't have it right now and might never have it.

He wrote back a beautiful letter, one he had worked hard on, and wanted me to realize that, in my disappointment, I had missed something I should have known: that people did love me and wanted me to stay. I had a home there. He told me what I already felt in my heart—and had nearly forgotten in my defeat—was that Rose's Creek was unlike anything I'd ever experienced before and, most likely, ever will again, because it was home for me. The people—Peggy, Bonnie, Cecil, and Otrel—wanted me to be part of their family, to be included in their lives. They were calling me home. I wasn't just a friend; I was family.

After I read his letter, my heart broke. He felt like family too, some integral part of who I was, and, even if I could not afford to go back, I might always feel that we belonged together, were part of a larger web of connections that neither of us entirely understood but would bind us for the rest of our lives.

This is what he wrote.

Dear Jason,

I will answer your letter I received the other day and I was glad to hear from you.

To let you no a little about my profile and to tell you I really like you as a friend. I am a friend to you, Jason, and I don't give a dam what you are that is your besness and I ant asking nobody for cherty and I talk to a lady in Knoxville and she informed me some informed some money is floating around somewhere or another and that we could make a comment and get money for facilities that is the way money progetes come off. So that way you and I and no one else on some bored has to spend any money.

But I do not want to get down on my knees to beg any one because I don't have to fret we have a show date at the High school in November.

By the way Erling was up the house the other day and jason, he says, is a friend I will say nothing but this I thin you are a fine boy and the family does to and watch and don't get into anything deep because this good old Unites States is good to ones it is free. We have our laws and we have our reading. We don't have to give nobody nothing unless we want to and for God Sacke lets keep it that way.

I ant got much education but I ant nobdy dam fool. Pleas do not quiston what I have said and I like you and I waont hav you feeling bad for nothing in this world so that bring us back to the music I like to play but I like to get paid of course to me it works just like another job.

Nobody in this world get something for nothing. Bill and Bobby caome to see me that other night to my family you is the best people we have every knone and don't say your arent coming to see Otreal, just say I am going home case when you are at my house its home case we like you like children. Jason I have a son about your age and he in VitNom and I would love something here worth it that he is dying against VitNon and I wont think that you would let me down and that is why I say you are my friend and we cant be friends in heavin if ther is sech place and sometimes I dout think ther is so I guss I am fetter find some thine but I don't mean to be ungodly but I would like to be able to pick my goalie and just go and play and sing and tell jokes and stories for always but I cant because have to make money so then you see why. But I wasn't asking you as you said in your letter for anything I am sorry you mis under stood the more money than you and I could get floating around some where now I know how to get it so good by and good luck come when you can and stay as long as you like caus I said this is home.

Sined Otrel Hamton and Family

I wrote back to him and thanked him for offering me a place to stay. In his heart, he would have taken me back just as, I was sure, when his son came back from Vietnam, he would welcome him into his home. When you have very little, it's strange how much you can provide and care for those in need. Peggy and Bonnie housed, fed, and sheltered me without hesitation. They didn't want to know what school I had attended, what pedigree I had, what I planned to do with my life. They accepted me at face value and told me I was family.

Peggy's kids wrote me letters inviting me to come home and stay with them for the Fourth of July, and they said a bed was waiting. Bobby talked about playing touch football and how I taught Milton, Eddie Terry, Rondel Hatfield, and him to toss the ball properly. He told me how he fell asleep in class, and the principal gave him five licks. He also mentioned that Lois, his sister, had a new car—a 1963 Chevrolet convertible, red with a black stripe—and that I could ride in it. After school, he shot twelve squirrels with his new rifle, which his mom planned to cook into a good meal. He wondered if I saw Johnny Cash because he liked "Ring of Fire." He also said that Erling came by to visit with O.J., a 6'2", 296-pound defensive end from Kansas State who kicked a soccer ball all the way across the road to the Folk School cabin. He asked if I had a girlfriend and what she looked like—does she have black hair? Is she tall but not too tall, around 5'8"? Skinny, but not fat; not too skinny, about 110 pounds? He told me how Erling and his Uncle Bobby walked around the Folk School property, and Bobby asked where they would build the next cabin this summer. Erling said he'd like to have one built by spring so they could have water for summer vacation, if he came up there. He wanted to know if I was coming up soon so I could help, because he was having trouble with science. He mentioned he was going rabbit hunting Saturday night. They only shot one and cleaned it, then put it in the freezer so I could eat it when I arrived. I would like rabbit.

He signed it, "Peace brother."

I wondered what Erling was doing in Rose's Creek and whether he was aware of the fiasco with the grant proposal. I wrote him, telling him the program was off, but got no reply.

Bobby's sister Lois wrote a surprising letter, given that, that first year, I'd insulted her belief in God. She told me about her new car, about how I'd helped her with her poetry, that she didn't want to kill herself anymore, but wondered if I ever did; then told me about her new nephew, and then:

You a sweet guy Jason what you said about being born when you met the Metzlers was really great, you're Beautiful Jason, you should always be so kind. It looks good on you. You know when I first met you I thought I wasn't going to dig you at all. You seemed so uptight like you were afraid. I thought you would be so snobbish, but you aren't. Maybe you were scared anyway you turned out to be a pretty nice guy. That's a compliment.

She was right. When I first arrived, I was scared. I thought I would never fit in. But I fell in love with them because they were genuine people. Lois shared what was on her mind —not following some polite script about what one should or shouldn't say about religion, but wondering whether God would accept her if she changed her religion from Baptist to Catholic. She wanted to know what I thought, even though, in those first weeks, I challenged her beliefs.

I told her in a letter (I was writing two or three a week now) that God was more interested in how caring a person was than in what church the person was affiliated with.

As the letters kept coming, I realized that my two years at Rose's Creek had changed me more than I'd changed anyone or anything in the hollow. I was part of their lives. If I wanted, I could go back and be accepted as part of their community and, if that were possible, find a home.

I wondered how often someone in Glen Ellyn, or at the golf club, ever bares their soul to someone they just met, or, for that matter, opens their door and offers them a meal, a bed, and a place in their home and lives. I suspected not often. Yet for those in Rose's Creek, with no fancy clothes to hide behind, no elaborately decorated homes to blend into, no strict codes of propriety, and no barriers to what polite conversation was, they spoke from the heart, and they listened when you said what concerned you.

In one final letter, Lois invited me to visit anytime. She mentioned that Peggy, her mom, wanted me to know she would be happy if I could come and not worry about how much I would eat. She also added that Peggy had thought about the board meeting and regretted not saying something, and that, in the heat of the moment, she wished she had supported the grant. The letter ended with

I hope you can spend Xmas here also it would really be great. We could go sledding. Winter in the country is a real blast. You could almost lose your heart to the world if you wanted to.

I had lost my heart there in the mountains. I wish I could find a way back. I wept as I read that line over and over. "You could almost lose your heart to the world if you wanted to."

I wanted to.

But how?

I thought that maybe Erling was staying with Marie if he was still in Rose's Creek. On a whim, I called Marie, asked if Erling was there, and he was. Before she handed him the phone, she told me how sorry she was that the grant had fallen through and that she was exploring other options. She also explained that now that everyone had calmed down, the board wanted me back and was considering whether we could reapply for the grant.

J.B. he had gotten into a fight with Cecil, threatened him, and Cecil told him off. J.B. quit the board and left for Chicago the next day. No one had heard from him.

When Erling got on the phone, he asked if I was angry.

I told him that I wasn't, but was disappointed and discouraged. "That seems to be my nature," I told him. "I'm slow to hate the people who have wronged me."

"Not a bad trait," Erling said. "But it must be hard for you."

"Yes. It is. Until I spoke with Marie, I wondered if I was the only one who cared about the loss of the grant. Everyone seemed to think it's no big deal."

"Oh, they do care," Erling said. "They're mad at J.B. now. I told them that, by and large, the grant was a good one. You may have added too much flowery language here and there. But it was good. And I let them know J.B. was way out of line."

"Thanks. But the grant deadline is gone, so it's dead."

"Too bad. You coming up for the summer?"

"No," I said. "I'd love to. But the church pulled the plug. I need to find work."

"Hope you're not running back to dad," he said.

"Lay off, Erling."

"You're not, are you?"

"Not sure. I hope not. I don't know what to do next. I want to get some distance from it before I make any decisions."

There was a pause at the end of the line. "Jason," he said, "that distancing may not be the best thing to do. It comes from your middle-class world, where everything is viewed at arm's length. I know you don't think much of religion, but I wonder when you will have a clear understanding that it's God who sustains us. You and I aren't the authors of compassion or concern because we're dependent on this worldly hope. Remember: 'There are men who cannot be bought,' which means there are men who affirm God before they put their hope in others or institutions. Maybe you need to step back and reconsider what your faith is grounded in."

I thanked Erling for his advice but told him I didn't need God's help. I needed to wallow in defeat and let it settle in before I moved on. Maybe this was the abyss he had spoken about years ago. If it was, I was definitely deep inside it, and I didn't see any way out. Still, I didn't want a way out because before I moved on, I needed to understand what I'd done, how I'd gotten caught up writing the grant, and lost track of what it would mean to the people I cared about.

Before he hung up, he invited me again to the Joseph Campbell Folk School in North Carolina. I thanked him. Yet I had to come to terms with what my father had said: the almighty buck came first. I had to find a job. To be sure, the invitations from the hollow were appealing. I knew I had a home there. The option to return there to live and find odd jobs was attractive, yet the rejection still stung.

With the daycare project off the table and no other options but to crash at Linda's apartment, staying in Nashville was no longer feasible. I needed to stop playing the role of a student, take the professors' ideas, and see what, if anything, actually applied to the real world. I'd already given up the notions that I had been studying in a Systematic Theology class about God being "greater than that which can be conceived." I was more worried that my life, as it was, was more than I could have conceived. It didn't matter that I could analyze different theological arguments and explain the nature of religion and the imagination. What mattered now was getting a job.

One evening, while we were getting stoned, Linda asked me to show her some of my books that I'd stored at her house. I pulled out texts on systematic theology, sociology, and ethics. She paged through them.

"Do these make sense to you?" she asked. "They're so abstract."

"They do," I said.

She laughed. "I work with kids. They're concrete. They want to know if you love them, when the snack is served, and if you can soothe a cut."

"They may be better off that way," I said.

Linda nestled next to me. "I'm sorry the proposal didn't work out," she said. "You seem down. Is there anything I can do?"

"Yeah. Pass me the joint!"

Later, we went to bed together. Her hands sliding under my shirt, and mine loosened her bra; one piece of clothing after another dropped to the floor. She took my erection in her mouth; I nibbled on her breasts. Neither of us spoke. Our hands, our mouths did the talking. As we held onto each other, the failed proposal, the months of work, the rising hopes, the brutal rejection, and the plans for being together all fell away in our long embrace. The next morning, a bit uneasy about our making love, I was quiet as I drank my coffee. If I didn't say anything, we could pretend it never happened. She sat across from me, dipping a doughnut in her coffee.

We drove to Helen's office to explain what happened. We wondered if the proposal could be revised and if Linda could work on it, maybe even resubmit it. Helen wanted me to know that it was a good, solid proposal. She didn't want me to take the blame for what occurred, but explained that the grant would need to be rewritten entirely for next year's submission.

When we got back to Linda's apartment later in the afternoon, she offered me coffee and a bagel.

"Want to resubmit it?" she asked.

"No," I said.

She leaned over the table, pressing her hands in front of her. "Can we talk about last night?" she asked.

"Sure," I said.

"Well, what happened?" she asked.

I sipped my coffee. The steam blocked my view of her. I set it down. "Nothing," I said. "We made love."

"Huh," she said. "That's it?"

I smiled. "Guess so."

She furrowed her brow. "It was more than that to me. I mean, it blew my mind. When I'm logical about it, I think, 'What blew your mind about that? When people go to bed, what happens happens.' Not that I didn't enjoy it very much. I guess it was just one of those things I never thought would happen, not between us. I remember how quiet we were this morning, and I wonder if I freaked you out or something?"

"Well, I admit I was," I said. "I mean, I didn't expect it. I told you about Ann. How mixed up I am about her. I still feel committed to Ann, so it freaked me out that I could do it. And yet, what can I say?"

"You don't need to say anything. It was fine. I'm fine. We'll let it be," she said, reaching across the table and pressing her hand to mine.

"Thanks," I said.

Later that night, when I was curled up on her couch, she came into the room and asked if she could sit on the floor beside me and just talk.

"Something wrong?" I asked.

"I'm feeling very blue today—really kind of deep purple, like a bruise. I can't remember if I ever told you about colors: it's one of my ways of understanding what's going on. Anyway, I'm purple. I got this thing about purple. It's not that it's royal. It's more that it's a mood, a feeling that pulls me into it, so I'm surrounded by it and dwelling inside this purple haze."

"Are you stoned?" I asked.

She slapped my leg. "No, silly. Do you have a favorite color?"

"Blue, a deep ocean blue," I said. "I like the feel of it; it's watery and quiet."

"Nice," she said, putting her head on my leg.

We didn't want to admit it, but we both wanted to make love again. She became quiet, and I did, too. Later, she slipped beside me on the couch. We made love again, this wordless drowning in flesh on flesh, the blue into purple, the purple into blue, that seemed to absolve all the loss each of us was feeling.

In the morning, Linda went to work. She had left a purple card with a note that read, "Lovely."

I sat at the kitchen table, feeling thankful for her and how easy it was with her. I pondered what I could do with my life. I couldn't return home. I didn't want to go east to Ann. My education, much as I enjoyed the intellectual challenge, was useless. I had to give up academia and the world I'd found in Rose's Creek. I had to find something else to do. But what?

I was used to being a student, spending weeks thinking about one text, discussing its meaning with others, and being deeply absorbed in thought. Switching to a regular job would be difficult. Maybe I'd become like others: using clichés, believing newsmen told the truth, subscribing to TV Guide, falling for a candidate, turning into an ordinary person, a public figure, holding a job, and earning a living. Perhaps I'd have to go home and find a job there. Be another Wallace Stevens. That seemed like the only choice. But I was afraid of it. I had no idea what my new face would look like.

Avoidance

DON BEISSWENGER, MY advisor, requested a meeting the following Wednesday to help me plan for my future. He encouraged me to write down my positive attributes and accomplishments beforehand and suggested I consider the arts.

That seemed unlikely to me. I knew no one in the arts. I wasn't an artist; I could draw, but not well. I had written a few poems. Some good. Some bad.

It was more likely that I'd have to work in a church. But churches gave me the creeps.

I never made the list Don requested. Instead, I made love with Linda, smoked dope, drank Jack Daniels on ice, and read Whitman. Time ground to a halt. I knew I should call my dad back and tell him when I'd return so he could set up the interviews.

Should, should, should rattled in my head.

My lack of direction muddled me. When I had to be somewhere, it meant that I had to be something. But when I had no place to go and nothing to do, and no role to play, no job to do, I could focus only on one thing: the moment, spending sweltering afternoons naked in an icy bathtub with my lover.

⁂

The weekend before I met with Beisswenger, I took one last trip east. The heat became intense, so Linda and I drove to the Blue Ridge Mountains to find a waterfall in a hidden valley that sounded like the one Erling had never discovered. We planned to camp overnight, skinny-dip in the stream, and make love on blankets under the stars.

On our drive to Boone, North Carolina, Linda told me about her two friends, both of whom starred in a production of the Daniel Boone story at an outdoor theater. One was a dancer. She wasn't sure I'd like him. He was a bit immature. But the other, a woman, was a fantastic singer and very thoughtful.

Her secret waterfall, one she used to go to as an undergraduate to sit under and bathe in its clear water while others skinny-dipped there, sounded idyllic.

Her old Ford roared across the state like a hound on a pleasing scent and wound down a highway to a country road, to a gravel road, to where North Carolina intersected with Tennessee and Virginia. Once in North Carolina, we drove down unpaved roads by furrowed fields to a muddy road with a bleached-out sign that said, faintly, "Waterfall."

The closer we came to her secret place, the more she talked about how we could sit around naked, get stoned, take walks, and make love—our haven.

"This will be so much fun. I've fantasized about doing this. But now it's real. I'm so glad I met you," she said, barely able to contain herself. She parked the car under a giant poplar, trekked down a wooded path, and mist hung in the air. I could hear a low rumbling sound.

Linda cried out, "Hear that? Not far ahead! It features a neat basin at the bottom and a small pool where we can relax. Clear as glass. You'll love it!"

We walked for a mile, heading toward a deep roar that grew louder as we drew closer. The ground shook. When we came to a bluff, she took me by the arm.

"Close your eyes," she said.

We stepped forward.

She cried, "Shit!"

Instead of a stream and a basin, massive waterfalls spilling over a rocky ledge with a torrent of water. They splashed into the basin below, sending up water clouds thirty feet high. Impossible to hear, her lips screamed, "Oh, my God" over and over.

We descended twenty feet to watch a five-foot-thick wall of water rush past us. A needle-sharp spray soaked us, chilling us to the core. I shivered and pointed upward, signaling that I needed to get out of there. She followed, glancing back several times as we headed to the car to warm up.

I held her while she wept over her fantasy being shattered.

"It's awful. What are we going to do?" she asked as if someone had died.

"Another time," I said. "Another summer."

We changed into dry clothes and thought about getting a room at a local motel, but decided to drive to the outdoor theater where we had one of the staff cabins reserved.

Once we picked up the tickets her friend had left, we went to the cabins assigned to actors for the summer. Robert, a tall redheaded dancer, greeted us and invited us to his cabin. His roommate, a lanky guy, jumped off his bed and offered it to us, saying he had to run some errands. We talked for an hour until Robert told us he needed to get into costume.

"You will be surprised," he said. "You will not believe how macho I am." He lowered his voice. "I'm a fierce wilderness guy." He struck a pose with his arms flexed like a weightlifter.

The production, a musical, portrayed Daniel Boone as a great explorer and Indian fighter, as well as a family man who wanted to do his best for his wife and children. It was a highly romanticized version of his life, but it provided good entertainment.

In jeans and red suspenders, Robert joined a chorus of dancers who portrayed mountaineers in one scene, British soldiers in another, and Indians in a third. In the final scene, they were pioneers heading west. Jumping, stalking, leaping, and pirouetting, he was incredibly agile, like a gazelle.

After the show, Robert invited us to a party. Linda's girlfriend, also a cast member, planned to be there, so we went. The party was held in a lounge inside one of the cabins.

Cast members had gathered in a semicircle. Robert sat beside his roommate on the floor and patted the space next to him. Linda grabbed my arm and said, "I hope you don't mind, but once Tracy comes, I'd like to spend some time with her. We haven't seen each other in years."

"Go right ahead," I said.

"You're a peach. Robert will take care of you. I already told him to watch out for you," she said, kissing me on the cheek.

At the party, the man playing Daniel Boone, a large, stocky man whose real name wasn't memorable, dominated the conversation, acting as if everyone had come into the room to idolize him. He told everyone that he was working on a Ph.D. in theater and aspired to be a director.

We sat around him as he discussed his career so far. His girlfriend, tilting her head to look at him, sat at his feet. He called on people as if he were a late-night talk-show host, asking them questions about their lives. I wondered if everyone was as impressed with him as he was with himself.

Linda nudged me and whispered, "Why doesn't someone tell him to shut up?"

Robert leaned over and whispered back, "His mother owns the theater."

The actor must have heard Robert because he pointedly asked Robert what he planned to do with his life.

Robert stood up, his drink in his hand, and answered, "I'm never going to grow up."

"You must be kidding," Daniel Boone said.

"No, I'm not," Robert replied and jumped into the air, landing a foot from Daniel, shoving his rear end at him. "Like Peter Pan, I'll be a child forever," and flapped his hands at him.

Daniel glared at Linda and me. We'd been delighted with Robert's performance.

"Grow up!" Daniel shouted at Robert. "You're such a fag."

"Damn right I am," Robert retorted and called out to us, "Come along, Tinkerbell and Robin," and skittered out of the room on his tiptoes. Unable to stop laughing, we picked up our drinks and followed Robert.

He went to the refrigerator to get another beer. While we were there, Linda's friend arrived, apologizing for being late. "They want me to do a solo dance number. Had to rehearse."

After a brief introduction, Linda informed me that she would return later.

Robert invited me to his room, where we drank and talked. Despite his histrionic flair, he actually worked hard and planned to get his B.A. in the arts. He lounged on the bed; I sat in a wooden chair by the window. His roommate dashed in, leaned over the bed, and whispered something in Robert's ear.

Robert said, "How lovely," and kissed his friend on the lips and, feigning shyness, raised his eyebrows at me. When his roommate left, he asked earnestly, "I hope you don't mind. We're—you know..."

"Gay?"

"You have it, dearie," he said. "Would you like another beer?"

I asked about his roommate's situation. As it turned out, he had a hot date with one of the leads. We drifted off to another room where two guys were in bed together, one lying on top of the other, completely clothed.

"I hope we're not disturbing you," Robert said to them.

"Oh, don't mind us. We're just rehearsing a scene," the man underneath said.

When we returned to his room, Robert asked me to get on his bed. It was much more comfortable than the wooden chair. He would sleep in his roommate's bed. Tired from the long day of driving, I dozed off and on, but stayed alert enough to answer some questions about what I had done and planned to do with my life.

"Oh, dearie," he said. "You're just a sleepy pie. Let me give you a massage. You can drift into la-la land," and, without asking permission, hopped on my bed, told me to take off my T-shirt and get face down on the mattress. He clambered on top of me and began kneading my shoulders, pushing with the heel of his hand. I melted into his touch, swooning for some time, just giving in to him. He turned me over and, sitting by my head, rubbed my face, cheek, and neck. His crotch, nestled by my head, had a bulge.

"You're a lovely boy," he said.

"So are you," I replied. "You touch like an angel."

"An angel?" he queried. "I'm more the satyr type."

I laughed. He leaned over and kissed me. With one move, he stretched beside me, his hand rubbing my chest and my legs. I put my hand on his cheek. Before long, he slipped out of his pants, shirt, and socks as quickly as if he were doing a costume change. He helped me out of my clothes.

We stripped off our underwear. He guided me to his lovely member, erect and proud. He held mine in his mouth. A ceiling fan swept air across us. I don't think either of us thought much about how it happened, but soon, moaning, we gave each other pleasure and fell asleep in each other's arms.

The door groaned. A light came on. I heard my name, "Jason." Disentangled from Robert's legs, I sat up.

Linda stood a few feet from us, agape.

Shit, I thought, and tried to wrestle myself out of Robert's arms. He awoke, turned, sat upright, and looked at Linda.

What could he say? I thought.

Not bothering to cover up, he stood up, walked right up to Linda, folded her in an embrace, and said, "Darling, no one owns anyone."

She wept. He patted her back. I scrambled to find my pants, underwear, shirt, socks, and shoes.

He comforted her. "Hey. He's a lovely guy, your Jason. He's still a man. I only borrowed him. Look, here he is: dressed, ready to be with you. I bet he'll please you as much as he did me."

"Oh, Robert," she said, laughing. "You always know the exact wrong thing to say!"

I came over to them. He stepped back. I hugged her.

She pulled back and stared at me. "What's going on?"

"It's all right," I said. "I just drank a little too much."

"Is that all?" she asked.

"That's all," I replied.

"You think I'm going to believe that?"

"Believe what you want." I was aggravated that she'd become upset and equally perplexed by how easily I'd fallen for Robert.

Robert stepped back from us and did a quick tap dance. "Liquor is the ruin of many a man," he said, waving his underwear over his head before he hopped into them and twirled around us, arms extended.

"Robert, you can make light of anything," she said.

"It's the Peter Pan in me," he said, offering her a beer.

She took it and turned to me. "You love me?" she asked.

"Of course."

"Okay," she said. I kissed her on the mouth.

The three of us sat on his bed, drinking.

At one point, he said, "You know, we could do a threesome!"

Linda shook her head. "Not with you, Robert. I'm not your type."

"You're right," he said. "But Jason here, he's a good little starter kit, and you never can tell. It may be another first!"

She pushed him back on the bed and held him by the arms. "You know, you drive me crazy," she said.

"It's because I love you," he said.

"I know," she said and let him go. He kissed her on the cheek and flopped against the wall behind the bed.

"You two love birds need some sleep," he said.

We had a room of our own. She held on to me all night. In the morning, I made love to her. It was different from what I had experienced with Robert. It felt more like I was an actor giving the best performance of my life. And I enjoyed it. But when I was with Robert, it felt like I was floating on a heavenly cloud, pulled deeper into a side of myself that longed to give it voice.

On the long drive back, we didn't talk as much as we usually did. I'd shattered some illusion of love we'd fallen into since the daycare fell apart. Back in Nashville, we slept together for several nights. We made love. It was all right. She had to go back to work and had a busy schedule. I knew I needed to get a job. Maybe Wolfe was wrong. Perhaps you had to go home again. That's where the jobs were. I didn't know what to do, but I knew I needed to get out of Nashville.

Unexpected

I AIMED THE VOLVO east on Route 40, the same path I took to Rose's Creek, the road that led toward where the Folk School blew up in my face. This time, I was heading further east: past Knoxville, beyond the Cumberland Mountains where Tennessee, North Carolina, and Virginia meet, along the Blue Ridge Parkway to the Cumberland Notch, where the eastern valley opens into West Virginia, and then to Nitro, a town north of West Virginia's Capitol, Charleston, right along the Kanawha River.

Mr. Beisswenger found me a temporary summer job so I could figure out what to do next and how to make a living. He let me stay at his house after Linda told me to move out; she needed time to think.

He had a "United Nations family"—two of his biological children, a boy and a girl, both blonde; one Native American child; one African American child; one Asian child; and one child from India. We ate dinner at a large picnic table in the kitchen. His wife, Margaret, managed the dinner crew: one set the table, one brought the serving bowls, one said grace, one cleared, one washed, and another dried. After dinner, we played board games—Scrabble for the older ones and Candyland for the younger ones.

The next morning, I met Mr. Beisswenger in his office. He sat across from me in a large armchair. I sat on a paisley sofa. Posters adorned his walls: Gandhi in his white khadi wrap; Dr. Martin Luther King Jr. at a march. He wanted to make our meeting informal. I told him what had happened at the Folk School.

"Too bad, too bad," he commiserated. "That would have been ideal for a guy like you."

"What do you mean?"

He pursed his lips and screwed them to one side, then took off his glasses and peered at them, rubbing one corner.

"Good question. Let me see how best to say this. You aren't like our typical graduates. They come here with a clear vocational goal: to be a minister, to serve the church or synagogue, or to go on to study and teach theology."

He laughed and leaned back in his chair, propping his feet up on an ottoman. "Let's face it, your graduate thesis was unconventional: on atheism, a broadside against God and established religion, using Dietrich Bonhoeffer to be sure, but not exactly as he might have wanted to be used. You proposed how to live your life, as he did, "in a world come of age," a world where God isn't necessary. It's not exactly your traditional thesis, given you've spent three years studying the New Testament, Old Testament, ethics, and theology, working in a local church, studying pastoral counseling—all preparation to work in the church business directly or indirectly."

I was surprised that he remembered what I had written and interrupted him. "Did you like my thesis?"

"I'm not sure that I liked it as much as I found it thought-provoking, but in a good way. It challenged many of the ways I see the world. That's not bad. But let's get back to your next move. You don't seem to fit the mold. You don't exactly seem like long-term ministerial material—at least not now." He furrowed his brow.

"That's true. I'm not the ministerial type," I said. "I never felt as if I fit the mold. I like to study theology. It interests me. However, it seemed like everyone who came here just wanted to do a job and make a living, and that was about it. They weren't here to ask questions or explore the deeper issues in their lives. I'm not interested in being a minister of God. I want to get people to think, to ask questions. I certainly don't have the answers," I said.

"Exactly," he pointed his finger at me. "You don't conform. You're not, at least not now, someone who could be happy in a traditional job. You need to explore, to find work that will allow you to sink into the muck and slime, as Thoreau said, and find your own answers."

The leaves on the trees out his window rippled with a gust of wind and tittered like fingers at a typewriter. My mind wandered to the afternoons in the Rose's Creek cabin where I'd sit and look out the back window at the dusty leaves of the cottonwoods and the small stream down the hillside. Peaceful days. I felt at home there.

I felt my legs rocking back and forth, and cupped my hands between them as if holding onto something that was slipping away from me.

"Hey. You all right?" Don inquired.

"Sure, sure," I said absently.

"Jason," he asked, "are you aware of your restlessness?"

"I suppose so."

"Do you know what you want to do?"

"My dad wants me to come back to Chicago. He's willing to set up interviews."

"With whom?" Don asked.

"Some of his friends, presidents of big companies like Sears."

"You want to work there?"

"It's a job."

"Is that what you want to do?"

"I suppose. It's the only option I can see right now."

"You serious?"

"Not really. I'd rather be doing something else. I'd rather write. It's sad because I'm not too good at it. But I feel at peace when I do."

"You could find a job as a journalist, but—I am afraid you're right—you don't write like a journalist. In fact, you don't even write like a minister," he chuckled.

"What do I write like?"

"Well, I guess you write like a poet."

"A poet?"

"Yes, you think in metaphors. Erling told me that was one of the reasons he liked you: as he called it, 'the poetic nature of your soul'."

"Erling never told me that."

"He told me. He said that you're a poet at heart. I think he's right. There's a certain restlessness in you."

"Maybe that's what Erling was driving at," I said, remembering his advice to break loose and let go.

"What'd he say?"

"He said that I should cut loose from my family. I should wander America as he does. But I just can't do that. I want to be able to make a living, to be on my own, and not be beholden to anyone. And, besides, traveling the country—what does that have to do with my finding work and having a career?"

Don rubbed his hands together, his cheeks puffed out, and then quickly expelled air.

"I'm hesitant to say this, and I wonder if you're ready to hear it. I've never shared this with anyone before, and it's not exactly good advice. But here it is: what you do for work, Jason, isn't all that important. Of course—don't get me wrong—you should find work that you believe in, that nourishes you, and does some good. But fundamentally, what you do for a living won't be as important as your quest—exploring who you are, what drives the world, and writing it down, making sense of it."

It took me a moment to comprehend what he said, but it made sense. I had to find jobs that would let me explore and discover new ways to see the world. But, even with that understanding, I was stuck: I needed work and needed it now!

I stood up and paced back and forth across the room. When I graduated from Divinity School, I realized that for the first time in my life, I would have to make it on my own. No dad to pay the bills. Independence. I didn't want to go back to school, nor did I want to return to the Chicago area and rely on my father and his connections to get me a job. I had to do that on my own.

Don sensed my frustration. "What's wrong?"

"None of this helps me," I muttered, shoving my hands in my pockets and quickening my pace. "Sure, I'd love to write. But right now, today, I need to make money. No one will hire me. I fucked up the one thing I cared about and worked to make happen. I destroyed it. It was mostly because of what I wrote—like Erling said, the flowery language I used. So I have no faith in my writing. I need a job, and no one is going to hire me because, as you say, 'I want to explore and delve into things.' " I felt steel bands tighten around my skull. I burst out, "That advice is all bullshit. I'm sorry, but that does me no good." I slammed my fist into my head. "Fuck. Fuck, fuck."

"Stop it!" Don yelled. He grabbed my hands. "Sit down."

I sat down for a few minutes, then stood up. He stood beside me and continued to probe about my writing.

"But that's who you are, isn't it?"

"What?"

"The delver and explorer," he said in a calm voice, gauged to calm me down.

I gazed into my palm, which stung.

"Yes, yes, I suppose so," I said. I couldn't figure out what he was driving at.

"Take a seat. You're pacing like a caged lion. Sit down. Let's talk," he told me.

I looked at the chair, which was as empty as I felt, went over to it, sat down, and realized that I was crying, tears streaming down my face. Soon enough, I was sobbing, convulsing like a little child.

Don came over to my side and patted me on the back. I felt like an idiot breaking down in front of him.

"There, there. I know it must feel awful to have lost the opportunity in Rose's Creek. You loved those people. You loved what you did. They loved you. You know that in your heart."

"I messed up. I shouldn't have let J.B. have anything. He should never have seen the proposal. I should have withheld it and only shown the board a summary. He was a criminal. He screwed me. He screwed their future, and I sat back and let it happen," I beat my fist against my forehead and cried out, "Damn. Damn. Damn. I'm such a fuck up!"

Don grabbed my hand and placed his other hand on my head, rubbing it. My skull felt as if it was going to crack open. "Come on. You don't have to be so hard on yourself. Sure, it could have gone differently. But give yourself a break. You're new at this. You didn't know. You trusted everyone. That's not such a bad thing: trust. And now you know what we all come to know: trust is something you give in small or large doses since not everyone is worthy of the gift."

I put my face in my hands and took several long breaths. He was right. The only problem was that I had let others down. I'd failed to see how words on the page are like the words in the Bible for some people who spend their lives feeling judged as sinners, cast out, denied. They can hurt as much as a punch to the gut. Marie had told me that the people missed me. But, even with all their wishes for me to come back, why did they vote down applying for the grant? Rather than an opening into life, adulthood felt like one door after another slamming in my face.

I heard a soft voice from what seemed like a long distance away. "Let's leave that for now, Jason. You have to move on. I know it's hard. But you need to find a way. What do you want to do now?"

Don was seated across from me again.

"I don't know what I want to do. I don't want to be a minister. I don't want to teach. I can't go into business the way my father wants me to. I can't go to war. It's just impossible. I have more don't-knows than do-knows. I have no idea what to do."

"Jason, what you do is not the issue," he said. "Did you hear me? It doesn't matter what you do as much as it matters that you let each job—the work you do—inform your deeper work. You need to have a job. We all do. That's a given. The job in itself will never entirely satisfy you. Do you see that?"

"I don't get it. Why is that? Why can't I just be like other people?"

He took the pipe off his desk, tamped down the tobacco with his thumb, then lit it, puffed on it, and stared out the window.

"You want to know why you're not like other people?"

For a moment, I wanted to say "no" because I thought that he'd sensed, as Will had, and just as recently Robert had, that I was different, not like other men. I didn't want someone else to tell me what I didn't want to know. But I also sensed that he knew something else I needed to hear.

"Yes," I said.

"You're different."

"Thanks!" I retorted cynically. "That really helps." Inside, I feared for sure that he had sensed that I was mixed up sexually. How could he know? I bit my lip.

"But you are!" he insisted.

I didn't want him to say what I feared most, my dreadful secret. Why did he want to confront me with that?

"What do you mean?" I pleaded, half-aware that I might be asking for more than I wanted to hear. "What makes me different?"

"You're an artist."

I was shocked, relieved, and flattered all at once. No one had ever called me an artist. I'd never seen myself as one. Confused, yes. Rebellious, yes. A poet, somewhat. A fag, maybe. Different, yes. But not an artist.

I had never created anything of any lasting worth—some drawings, several poems, lots of journal entries with my rambling thoughts, many pages filled with laments about my desires, resentments, and fears—but never any art.

I wanted to believe my ears and asked, "I'm an artist?"

"I believe so."

"So what does that mean?"

"You must pursue your art—whatever it will be—throughout your life. You have no choice. That's what's in you. And that means that, as I have said, don't worry about the work. It will come. You're personable. You're articulate. You're skilled. You're sensitive. Let's face it, you're also good-looking and that never hurts in our society!"

We laughed, and he went on with his point.

"Find work and do it well, but keep your heart focused on your larger calling, which is your art. Don't worry about your location. It could be here in Nashville, Boston, Tampa Bay, or even, heaven forbid, Chicago. Your location doesn't matter. Don't search for it there. Based on conversations I've had with other artists, you will find a home not necessarily in a place but among the other artists who live there. What I am saying is that your home will become a community of artists. Your true home will be in the arts. Your calling will be fulfilled through being with them. In a sense, that will be what the clergy refer to as the sacred community."

"You're serious, aren't you?" I asked, disbelieving, yet wanting to hear more.

"Most certainly I am. Do you know what I mean by 'calling?'"

"Not exactly. I find the term weird. Whenever some guys say that 'God called me,' I think they're deranged. I imagine God dialing their phone and saying, 'This is God. I'm calling you. Are you there, Jason?' 'Hang on, He's on another line…'"

Amused by my example, Don agreed that, indeed, the term sounded weird, but, as he went on to explain, "A calling at its best is not some voice from some fiery bush calling to us. It's more what's in our nature—part of us we may not entirely understand, but we must honor. It demands that we surrender to it because we have no other choice. It requires that we delve into ourselves to find out what it means and where it is directing us."

He puffed several times on his pipe, tapped it in the ashtray, and put it down.

"I guess the only analogy I can give is falling in love. I felt, when I saw Margaret for the first time, that I had no choice. And each time we had a child, the moment I saw them, I fell in love again. They're my calling. This work is part of my calling, too, but if you pressed me —if you wanted to know what truly nourishes my soul —it's being a husband and a father. Did I know that would be my calling when I was young? No. Did I fight against it as a young man? Yes. I was ambitious and competitive. I should make a lot of money. Be a professor. Write articles. Publish books. And move up the academic ranks. The academic dream machine. But after I met Margaret and I started learning more about myself, I realized that family was my reason for being. As you may see from my work with students, creating family is what I do at work and at home, too. For you, I think your calling will be your poems, your art."

He stopped and let what he said sink in, and then continued.

"And, too, as you find your way with it, the relationships, like those with Erling and the people of Rose's Creek, will help you discover your voice and a way to express yourself. Eventually, you will find a family of artists, and wherever they are, that will become your home. They will be your home. Until then, from what I know about artists, it will be a lonely journey. You must find your own path. It's not easy. But one thing is for sure: if you deny the artist in you, you'll never be happy. Eventually, as I mentioned earlier, you'll find other artists—poets in your case—and that will help ease some of the loneliness."

I wanted to ask him more questions, but he looked at his watch. I knew that he had another appointment. He moved to the side of his desk. His demeanor changed. He took on an official air.

"Let's get down to business. You need work, and I think I have something that will tide you over." He picked up a piece of paper with a telephone number and a name. "Reverend Robert J. Highbottom, First Methodist Church. Nitro, West Virginia."

"With a name like that, I'm not sure I can keep a straight face if I met him."

Don chuckled. "You'll manage. He's a person, after all, despite the name. he's a Vanderbilt graduate, a respected minister, and he is coming here with his family for a month in a post-graduate program we offer each summer. He needs someone to serve as an interim minister, oversee the church, and conduct services while he is away. They provide room and board and a good salary in the short term.

"Being a minister?" I exclaimed. "Being a fucking minister? No way!" I shoved the paper back to his desk.

Expressionless, he picked up the paper. "I wouldn't be so hasty." He pressed the paper back into my hands. "Jason. It's only a job. Work. Do you hear me? Work. It's not a life sentence. You'll not die. You did an internship at a church. You survived. It will get you on your way. Give him a call. I've told him about you. I've also heard from a former student, Ken McDonald. You remember him?"

"Yeah, we went on a march together in Mississippi. I gave a sermon once at his church. I was terrible, but he thought, for a white guy, I did all right."

"That's him. He's the director of a community action program in eastern West Virginia. I told him about you. He says that there may be a job in the program. Give him a call. That may give you a long-term job not in the church, something that may, after this summer, better fit you."

As June bled into July, my money would run out. I had to make that call. It was a step. A job. This job was like a stopover on a long flight across the country. Maybe Don was right. My mistake was to look for a home in a place instead of seeing it as a way of being.

"You going to make that call?" he asked.

I didn't like the idea of being an interim minister, but it was an opportunity that I had to accept, and if Ken had something better, I could call him. I took the sheet of paper, folded it, and told him that I would think about it.

He squinted, "Think about it?"

I smiled, "All right, all right. I'll call him."

"There, you've got it. You're on your way. It's not a lifelong commitment. It's a steppingstone. In time, you'll find another—Ken's looks like a possibility—and another, and so it goes," he said, grabbing me by the shoulder as we walked to the door. He shook my hand. "Keep in touch."

"I will," I said and headed to Linda's apartment, which I knew would be empty since she was at work. I wrote short letters to Erling and Ann, and longer ones to Marie and Peggy, asking them to pass the word to the other members of the board that I had a job. After that, I had to write the most difficult letter—to my parents to inform them that I wouldn't be coming home. My father had called to let me know that he had set up job interviews with several of his friends—Mr. Ayres, chairman of the Board of Commonwealth Edison, and Mr. McCalf, president of Sears and Roebuck. He expected me to be home on time to do the interviews. I needed to explain how the daycare program had fallen apart and what my plans were, and in the process, reveal who I was—something that Erling had said I needed to do if I was ever going to be independent.

I'd given some thought about what it meant to be an artist, and at least how it clarified why I felt as I did and why I couldn't go home again. I knew I was happiest when I had a pen in my hand. What I didn't clearly understand was how my decision to be an artist justified my departure from my father and his hopes for my future.

Dear Mom and Dad,

After considerable time, the ending has come. Government funds will not be allocated for the daycare and summer programs. The Rose's Creek board withdrew its support. To be honest, I knew this weeks ago.

I've spent time deciding on a direction. Several options were available to me. Some required both clarity and ambition that I no longer have. I don't want to apply for an 8-5 job, to feel like everyone else just struggling to make money or, as you say, Dad, "contributing" to the GNP, or some variation of that broad theme.

That wasn't a good beginning. I had to be more positive. I needed to state my position.

I met with an advisor who helped me determine, based on my graduate education, which job options are best for me. I have accepted an interim minister's position for 8 weeks in Nitrate, West Virginia. There, I hope to focus on writing or working on my writing and to get away from Nashville (escape, really) from the failure of the Rose's Creek projects. I also want to escape the ambition that drove my earlier years—to be a big success and make a lot of money. Maybe I can gain some insights into myself and who I am as an artist.

It's not that I want to dismiss your concern for my well-being or your wish for me to be happy and prosperous. It's much more fundamental. I need to be alone to discover my talents as an artist. e.e. cummings said there are three kinds of people—artists, merchants, and warriors. If you're an artist, you must focus on your craft to be as creative as possible. If you're a warrior or merchant, you need to compete against others or external challenges to prove your strength.

Each person must develop a set of skills and a reliable reservoir of knowledge to do their work. An artist depends on their own internal makeup and a shifting reserve of knowledge that they must draw on in whatever art form they have chosen as their life's work.

That's one way to say my ambitions are more about becoming an artist than about opposing you. I just picked a different career path. That's all.

But for you and me, Dad, the differences go beyond just our careers. It's about what we believe is valuable in this world. Once, after I wrote to you from college—the day after Dr. King's assassination—I shared my thoughts on civil rights, not to argue with you, but to express my views. Later, my brother Jack called to tell me you were upset and that you didn't really care what I thought. You cared more about what I did, who I dated, and how I planned to earn a living. I could keep my thoughts to myself. I could accept that something I said was wrong, but I couldn't abide the option being given secondhand.

I put my pen down. What was I trying to do? Complain that Dad was the way he was? I had to take a different tack. Dwelling on the past would do no good unless I could explain why it bothered me.

I knew you wanted me to have the freedom to do as I pleased, but that freedom came with a cost. If I dared to go against what you believed was right, I was cut off and had to pay for my graduate education myself. Back then, I followed my brother's advice and stayed silent.

Later that summer, we talked, and you said, "Do what you like, son, but don't bother telling me what you think. Quite frankly, it upsets me. Your mother and I are set in our ways and have been as good as we can to you."

What you said was true. I also felt that I shouldn't explain why I did what I did or what led me to go to Divinity School and to take poetry courses there. Literature and writing, even if they are things you value in your own way, are only secondary concerns to you. But for me, they are primary. You don't associate with writers; they aren't part of your life. Back when Jack was in college, he once told me tearfully that "Dad doesn't even care that I write short stories. All he cares about is that I make a good living."

He was right, but I also thought he was wrong. How can someone care about something they know little about as a career? All the people you know are successful businesspeople who make a living selling products and earning profits. You don't know any artists or writers. It seems that in this country, the arts exist in their own world, while big business is in another. They might as well be on separate continents, speaking different languages.

Years later, Jack decided to work at Sears as a salesman, a career that pleased you. He shares common ground with you. He's becoming, as you told me, a good businessman, climbing the corporate ladder as a division manager. I'm glad he's achieved what you wanted. He's become a success, as you understand it.

On the other hand, I know I'm not going to please you because I want to write. A merchant's life isn't in the cards for me. Of course, I'll need to earn a living; I'll have to work hard. I will search for jobs that fit a writing life, which is, in many ways, about seeking a form of expression. I do realize that all jobs are a form of expression, but few jobs require that the end product and the profits of one's work stay inside oneself, rather than in external monetary gains.

How, then, do I find a common ground with you? I'm not sure. Maybe it's not for me to decide completely, nor for you. I must be certain that I can be respected for going down my own path….

I found that I couldn't go on. I was befuddled. What I felt stir inside me was an amorphous anger. Furiously, I scratched out a list to sort out what I was feeling:

Jason is in need of recasting, Jason who will never please his dad

He isn't the dutiful son

He isn't a clean-cut American youth

He isn't happy with the world

He dislikes chatter and idle talk

He is a long-haired man most of the year and, no, doesn't want to get a haircut while at home

He loves his mother and dad, but doesn't care to love someone who expects him to act in ways that are contrary to what he wants, or needs, or values

He doesn't need (ever) to keep up appearances that satisfy their friends and members of the club…

I found that I couldn't make that list without second-guessing myself, without considering my parents' point of view, without hearing "but all we've done for you" and "how can you say such things?" It was as if they had crawled inside my head and were speaking to me even though they were hundreds of miles away. I kept trying to anticipate what they would say.

Stating these things might seem petty. Why can't I do these things, you ask—look presentable, dress properly, think the way I should (at least in public)? Isn't that a small request for my parents, who paid for my education, both undergraduate and graduate?

I reply, "Yes, it is." But I add, "What if you reverse the question and see it from my point of view? Why can't you accept that I am different? Just because I think and feel differently from you doesn't mean I'm asking you to think and feel differently than you already do. I want you to acknowledge that I do. I don't even need to mention my ideas. I don't want to feel as if you're always trying to keep me in my place."

Yes, I am your son. That's obvious. But how I am and how I appear aren't under your control. However, how you come to accept me as I am is under your control. The point is that I don't want to wag my tail like our dog, Tana, because I appreciate all that you've done. I want to be myself and ...

Once again, I found myself going in circles and tossed my pencil across the room. It pinged against the wall and then dropped onto the couch. I folded the letter, placed it in my journal, and left it for another day. For now, I would make a quick phone call to let them know where I was, where I was headed, and what I was doing once I arrived.

My parents might not understand what I was about to do—to head off on another voyage to a strange land—any more than I did. But Don had given me a way to think about myself, and, although I hadn't figured out how to bring that up with my dad, I decided to take an interim job in a state and town I'd never been to, trusting that whatever happened was meant to be. I would make the best of it regardless of what it was.

I had hoped to find a new home when I came to Vanderbilt. I even thought I'd found one in Rose's Creek. But I was still a wanderer, and that was okay. I had decided not to return to my parents' house. I would go wherever my next adventure took me and find my home—like Don—

within whatever I could create in the depths of my soul. Of course, I had to discover what that was, but at least I had a destination. It wasn't an outward one; it was inward. I could live with that. It's what I had to do—a calling.

I remembered what Mr. Hook said about painting, how it provided a refuge from having to make a living. I also heard Erling say, "Good lad," and saw him puffing on his pipe and nodding, "That's the way! Make your own way."

I never expected to be like him, venturing into the unknown and figuring out what to do next. I wanted to call him and tell him, yes, I'd broken with my past, but I knew I hadn't done anything drastic. I still hadn't confronted my dad. I had a long way to go to achieve real independence. But I could see—and it made me smile—that squirrel in the oak outside my room sitting up, paws together, nodding, and saying, "You're getting the hang of it." I would have to find out what's ahead for me, piece together my fate, and take that next step.

I called Reverend Highbottom. He told me in a booming voice how much he'd heard about me.

"Delighted," he said, "simply delighted to have a man of your character working with my church."

He invited me to drive over and have dinner with his family. He told me that it was a perfect fit—the kind of job that would meet all my expectations: to serve as an interim caretaker, lead Sunday services, and work with the church youth. I wrote down the directions to his house and headed east.

About the Author

As a former Poet Laureate of Portland, Maine, Bruce P. Spang has published three novels, *The Deception of the Thrush,* (2015), *Those Close Beside Me* (2019)) and *The River Crossed* (2024). He has a new memoir: *Dear Teen, Dear Poet: A Coming of Age in Letters.* Warren Publisher, 2026. He wrote the libretto, "Charlie!", a musical drama about a gay man murdered by three high school boys in Bangor. He's the author of seven books of poetry, including, *Twist* (2025), *All You'll Derive: A Caregiver's Journey* (2019), *Not Just Anybody* (2016), *Boy at the Screen Door* (Moon Pie Press, 2015), *To the Promised Land Grocery* (Moon Pie Press, 2008*), I Have Walked Through Many Lives: Young Voices—Scarborough* (Moon Pie Press, 2009) *The Knot,* (Snow Drift Press, 2005), and *Tip End of Time* (Snow Drift Press, 2004).

He teaches writing at the Great Smokies Writing Program at UNC in Asheville. He is a lead writer for Asheville Poetry Journal and poetry editor for the Smoky Blue Arts and Literary Journal. He lives with his husband, Myles Rightmire, and their two dogs, fifteen birds, and ten fish in Chandler, NC.

For more about him, contact him at Brucespang.com or bspang4@gmail.com.

www.ingramcontent.com/pod-product-compliance
Lightning Source LLC
LaVergne TN
LVHW050926080826
845145LV00001B/227

* 9 7 8 1 9 5 8 6 6 9 9 8 3 *